ROUTLEDGE LIBRARY EDITIONS:
EARLY YEARS

Volume 5

NURSERY LIFE
300 YEARS AGO

NURSERY LIFE
300 YEARS AGO

The Story of a Dauphin of France, 1601–10.
Taken from the Journal of Dr Jean Héroard, Physician-in-Charge, and from Other Contemporary Sources

LUCY CRUMP

Routledge
Taylor & Francis Group

LONDON AND NEW YORK

First published in 1929 by George Routledge & Sons, Ltd.

This edition first published in 2023
by Routledge
4 Park Square, Milton Park, Abingdon, Oxon OX14 4RN

and by Routledge
605 Third Avenue, New York, NY 10158

Routledge is an imprint of the Taylor & Francis Group, an informa business

British Library Cataloguing in Publication Data
A catalogue record for this book is available from the British Library

ISBN: 978-1-032-34369-3 (Set)
ISBN: 978-1-032-35000-4 (Volume 5) (hbk)
ISBN: 978-1-032-35053-0 (Volume 5) (pbk)
ISBN: 978-1-003-32506-2 (Volume 5) (ebk)

DOI: 10.4324/9781003325062

Publisher's Note
The publisher has gone to great lengths to ensure the quality of this reprint but points out that some imperfections in the original copies may be apparent.

Disclaimer
The publisher has made every effort to trace copyright holders and would welcome correspondence from those they have been unable to trace.

THE DAUPHIN AT SEVEN MONTHS

From the Pepys Library, Cambridge

NURSERY LIFE
300 YEARS AGO

The Story of a Dauphin of France, 1601-10
Taken from the Journal of Dr Jean Héroard
Physician-in-Charge, and from other
Contemporary Sources by

LUCY CRUMP

Editor of " Letters of George Birkbeck Hill," Translator of
Phillip de Mornay's " A Huguenot Family in the XVIth Century "

WITH 16 FULL-PAGE PLATES

LONDON
GEORGE ROUTLEDGE & SONS, LTD.
BROADWAY HOUSE: 68-74 CARTER LANE, E.C.
1929

PRINTED IN GREAT BRITAIN BY THE EDINBURGH PRESS, EDINBURGH

CONTENTS

LIST OF ILLUSTRATIONS

NURSERY LIFE
THREE HUNDRED YEARS AGO

CHAPTER I

THE BIRTH OF A DAUPHIN

IT is more than thirty years ago since I took from the
shelves of a great library the *Journal* of Jean Héroard
concerning the childhood and youth of Louis XIII.
I can see now the rows upon rows of books, smell the
scent which seems inseparable from a mass of books
gathered together in the still air of a library. Often it
seems a singularly dead scent, but now and then we
take some book from a shelf which in itself is so alive
that we feel the sudden quickening of the very air
around us. For me this old French journal was such
a book. Was there any other like it in all literature,
any other similar record of the doings and the sayings
of a little child ? As I stood reading slowly a sense of
a satisfied wish came over me. I could see myself again
a small girl in a schoolroom, see the June garden outside
drifting the scent of white magnolia and the hum of
bees through the window, hear the squeak of my
brother's slate-pencil as he did his sums, and myself
reading aloud slowly and with some help over difficult
words, *Little Arthur's History of England.* It had its
thrills. There was the scene with Hubert and a very
boyish Arthur of Brittany, the Princes in the Tower
and, though I was a staunch roundhead, an affecting

farewell of Charles I to his little son and daughter. But where were the children in the centuries between? I never asked the question, and if I had my governess —she wore a chignon and a much befurbelowed dress— would have replied that children were not generally of much importance and very little was therefore known of their doings. And here in my hand was the story of a little boy whose every act and word was thought worth recording and, because of their childish triviality, could hold me spellbound three hundred years after his childhood was past and forgotten.

Jean Héroard's journal is often quoted by French writers. In England it is less familiar, nor would there be many who would care to read it all. Its repetition of small details would be tedious to some readers, its occasional coarseness would repel others, and even its language might be a deterrent. But among those who like wandering along the little by-ways of history, not seeking overmuch scholarship nor desiring to do more than realize the living reality of past days, this story of a child may appeal to them as something different to other intimate records of bygone times. For these I have made this book, not purporting to be a complete translation, for those who desire the complete book will go to the original. But Héroard's journal is the principal source of information in this study of children and his words are given wherever possible. Other books, mostly contemporary, have been used where the entries made by Héroard seemed too meagre to tell their story, very much as when in an old tapestry subsidiary scenes are introduced to complete and enhance the interest of the main subject. The skill of the weavers lay in making one composition out of the component parts. It is a skill not easily attained by either weavers of tapestry or writers of books.

The Birth of a Dauphin

The journal of Dr Jean Héroard covers the events of twenty-seven years, from the dauphin's birth in 1601 to the writer's own death in 1628. Only the first ten, however, fall within our scope for our purpose is the study of a little boy's daily life in the early years of the seventeenth century. With contemporary history we have not much concern but since this boy was a king's son, and heir to a throne, his life, even as an infant, was profoundly influenced by his royal birth. We must, therefore, realize something of the big world outside his home if we would understand the meaning of many of the scenes described in this curious record. The extravagance of the rejoicings at the child's birth, the singular family life in which he grew up, the influences which shaped his character would lose their significance had we not some slight knowledge of contemporary France. We must indeed go back to years anterior to 1601, and recall the strange fact that no son had been born to a king of France for close on fifty years; nor, when Henri IV succeeded Henri III, the last king of the House of Valois, did there seem any likelihood that he, any more than his three immediate predecessors, would leave a son to succeed him. Since the tragic eve of St Bartholomew in the year 1572, Henri de Navarre had been bound in an unwilling marriage with Marguerite de Valois. The best years of the lives of both had been passed by Henri in fighting and by Marguerite in a small independent court of her own in remote Auvergne. For twenty years neither had met, nor wanted to meet, the other. There never had been any child born of the marriage, but Henri had a mistress to whom he was ardently attached and she had borne him two sons and a daughter. Gabrielle d'Estrées, no less than Marguerite, stood in the way

3

of a legitimate heir. Had it not been for a widespread opinion that Henri would marry Gabrielle, were he free, Marguerite might have sooner consented to join him in a petition for the dissolution of her marriage, but she would not do it to see the king's mistress queen in her place. Henri refused to give Marguerite herself the title of queen of France, nor even after the civil wars had come to an end, to allow her to leave Auvergne. The wrangle between the husband and wife, who had never done anything but wrangle, came to a final end with the death of Gabrielle in 1599. The greatest obstacle to a fresh marriage was gone ; other difficulties could be met and overcome. Henri passionately wanted an heir; Marguerite wanted payment of a vast accumulation of debt, control of her estates and above all leave to live once more in Paris. Both were ready to bargain and both desirous to come to an agreement, perhaps for the first time in their lives. In 1599 the marriage, entered into twenty-seven years before, was declared null and the following year a new bride set out on her way to France to wed a now elderly bridegroom. The choice of the bride, Maria di Medici, may have facilitated the decision in Rome; her wealth secured her a welcome in the impoverished court of France. She certainly had no great share of good looks or good temper to recommend her, and in contrast to Gabrielle d'Estrées, who had possessed a large measure of both, she must have proved a sad disappointment. In the matter of children, however, she did her duty for she bore three sons and three daughters to the king in the nine years of her married life; so far as temper went she surely had enough to sour it and as for her looks she was as God made her.

The marriage was celebrated in Florence by proxy

and the new queen immediately after sailed from
Livorno for France. L'Estoile, the diarist of Paris,
whose opportunities for hearing the news of the day
kept his pen busy for forty years, jotted down what he
could learn of the queen's voyage. In its mingled
luxury and discomfort, its magnificent ceremonial and
storms it was very typical of the new life awaiting her
in France. "18th Oct. 1600. The queen went on
board the *admiral* of the Grand Duke, one of the most
beautiful and richest galleys ever seen on the sea. It
was escorted by five Papal galleys, five galleys of the
Knights of Malta and six others belonging to her
uncle, the Grand Duke . . . on the 19th she reached
the port of Esperies (Spezia) where the Genoese
ambassadors met her with the offer of their galleys in
addition. On the 19th October she arrived at Portofino
where she was forced to stay for several days by stormy
weather. The aforesaid ambassadors pressed her to
land and take shelter in the neighbouring town from
the storm, which even daunted the sailors. She steadily
refused saying that she had no permission from the
king to land, ' on foreign soil '." Portofino, in Genoese
territory, could, however, shelter her very effectively
in its almost land-locked cove, deeply cut into the
olive-clad hills. Beyond the sheltering cape and the
guardian shrine of St George the waves can be very
wild indeed; but the queen's galley would have ridden
the green water of the little harbour in reasonable
quietude. Her ladies, hampered by no scruples, went
ashore and no doubt visited the fine castle above the
cove, and possibly made their way along the mule road
to the other little cove and the castle of Paraggi,
where François I was brought, a prisoner, and em-
barked for captivity in Spain. For nine days the galleys
tarried, and some of them must have had to toss

outside a harbour far too small to shelter so large a number. On the 28th October she set out again and on the 3rd of November she at length disembarked at Marseilles. There she loitered amidst a succession of fêtes held in her honour. There was no need to hasten northward for Henri was busy with a small war in Savoy, but early in January the king met his new queen at Lyons. He rode into the city late in the day and found her at supper surrounded with a crowd of onlookers, and peeped between their shoulders to see what manner of lady she was before his arrival was made known. He seems to have been content. She had not the beauty of Gabrielle, nor the malicious charm of Henriette de Balsac d'Entragues, his new mistress; but Gabrielle's son could not succeed him, nor could Henriette, in spite of the written promise of marriage she had extorted from him, give him a legitimate heir. So he welcomed Marie with kindly words, gave her a great place in the world and took from others the amusement she was incapable of giving him.

It was the beginning of a complicated family life such as would have daunted most men, and it was certainly not free from trouble. However, the expectation of the birth of a child, and the passionate hope that it would prove to be a son, must have made the summer of 1601 a golden time. The king had chosen Fontainebleau, his beautiful palace in the forest, for the place where his child was to be born, and in August 1601 he and the queen were busy making all the necessary arrangements before they left Paris. The most important of these was the choice of a midwife whose experience and repute would best suit her for the immense responsibility to be laid on her, and many were the discussions and intrigues in which the choice involved the court. By the end of the sixteenth century the midwives, or *matrones*, of Paris were a well-organized body and some among them had attained a position of considerable distinction. None might assume the name of *matrone*, nor hang a sign of her profession at her door, who had not given proof of her fitness to a physician, two surgeons, and two experienced midwives; she was, moreover, required to have received a certain amount of instruction and to have attended a certain number of cases. The best known of these recognized midwives at this time was an elderly woman named Dupuis, who, in her day, had been very popular among the ladies of the court. The king himself knew her well for she had repeatedly attended his beloved Gabrielle, Duchesse de Beaufort, and he took it for granted that the queen, in her turn, would engage her. But the duchess had died in childbirth and the tragedy of her death was still fresh in people's memories. Some of the ladies about the queen told her that they knew of a worthier woman, younger and of a better class and who, moreover, had gained a well-deserved popularity among the ladies of the court and city. Marie listened willingly although nothing was said hastily on the subject to the king.

The woman thus recommended, called indifferently Louise Bourgeois or Boursier, one being her maiden and the other her husband's name, wrote a book entitled *Les six couches de la Reine*, which contains a very detailed account of the dauphin's birth. This portion of the book has been often quoted by French writers but the part relating to her own early life is less well known; it is interesting, however, to see what was the origin of so noted a woman and how she obtained her position. She tells us that she was the wife of a surgeon, a good match for him for she possessed house property just outside the walls of Paris. Her husband, who had been a pupil of Ambrose Paré, had an appointment in the army of Henri III and after that king's assassination had stayed on in the service of Henri IV. During the years of the civil war he had small opportunity to look after his wife and children. Up to the year 1590, however, Louise got along well enough, but in that year Henri IV's troops came before Paris and sacked the suburbs outside the walls, Louise's houses among the rest. She tried to keep off starvation with her skill in embroidery and fine sewing but there was little to be gained in that way, and at last encouraged by her success in the care of several of her neighbours in childbirth she made up her mind to take up the work as a regular profession and to seek admission into the recognized company of midwives. She describes her examination very amusingly. She seems to have had no difficulty in satisfying the three doctors as to her fitness but the interview with the two qualified midwives was a more troublesome matter. "I was sent before Dame Dupuis and Dame Peronne," she tells us. "They asked me what my husband's calling was and hearing he was a surgeon Dame Dupuis had no wish to admit me. 'Heaven help us! neighbour,' she said, 'that would never do for us, for if she is the wife of a surgeon she will be as thick with the surgeons as thieves are at a fair. We ought only to admit the wives of craftsmen who have no acquaintance with people of our calling.' She told me that my husband ought to be able to support me without any need of mine to work for my bread." In the end Louise was admitted for "having been accepted by all the others Dupuis had to accept me too, although to her great regret." Louise comments on this, "I mention it to

8

show how God sends his vengeance on those who do ill to others."

Henri, as we have seen, had taken the engagement of Dame Dupuis for granted. Louise, who had plenty of opportunity for hearing all the court gossip on the momentous decision, gives the following lively account of the discussion between the king and queen. Henri was on the eve of leaving Paris and before he left was desirous to see all the last arrangements for his wife's comfort finally settled. " ' You have,' he said to her, ' M. du Laurens, your physician in chief, M. Guidi, your physician in ordinary and Dame Dupuis, your midwife.' The queen shook her head. ' I don't want Dupuis.' The king looked much surprised. ' What, my love, you have waited till I am actually on the point of starting for Calais before telling me you don't want Dupuis. Who do you want then?' ' I want a woman who is young, tall and active, who nursed Madame d'Elbeuf, and whom I saw at the Hotel Gondi.' " This meeting had been carefully arranged, as if by chance, by the ladies who favoured Louise with the hoped-for result that the queen took a fancy to her. The king was troubled and " sent for M. du Laurens and told him what the queen said. The doctor let the king know that he was well aware of the queen's wishes and that he had in consequence consulted with several doctors and they all thought the woman suitable. ' Who were they,' asked the king. ' There was M. Malescot, who is the oldest doctor in the city, M. Hautin, one of your Majesty's own doctors, M. de la Violette and M. Ponçon.' ' Their opinion is not enough. Go and find the woman at once and tell her to give the names of a dozen ladies of quality whom she has attended, and find out whether she gave satisfaction.' " Louise named thirty of her

9

most recent cases and sent her serving-man to take the doctor to call on six ladies, five wives of high officials and the sixth a rich merchant's lady. Every one of them spoke well of her and the king gave way.

The vengeance of Heaven had indeed fallen. Dupuis' day was over and Louise Boursier had won the great prize of her profession. She at once entered the queen's service, and when two days later the move to Fontainebleau took place she travelled in the same coach as her royal mistress. It was a roomy coach and, beside the queen, held the chief lady-in-waiting, the queen's foster sister and favourite, Leonora Galagai, and the court fool; but he, it seems sat on the box with the coachman. A string of other coaches followed with ladies, serving women, and the household gear needed on a journey. The account Louise gives makes curious reading. To us it gives a most comfortless impression, but lack of comfort was the last thing noticed in those days. "The journey from Paris to Fontainebleau took two days. Our first resting place on the first day was at Corbeil, in an inn where there was only one wretched little room for the queen, with a low ceiling and very stuffy. The chamber-women and I were put to sleep in what was meant for the queen's dressing closet; there was nothing between her bed and mine but a slight partition of daub-plaster. I had the honour to be present at the queen's rising. We dined at Melun at the house of M. de la Grange le Roy. His house was very scantily furnished and it was specially noticeable that there were no proper fire-dogs, but only some big stones on the hearth. A fire had been lighted for though it was the end of August the weather was not too warm. Three big logs had been laid on the fire and, as the queen was standing by the hearth with her back to it, these logs, which were enormous, began to slip down. I was standing by the chimney-piece at the side and I flung myself down just in time to stop a great round log from hitting the queen on the heels. Had it done so it would certainly have knocked her down. This was the first service I had the honour to do the queen and to the future king she bore."

If Louise Boursier thought the house bare it would have looked doubly so to our eyes. Houses in 1600, even palaces, had but little furniture compared with those in the twentieth century, and such furniture as they had was not so much of a fixture. If M. de la Grange le Roy had a house elsewhere much of his furniture would be moved when he himself moved. Beds, table appointments and kitchen utensils all formed part of a great person's usual travelling equipment and might, indeed, be as necessary on his arrival at home as on his journey. Only those who were too hurried or too poor to bear the cost and the tediousness of transporting heavy goods put up with such accommodation as inns offered, a share of a bed, a shakedown by the hearth or a bundle of hay in a loft often crowded and evil-smelling. Undoubtedly the queen would have had her bed with her and since she probably had her table and kitchen appointments and possibly her food she may have given very short notice to her host at Melun. She wanted the shelter of a roof and little else. By the end of the second day Fontainebleau was reached and there the queen awaited the arrival of the king and the birth of her child.

The king reached Fontainebleau in the beginning of September and immediately busied himself with arrangements for the care of the child about to be born. Just to keep off ill-luck he had a bet with Zamet, the rich financier and unofficial minister of his pleasures, that the child would be a girl, but at the same time he behaved as if he believed that the very intensity of his hopes must bring their realization. That this was so was shown by his words to the two persons to whom the care of the infant was to be chiefly entrusted. " I have chosen you to take charge of my son. Serve him well." One of these was Mme de Montglat, the child's *gouvernante*, the other Jean Héroard, his physician. The choice of Mme de Montglat was not a wholly fortunate one, although the king never regretted his selection. Those who lived with her thought her greedy and mean; she certainly was coarse in language nor did she ever win the affection of the children under her care. Her character, as Dr Héroard saw it, unfolds itself in the pages of his journal and we shall frequently meet with her. The contrast between her and Jean Héroard is very strong and happily so, for the qualities of the kindly, sympathetic physician made up for the many defects in the *gouvernante*.

It is not easy to reconstruct Héroard's background from the meagre and sometimes conflicting accounts now available, but certain facts do emerge with clearness. The manner of man he was is best shown in his writings. M. Eud. Soulié and M. Ed. de Barthélemy, the editors to whose enormous industry we owe the edition of the journal published in 1868, gathered almost all that could be known of Héroard's life up to his appointment in 1601 as physician to the dauphin. His father, Michel Héroard, was a surgeon of Montpellier. In a diatribe written against his son Jean, by a fellow court physician, one Guillemeau, who spared none of the abuse natural to an embittered rival in that age, this Michel is said to have been a mere barber, and his family is accused of

belonging to the *religion pretendue reformée*. The latter
statement receives confirmation in the journal of a
young medical student who travelled from his native
city of Bâle to study medicine at Montpellier in the
year 1552, but it is also clear from this journal that
Michel Héroard's position was much above that of a
mere barber-surgeon. The young Swiss, Felix Platter,
came to Geneva on his way south. " I waited," he
says, " on M. Calvin on my arrival, to whom I gave
a letter of introduction from my father. So soon as
he read it he said to me, ' M. Felix everything is
falling out for the best. I know of a most excellent
companion for the journey for you, without making
any search, a surgeon, one Michel Heroardus of
Montpellier. He is setting out to-morrow or next
day. You couldn't want a better companion.' " Felix
Platter travelled with Michel Héroard down the Rhône
and from what he says of him both on the journey
and later in Montpellier it is clear that the surgeon
occupied a good position. Montpellier, during the
seven years that Felix Platter studied in it and when
Jean Héroard was a little boy, was a catholic city,
but there were already many huguenot families in it.
Later the huguenots outnumbered the catholics and
Montpellier became one of the most savagely disputed
cities between the two religious parties. Jean seems
to have become a catholic in later years but his writings
continued to show the strong influence of his huguenot
upbringing. He is said to have matriculated in 1571
and to have taken his degrees in 1575. The dates are
difficult to adjust to other known facts for he was
certainly in Paris early in 1574. As the lapse of a
statutory time was necessary between the taking of the
lower and higher degrees it is probable that he had
finished his medical studies some time before he could

take his final degree. He may have returned to Montpellier in 1575 for this purpose. However this may have been he was certainly in Paris in 1574 for Ambrose Paré, commissioned by Charles IX to find a doctor ready to devote himself to the diseases of horses, selected Jean Héroard for the post. Charles died in the May of that year and Héroard laments that this untimely death "frustrated my hope of showing my ardent desire to please my king and obey his wishes," in pursuing his studies among the horses of the royal stable. His jealous and angry colleague of later days considered himself justified in speaking of him as "a doctor of horses not men." The appointment of royal veterinary surgeon was confirmed by the new king Henri III who bade him finish his book on *Hippostologie*; the work, however, was not published until 1599, long after the death of this second royal master. In the intervening years Héroard had devoted himself to the diseases of his fellow-men and by the time his book on horses was published he was already a court physician. He had his heresies in medicine even if he had lost them in religion. One of them, a disbelief in the use of bleeding, may have endeared him to patients ; it undoubtedly made him enemies among doctors, one of the most noted of whom boasted that he "would bleed an infant two weeks old or an old man of eighty cheerfully and with confidence." I cannot recall any occasion in the dauphin's childhood when Héroard used his lancet for bleeding, a truly extraordinary thing in those days.

Jean Héroard's fortunes advanced steadily if slowly. When he was fifty he was in a good enough position to marry an heiress, and was henceforth entitled to call himself the Seigneur de Vaugrieuse, in right of his wife's estate. Two years later the king summoned him to Fontainebleau. Héroard himself describes the meeting. " On Sep. 21st, about four o'clock in the afternoon I met the king returning from the chase at the entrance of the water garden. He called me to him and did me the honour to say, ' I have chosen you to be in attendance on my son. Serve him well.' " On the 29th of January 1628, the last entry of this unique diary was made. The dauphin, king he had been since he was nine years old, had been very truly served by his physician. Héroard was over fifty when he began his long years of service and not far short of eighty when it ended. True to his duty he had followed the king to La Rochelle, which the royal army was besieging during a small recrudescence of civil war. It was a long road from the old man's childhood in Montpellier, where a huguenot could only worship in fear and in secret, to his death before the defiant city making a last struggle not for huguenot tolerance, for that it had, but for huguenot independence of the royal government. But we have nothing to do with the days of Louis XIII's kingship. In the days of his childhood the wars between the two religions were over, as men hoped for ever, and their hope seemed to receive its seal in the birth of an heir to the king who had brought them peace.

Here then in September 1601 were gathered together at Fontainebleau the king and the queen, the princes of the blood, Mme de Montglat the appointed *gouvernante*, Jean Héroard the doctor, Louise Boursier the midwife, courtiers of all ranks and both religions, their attendants and domestics innumerable, couriers ready at a moment's notice to gallop off to spread the great news, and among them all a little boy of three years old who though petted and played with by every one, was soon to learn the enormous difference between

15

the son of the king's mistress and the dauphin of France. We shall often hear of him again, first as Alexandre Monsieur, and later as the Chevalier. He was Gabrielle d'Estrée's second son. On the 27th of September Héroard could at last begin his journal in good earnest. " At the fourteenth hour of the new moon, at the half hour and half quarter after ten o'clock in the evening according to my watch made at Abbeville by M. Plautard, the queen gave birth to a son." How many of us know where and by whom our watches were made? We feel sure that M. Plautard's was a good watch and that the doctor liked to give credit where it was due. He tells us much about the dauphin's birth and Louise Boursier tells us still more; by taking something from both accounts a very vivid reconstruction of the event can be made. Louise tells us that the baby was born " in the oval room which is near the king's room, and which had been prepared for the queen. There was a large bed hung with crimson velvet embroidered with gold and near it the small lying-in couch for the queen. The hanging pavilions, both the big and the little one, which had been draped in festoons against the ceiling were let down. The big pavilion was stretched out at the four corners like a tent and kept taut with cords. It was made of fine holland and was fully twenty ells round; in the middle was the small pavilion, made of similar material, draped round the small couch. The ladies whom the king had chosen to attend the queen were summoned and folding seats and stools were placed within the big pavilion for the king, Madame his sister and Mme de Nemours." Héroard says Mme de Guercheville also had the honour of being present. " Two elderly Italian ladies," Louise continues, " both mothers of large families, were in attendance as chamber-women. The reliquary with the relics of Madame Sainte Marguerite stood on a table in the room outside the pavilion and two monks from Saint Germain des Près prayed before it without any pause. . . . The king only left the queen to eat and even then he sent for news and Madame, his sister, did the same."

The oval room is one of the most charming rooms in the beautiful palace of Fontainebleau. It is known nowadays as the Salon de Louis XIII. Happily it has been less changed by later kings than many of the other rooms. It forms part of the suite looking into the Cour Ovale and it would seem that its shape purposely mimics the shape of the court below into which its windows look. At one end is the fireplace not altered in form although its old woodwork has been replaced by marble. The panelled walls, although retouched, remain the same as when Henri IV had the room redecorated in commemoration of the dauphin's birth. The square mirror that was fixed into the wall for Catherine di Medici, the first mirror to reach France from Italy, is still in its place and marks the spot where the second Medici queen's bed stood with its tent of fine holland " twenty ells round " draped over it. The oval room is not very large and one wonders how so many things and so many people as Louise describes ever got into it. In most rooms where a birth was to take place it was the custom, down to the seventeenth century, for a dresser to be set up on which a display of silver vessels and other valuables was made; if a household had not enough to satisfy its vanity relatives would lend what they could spare for a few weeks. Sweet-scented flowers were strewn on the ground and flagons of wine and dishes of sweetmeats were placed among the silver ready for the constant stream of neighbours and friends who made merry in the house, cheered up the mother and admired the baby. Citizens' wives copied the noble-born ladies, making the best display they could while the poorer women had at least a dish of spiced comfits and some pungent scented herbs to welcome their gossips. We do not hear of any display of royal gold and silver in the queen's room; possibly the golden reliquary of Saint Margaret made show enough, but we do hear of the extraordinary number of people in the room. Even within the pavilion the queen was allowed no privacy, for according to the custom of the royal house the three princes of the blood, Soissons, Conti and Montpensier, were called behind the curtains immediately after the birth of the child ; five doctors were also in attendance and in addition to these we must add the king, his sister and three or four ladies-in-waiting. It is clear that a circumference of twenty ells was none too much for there to be room for every one.

After the birth of the baby, which was a protracted affair, Louise thus continues her story. " I held the child on my lap rolled up and hidden from view, but I could see by its face it was very feeble. I asked one of the gentlemen of the king's chamber to bring me wine. He brought a bottle and I asked for a spoon. The king took the bottle and I said, ' Sire, if it were any other child I should first fill my mouth with wine and give it to the child from my mouth.' The king held the bottle to my lips. ' Do as you would do to any other child,' he said. I filled my mouth and emptied it into the baby's and he looked better at once. I saw the king looking sad and worried, for he did not yet know the child's sex, so I said to Gratienne, the chamber-maid, ' bring me a warm towel,' for that was a signal I had arranged with her

to show it was a boy. She went up joyfully to the
king to tell him but he pushed her away and would
not believe her, saying he knew it was a daughter
from my down cast looks. Gratienne replied ' But she
said she should look down cast for fear of exciting
the queen.' ' That's true,' he said, ' but if it were my
son she *couldn't* have done it.' He then came up and
put his mouth to my ear. ' Midwife, is it a son?'
I said ' Yes.' ' Don't give me short lived joy. I
should die if you did.' I showed the child to him; he
raised his eyes to Heaven, clasped his hands and gave
God thanks. Tears ran down his cheeks as big as
peas. He asked me whether there would be any
danger now in telling the queen and I said no, but
I begged him to do it with as little emotion as possible.
He went to kiss the queen and said, ' My love, you
have suffered much but God has been very gracious
to us and given us our desire. We have a fine son.'
The queen raised her eyes to Heaven, joined her hands
together, wept great tears and sank back fainting. . . .
The king kissed the princes without noticing the
queen's condition and then went to open the door of
the room and let every one waiting in the antechamber
come in. I am certain there were two hundred of
them so that we hardly had room to attend to the
queen. I was extremely annoyed and said that it was
most improper to let in all these people before the
queen was ready. The king heard me and slapping
me on the shoulder said ' Hold your tongue, midwife,
and don't be cross. This child belongs to every one
and every one must rejoice with me.' . . . Having
revived the queen from her faint I next saw to M. le
Dauphin under the eye of M. Héroard. He made me
wash him all over with wine and water." Héroard
himself says it was red wine and oil of red roses. His

account differs in certain other small matters from Louise's; he says for instance that the wine which revived the baby was given by Dr Guillemeau, but Louise's words have an air of such naïve truth that it is pleasant to accept what she says. Héroard gives a long and extremely detailed description of the baby noting among other things that he was " a large boned child, very muscular, well nourished and a good red colour. His head well formed, black haired and hazel eyed with a snub nose, large ears and a pretty mouth . . . his feet large, very wide at the toes with a small pointed heel just like his father's feet."

The use of oil of red roses for new-born infants was a custom centuries old. As far back as 1350 it was advised that the newly born " should be rolled in red rose leaves first sprinkled with salt to comfort their limbs and that after they should be washed and often rubbed with oil of red roses." Ambrose Paré, two hundred years later, still had new-born children washed with a decoction of red roses, myrtle leaves and salt, so that Héroard only carried on the old tradition. We shall find him later on ordering a bath for the dauphin with red roses in it " to make it wholesome." We still sprinkle our rose petals with salt when we make potpourri. Did our grandmothers fill their jars with the sweet-smelling mixture so that they might always have a handful of salted rose leaves ready to make water for washing wholesome? While the baby was being washed and swaddled over by the fire at the further end of the room, the happy king led up little groups of courtiers to see him. " The joy," says Louise, " was greater than could be expressed. Every one was kissing every one else and I heard it said that ladies kissed their serving men in their transports of joy without knowing what they did."

The Birth of a Dauphin

At last Mme de Montglat bore the baby off to its own room followed by Dr Héroard and the women appointed to wait on the dauphin; the queen was settled peacefully in her big crimson-curtained bed, the king "had his bed set up by hers where he slept till she was about again," and we must hope that they both rested well after a harassing thirty-six hours. Possibly in the Cour Ovale all the noise of rejoicing did not penetrate, the salvos fired, the fireworks in the Cour du Cheval blanc, the couriers clattering out of the palace precincts; they would not have hurried if it had been a girl, they said; the bells in the little town, the drums and trumpets, the broaching of kegs of wine and the shouts of a people delirious with joy.

Only one person among all the noisy throng found the commotion very bewildering and even he, Gabrielle's little son Alexandre, caught the fever of excitement. Louise found him outside the queen's room shortly before the dauphin's birth. " Midwife," he said, " is it a boy? Do make it a boy and I'll give you all I've got." The following day she came across him again. " In the afternoon I found M. Alexandre de Vendôme alone at the door of the antechamber. He had hold of the curtain before the door which led to Monseigneur le Dauphin's appartement, and he had stopped there quite puzzled. I said to him, ' Why, Monsieur, what are you doing here?' He replied, ' I don't know why it is, but everybody used to talk to me and now nobody says anything.' ' Monsieur, every one has gone to look at M. le Dauphin, who has only just arrived. When they have paid him their respects they will talk to you again, just as before.' I told the queen what he had said and she was full of pity. ' It is enough to drive the poor child into his grave,' she said. ' The reason is that every one is full of my son and nobody thinks any more of the poor child and he must feel it very strange.' She at once gave orders that he was to be petted as much, or more, than formerly." Héroard, in his journal, rarely speaks of any feeling shown by the queen for even her own children, of whom she really saw very little, and this makes her kindly thought for the little Vendôme boy all the more pleasing.

One more extract from Louise's story, too long and too detailed a story to be quoted in full, will bring our indebtedness to her to a close. " On the 29th September I went to see M. le Dauphin. His usher, M. Birat, opened the door of his room to me. I saw the room was full, the king, Madame, his sister, the princes and princesses of the blood royal were all gathered together for the baptism of Monseigneur. . . . I drew back but the king called to me, ' Come in, come in. You are not the person to be kept out.' Then he said to Madame, his sister, and to the princes, ' I'll tell you what. I have seen plenty of people in war and in peace but never anyone so resolute as this woman here. She held my son in her lap and looked about her as calmly as if she held nothing at all. Why it is eighty-four years since a child was born dauphin of France.' I replied, ' I told you, Sire, that it was most important for the queen's safety to keep calm.' " Henri II's eldest son had been born in his grandfather's lifetime and Henri IV had to go back to the birth of the eldest son of François I in 1517, to reach the last child " born a dauphin."

The baptism which Louise interrupted was a private ceremony such as was customary in the French royal family. The full rites were reserved for a future public ceremony, when sponsors were chosen and the child named. We shall hear about this christening five years later, until which time the baby, although a baptized Christian, was a nameless little boy.

The grateful king offered Louise the post of dresser to his son, but she refused saying that she must continue to practise in her proper profession to keep her hand in for the queen's next need of her. And here she passes from our story although from time to time she visited the dauphin. The homely simplicity and occasional humour of her narrative carry with them a conviction of its truthfulness. Without Louise's account we might be tempted to believe the gossip of Paris as recorded by L'Estoile. " On the 27th September the queen, being at Fontainebleau, gave a dauphin to France. The king who was present, together with the princes of the blood royal, as soon as the baby was brought to him, gave it his blessing and putting his sword into its hand said ' May you use it, my son, to the glory of God and for the defence of your crown and your people! ' " We, who have heard the anguished whisper, " Don't give me short lived joy, midwife," can feel, in contrast to L'Estoile's bombast the exquisite reality of Louise Boursier. The birth of the dauphin as she tells it is a homely living story. L'Estoile's entry in his journal is history as it is too often written.

CHAPTER II

THE CHILDREN'S HOME

So far we have not learnt very much from Dr Jean
Héroard's journal but henceforth he will be our chief
story-teller. Other writers will be used to illustrate his
pages, amplify passages which are too brief to tell
their story clearly, but generally his observation was
so minute, so sympathetic with childhood that his
journal can stand alone, each entry, however short,
drawing its own vived and illuminating picture of a
moment in the dauphin's life. Our only regret is that
he concentrates his attention so exclusively on his
special charge to the neglect of the other children
surrounding the dauphin. It is clear that he watched
over them too, noticed traits of character, recorded
sayings and little events which concerned them, but
the journal was the journal of the dauphin, whose
importance was of immeasurably more importance than
that of any other little boy in the world. So much
was this the case that Héroard rarely uses the child's
name, contenting himself with a pronoun only. " He "
and " him " can only mean the dauphin and this, for
the most part, is the way in which the child is spoken
of throughout the diary. If any further designation is
needed the simple word Monsieur is used. " Monsieur "
the child was to everybody from the moment of his
birth, and indeed he had no name of his own till his
public christening when he was five years old. So
remembering these things we will read what Héroard
has to say on the earliest days of the dauphin's babyhood.

"LA NOURRICE"

From La Céramique Française. M. J. Ballot
By permission of Les Éditions Albert Morancé

[face p. 24

" Sep. 28th. His nurse was damoiselle Marguerite Hotman and as he seemed to have some difficulty in sucking his mouth was examined and it was found that he was tongue-tied; so at five o'clock in the evening M. Guillemeau, the King's surgeon, cut the tendon three times." The operation was obviously successful for a fortnight later Héroard writes, " when he sucks it is in great gulps so that he swallows as much in one gulp as other babies in three. His nurse never had enough for him." This failure on the nurse's part was a cause of constant anxiety to the doctor in charge of so precious a morsel of humanity. On 14th October things had got to such a pass that the child " was ravenous and never satisfied. He was given some broth which he swallowed eagerly." The use of broth for infants was much recommended by many doctors, but Héroard greatly regretted the necessity of any supplementary feeding. On 17th October we read " because he was never satisfied the fussiness of the women made them rub his gums with a bit of fresh boiled bacon. He bit off a piece and nearly swallowed it." On 19th October matters came to a head. " As the nurse had been short of milk several times," although she had tried to remedy the defect by over-eating herself, " Messrs de la Rivière, du Laurence, Guido Guidi and I held a consultation by command of their majesties and it was agreed that the second nurse should supplement the first." But the trouble went on and two months later Héroard bitterly records that " anyone could see that he was not being nourished; the muscles of his chest were all wasted away and the great fat fold round his neck nothing but skin." For some reason, though it must have been sorely against the doctor's will, Mlle Hotman remained the child's wet-nurse for the first three critical months of its life. I have retained here her title of *Mademoiselle*, for the fashion of calling all married women *Madame* had not yet come wholly into fashion, although in Paris it was already well established among the bourgeoisie. In court circles only ladies whose rank or position entitled them to the distinction were called *Madame*; others, married or unmarried, were *Mademoiselle* after as before marriage. Almost all the women in attendance on the dauphin, or on the other children brought up with him, were married; indeed the husbands of many of them had also their appointments at court; but Héroard speaks of all of these women as *Mademoiselle*. So Mlle Hotman, a married lady of respectable family, stayed on with the baby weeks after the doctor would have liked to send her away. One morning early in December she sat " nursing him by the hearth and playing with him on her knee. ' Monsieur,' she said, ' when I'm old and hobble with a stick will you still love me? ' He looked up into her face very straightly and then, as if he had thought the matter over, said ' No.' I was close by and had been watching him while he was suckled. I was greatly astonished, as were all those standing on the other side of the balustrade."

And well might they all be astonished seeing that the baby was but nine weeks old! But Mlle Hotman took it very ill and, when soon after the king wrote to Mme de Monglat that a change of nurse was to be made, the poor lady " made bitter complaint bethinking herself of the ' no' M. le Dauphin had said to her." Héroard says " he had never been suckled by Hotman without getting into a temper." So on 27th December she went away weeping bitterly. Unfortunately for the baby the nurse who followed her was also dismissed because, owing to mischief-making in the court, the

queen had taken a dislike to her. "She was," says
Héroard, "a very worthy woman, sweet tempered and
with plenty of good milk. Would that it had pleased
God that Monseigneur had been suckled by her from
the beginning. It would have been better for his
health and he could have been nourished with one
milk only. God pardon those who contrived it otherwise." A third nurse was installed but was not clean
and so she followed the others. The fourth nurse
stayed, not only till the child was finally weaned at
two years old, but for many years afterwards. She
had for a pet-name Maman Dondon. She must have
been the nearest thing to a real mother that the dauphin
had and she is often mentioned in the journal, always
unfailingly kind and watchful.

But we must go back to the first days in the dauphin's
life. Héroard gives us many glimpses of bygone ways.
He shows us, for instance, how a new-born baby was
carried about. "Oct. 5. Carried to see the queen.
The king was with her. The king lifted him up as
he lay on his cushion of smooth pile velvet, meaning
to kiss him before handing him back to his nurse.
The baby slipped and the king kissed the cushion
instead. M. le Dauphin would most certainly have
landed on his feet on the floor if his nurse had not
clutched him. A strip of velvet was at once added
to the pillow to make a pocket into which he was put
whenever he was carried out of his room. But the
king did not carry him again or take him up into his
arms." It sounds droll to be told that the week-old
baby nearly landed on to its feet but we must realize
him as a stiff little bundle with his limbs kept straight
with swaddling bands. Such a morsel might easily
slip from a cushion if it were clumsily held by an
elderly father, and not be too easily caught either. It

27

must have been a bad moment for the king and we need not wonder that he made no further attempt to hold his son, not even after the piece of velvet was added to make a pocket. The child only stayed for the first month of his life at Fontainebleau. At the end of that time the queen was fit for the court to move to Paris and the dauphin old enough to be taken to St Germain-en-Laye, the home of other families of little princes and princesses in bygone days.

And here we must leave, for a time, Héroard and his journal if we would know anything about this home of the king's children, for he naturally only mentions castle and gardens as they affect the scenes he describes. Neither in the building of the castle or the planning of the gardens had he any special interest, but for us, who want to visualize the child-life lived in them three hundred years ago, it is important to know something of both. The history of St Germain-en-Laye lies very far back and many have been the castles built by kings of France between the river and the vast forest. It is a great and beautiful forest still, lying within one of the wide sweeps which the Seine makes below Paris; in old days it was very much larger and full of wild creatures and birds fit for the chase, and a favourite haunt of a race of kings passionately fond of hunting. In Henri IV's time the building, still existing, was already known as the old castle, although it was in truth scarcely more than fifty years old. François I had built it on the site of earlier castles, a sample of the fine brick and stone architecture that makes the *châteaux* of his day so famous. He left the gothic stone chapel of St Louis' castle standing in its odd oblique position at one end of the curiously-shaped courtyard, and the keep of Charles V's castle also still stands at one angle of the newer building, although so carefully incorporated with it that it is in no way incongruous. The massive brick and stone of the old castle can have acquired little appearance of age when Henri IV became king, but, comparatively recent as its construction was, there was a yet newer building rising on the sloping ground above the Seine. As far back as the reign of Henri II a small pleasure-house had been planned, and partly built, on this site but the civil wars lay between its earliest beginning and its final construction. Not much of this last of the many *châteaux* of St Germain-en-Laye remains to-day; just one pavilion, now converted into a restaurant and part of another enclosed in private grounds. The whole position of the little palace has been so altered by the later construction of the famous terrace of St Germain that it is difficult to imagine it as it once stood. A modern road runs where great flights of steps led down from palace to river, and vineyards and market-gardens have engulfed the alleys and the flower-beds. The whole place was hastily and flimsily built to satisfy the fancy of a king who shared the tastes of his predecessors but who had inherited a kingdom impoverished by years of war. *Château* and terraced gardens showed signs of decay almost before they were finished, grew shabby and at length unsafe, and at last were swept away in the eighteenth century as useless to kings who could choose between Versailles, Trianon and Marly. It was never much more than a pleasure-house and the gardens pleasure-gardens, greatly admired in their day and full of new experiments in the Italian art of marvellous fountains and in new methods of laying out flower-beds. The children lived so much in the gardens and in the park round their home that it is worth while to try and visualize their play-place before

29

we enter the old castle and trace out the rooms they occupied there. There are not a few descriptions of the gardens at St Germain-en-Laye but, perhaps the best, because written by one who marvelled most at all he saw, is that written by a young medical student on his way home from Montpellier to Bâle. Thomas Platter was his name, a much younger half-brother of that Felix Platter whom Calvin recommended to Héroard's father as a fellow-traveller from Geneva to Montpellier. The younger Platter was interested in the new *château* but his real enthusiasm was for the gardens. He wrote in a journal, which is full of interesting matter, " On leaving the *château* I saw a gallery from which the gardens were reached by two wide flights of steps. The gallery, or terrace, was so wide one could have driven or ridden down it. On the right hand under these steps a grotto had been most artfully contrived in the middle of which a fountain had been made of sea shells and coral. A griffon spouted out water and nightingales, by a contrivance worked by the water, sang most charmingly. All sorts of shells were to be seen, and coral mingled with lovely coloured stones. When the water was turned on it gushed out of the rocks and out of all the statues which had been most tastefully placed in various positions, so that the spectacle was at the same time curious and charming. The floor, so far as I remember, was made of coloured pebbles which were so set that they formed innumerable little pipes through which the water was forced up to the vaulted roof from which it fell again like heavy rain, so that one could neither stand above nor below without being wetted. The walls were full of recesses in which all sorts of figures stood, in metal, in marble, in shell-work, nearly all of whom spouted out water. Many of the figures moved, such as smiths striking on an anvil, birds who sung and flapped their wings, lizards and frogs and serpents poised on the rocks, spouting water with many curious movements. If I remember aright in the middle of the grotto there was a figure of Neptune, with his trident who came out of a pool riding in a chariot. We could see him emerge on the surface, turn right round and disappear anew under the water. On the left hand of the steps another grotto had been constructed in which a water-organ had been placed. Against the walls yellow roses, made of shells were seen against a black background. In short there were so many lovely things that one could not notice them all in a brief visit. . . . On leaving the grottos we went into a courtyard where there was a superb fountain with a single jet of water flung up the height, at least, of two men. The water falling from it made so loud a noise that one might have thought it was the sound of a musket firing. The king had sent for an Italian to make all these marvels for him." The Italian, Tomaso Francini, was a famous man in his day before the wonders of Versailles came into being. The dauphin was fond of him and kept him in his employ all his life, and indeed Francini outlived his master. In illustration of the current opinion on the building of the new *château* and of the fountains in its gardens we may anticipate Héroard's journal by several years, and give here two little anecdotes of the dauphin, one when he was four years old and one when he was six. " March 27th, 1605. After breakfast the dauphin gave three jumps, one for Papa, one for Mamma and a little one for Madame, his baby sister. Was taken to the grottos. Made a great fuss at going in. They promised he should turn on the taps so he went in for the fun of wetting every one inside." The grottos with all their strange beasts might in any case have scared a child but the dauphin's fear came from overhearing they were too hurriedly built to be really safe. The same fear recurred about the new *château* in the following year. " I told him," says Héroard, " he was to go to the *Nouveau Château*. He said ' No, no. I don't want to go. When the frost comes it will all tumble down.' He had overheard some of us saying this for he listens to everything and remembers what he hears." The new palace, at any rate, lasted through the dauphin's life. It was a favourite residence of his, as it had been with his father, and in it he died in 1643.

But the grottos and fountains were not the only marvels of the new *château*. Below them were many walks, alleys of trees, trellises of roses, peaches, quinces and other fruit-trees brought from the royal gardens at Pau, for the king of France had no further use for the gardens of the king of Navarre. M. Houdard in his exhaustive study of the two castles has collected everything that can now be known of the vanished gardens. Perhaps the most interesting thing for us to notice is the novel laying out of the beds in the level strips of garden by the river side. The king's gardener was a man of imagination and initiative, and he boldly filled his beds with flowers, trusting to his skill in so contriving their seasons and their colours that the intricate patterns in which they were planted should remain intact throughout the summer. It may not at first sight seem so novel a matter to plant flowers in a garden, but a little study shows what an advance on many contemporary gardens those at St Germain-en-Laye were. The knot-garden was still a favourite fashion in spite of Bacon's scorn of them as " toys ;

you may see as good many times in tarts." Milton,
later in the century, would have none of them for in
Eden there were only:—

> " Flowers worthy of Paradise, which not nice Art
> In beds and curious knots, but Nature boon
> Poured forth profuse. . . ."

Clearly the skill shown to such perfection by Henri's
gardener must have slowly driven all other styles into
disrepute by the time Milton's later years were reached.
The older knot-garden was so quaint a phase of
taste that we may well linger a while to see how two
contemporary writers describe it; both were writing
for English gardens but the fashion seems to have
been nearly identical in both France and England.
John Parkinson, in his delightful book *Paradisi in
sole paradisus terestris* best describes the first laying-out
of the plot.   A garden, we learn, was first divided
into beds by broad straight walks; these beds, more or
less in number according to the size of the garden,
were enclosed with low hedges, of sweet-briar, privet,
yew or pyracantha, well and evenly clipped; privet
was best for the housewife to bleach her linen on,
pyracantha most pleasing for its white blossom in
spring and its red berries and glossy leaves in winter.
The large beds within these hedges were then marked
out in patterns " according as every man's conceit
alloweth it," geometrical patterns, armorial bearings,
birds and fishes, leopards and lions, allegorical figures,
all marked out by low borders of germander, hissop,
which was good to strew floors with, thrift, gay and
pleasing but apt to overgrow other plants, marjoram,
thyme and yellow cotton-lavender, and best of all
Dutch box if from time to time you take a sharp knife
and cut all its roots on the bed side.   Such are the

living borders that the old gardeners preferred, but
" dead material," as they call it, was also recommended
as a saving of time and labour; lead, handsome but
costly; the polished bones of sheep set upright in the
earth, an economical method this; tiles and, perhaps
prettiest of all, large white or coloured pebbles. The
patterns thus made, whether they were marked out in
living plants or " dead material " might be filled in
with plants bearing flowers of appropriate colours, and
this is the method recommended by Parkinson. Gervase
Markham, on the other hand, writing somewhat earlier,
recognizes the difficulty of keeping the beds gay all
through the summer and he relates a method of over-
coming it by replacing flowers with coloured earths; a
method particularly suited to those who " may beare
coate-armor." The knots were designed in amorial
bearings with germander, hissop or other herbs and " you
shall understand that your colours in armory are to be
thus made. First for your mettalls, you shall make your
yeallow either of a yeallow clay, usually to be had in
every place, or of the yeallowest sand, or for want of
both of your Flanders Tile, which is to be had of every
Ironmonger or Chandler and any of these you must
beate to dust: For your white you shall make it of
the coursest chalke beaten to dust, or of well burnt
plaster, or, of necessity of lime, but that will soon
decay. Your Blacke is to be made of your best and
purest coale-dust, well clensed and sifted: your Red is
to be made of broken uselesse brickes beaten to dust:
your Blewe is to be made of white chalke and black
coale-dust mixed together till the blacke have brought
the white to a perfect blewnes: lastly your Greene you
shall make of camomill, well planted. For the rest of
the colours you shall sift them and strew them into
their proper places, and then with a flat beating-

Beetell you shall beate it and incorporate it with the earth, and as any of the colours shall decay you shall diligently repair them, and the luster will be most beautiful." But Markham too feels that flowers would be preferable for he goes on to say, " there is another beautifying of gardens which although it lasts not the whole year yet it is most quaint, rare and best eye-pleasing, and thus it is. . . . You must understand that in this case the plainest knot is best. . . . Plant in every thrid (that is thread of the design) flowers of one kind, as for example: in one thrid plant your carnation Gilly flower, in another your great white Gilly flower, in another your mingle coloured Gilly flower and in another your blood-red gilly flower. . . . You may in this sort plant your severall coloured hyacinths as the red, the blew and the yeallow, or your severall Dulippos (Tulips) and many other Italian and French flowers . . . the grace of all which is that so soone as these flowers shall put forth their beauties if you stand a little remote and somewhat above the knot you shall see it appeare like a knot made of divers coloured ribans, most pleasing and most rare."

The knots at St Germain were designed by no means in the plainest way, but in intricate scrolls and arabesques, heraldic figures and interlacings innumerable, and if the king's gardener could lay them out with flowers of " appropriate colours " and so keep them blooming all the summer he was indeed a past-master in his art. Carpet-bedding in the Victorian age was child's play to knot-gardens laid out with growing plants. But the result at St Germain seems to have been so successful as eventually to drive out the curious device of coloured earths.

But we must not loiter overlong outside the home of the dauphin and the big and complicated household in which he grew up. This, as we have seen, was established in the old castle, the new one being reserved for the use of the king and queen when they stayed at St Germain for the sake of the children and the hunting. The old castle has suffered many vicissitudes in its three hundred and seventy years of life. It amply served the needs of François I and was even big enough for his son, Henri II, and his large family; nearly all Henri IV's children were brought up there with as much space to house them as anyone asked for in those days; but for Louis XIV it was too cramped. It is true that Henri IV and Louis XIII had the new *château* to spread themselves and their court in, whereas by the time Louis XIV came to manhood much of the structure was scarcely safe to live in. So the fourteenth Louis added large wings on to each of the four corners of the solid old castle and considerably altered the exterior façade. The interior of the courtyard he happily did not touch and it remains to-day very much as when it was first built. Nor does the whole building greatly differ from its original plan. Perhaps only the French nation can so laboriously restore old buildings, spending long years of minute effort in the preservation of their noble monuments; the work on St Germain-en-Laye, begun in 1862, was not completed until 1907. Louis XIV's additions were swept away, the chapel, threatened with collapse, was rebuilt stone by stone and, thanks to these years of labour, we can now find our way about with some degree of certainty as to the arrangements of the rooms as they existed three hundred years ago.

We know, for instance, which was the king's room given over for the dauphin's use; the balcony where stood his aviary; the big hearth by which Marguerite Hotman sat dandling him on her knee when, at three months old, he so grieved her by his "no"; the small room close by where Nurse Dondon lived; the turret-room and the stair in the wall leading to Dr Jean Héroard's study where the picture-books were kept and the journal was written; these we can all identify. The windows of the dauphin's room faced both north and east, looking north across the garden of the old castle into the depths of the forest and east across the small park and bowling-green to the new castle and the wide view of the Seine. The south side of the quadrangle had always been set aside for the use of the royal children, François' children, Henri II's children, and more recently the children of Gabrielle d'Estrée, Duchesse de Beaufort. There are a number of small rooms in this part of the castle, but even so it must have been difficult to find room for every one. Henri IV's notion of a family was oriental and it mattered little to him that his children had different mothers. So far as affection went he was fond of them all and liked to see them all together when he rode out from Paris to St Germain to visit them, but there was always an unforgettable gap between the queen's children and his mistresses'. Probably the dead Gabrielle's children lay nearest the king's heart though he delighted in the wit inherited from Mme de Verneuil by her little son and daughter. But for the dauphin his feeling was not only a father's love; a dauphin was something apart, infinitely precious, a guarantee for his dynasty, for France, for the peace and prosperity which only an undisputed succession could procure.

The queen's children were six in number, all of whom were brought to St Germain in their earliest infancy: Louis, the dauphin, Elizabeth, Christienne, Orléans, Gaston and Henriette Marie, whom we know as Henrietta Maria, Charles I's queen. The second son died at four years old unnamed and so was never anything but the *Duc d'Orléans*. Gabrielle's three children had lived at St Germain for some years before their father's marriage. Henri could not make her eldest son, Cæsar, dauphin but he gave him his most valuable Bourbon possession, the Duchy of Vendôme, and since he and his brother and sister could not be *enfants de France* they were all three known by the name of Vendôme. Little Alexandre we have already met at Fontainebleau, Cæsar and Catherine were at St Germain when the baby dauphin first came there. But the list of the king's children does not end here. Henriette de Balzac d'Entragues succeeded Gabrielle as the king's mistress and was known as the Marquise de Verneuil. Her son, Henri, was born just a month after the dauphin's birth, and her daughter, Gabrielle, came between the queen's children, Elizabeth and Christienne. The Verneuil children were presently added to the family group, but " le petit Moret," Jacqueline de Buel's son, whom the dauphin scornfully refused to recognize as a brother, never lived with the others, nor did the two daughters of Mme des Essarts. The king legitimized them all three but his liking for their mothers was mere caprice, or perhaps a consolation during one of his frequent quarrels with Mme de Verneuil.

These children of the king did not, however, include all the children who crowded the old castle in the early years of the seventeenth century. Quite a number of the great nobles sent their sons to be brought up with the dauphin and learn all the things necessary to a gentleman's education, much as a boy might to-day be sent to a great English public school. We find, too, other children, sons and daughters of the various nurses attached to the royal babies, of Mme de Monglat, the *gouvernante*, of ladies in employment about the children whose husbands also belonged to the castle staff. Little nobles, foster brothers and sisters, children of the castle staff all grew up and played together, for manners were easy and the royal rooms very accessible. Undoubtedly it was a very complicated household over which Monsieur and Madame de Monglat held sway, she as *gouvernante* to the children and he as *intendant* of the old castle. It is not easy to reconstruct such a household, it was so vast, complicated and, to our modern notions, so uncomfortable because so crowded. Although there was a large *basse-cour*, now entirely vanished, without the castle itself with buildings devoted to domestic and garrison purposes, yet the interior quadrangle was not free from matters we might well suppose would have been banished without the walls. Just within the entrance stood the smithy, nearby stables, storage rooms, the guardroom, kitchens for the private household, and various offices, such as a shed for plucking poultry, and very rudimentary sanitary accommodation. In the entresol was housed the armoury and the " king's wardrobe " and the wardrobe officials in charge of his stores and his accounts. Maybe there was also accommodation for inferior servants. The first floor was reserved for the king and his family and such of their personal attendants as there was room for. On this floor too was the great hall where many a famous ballet had been danced when Catherine de Medici lived at St Germain as dauphine and as queen. Many of these rooms are now filled with the Musée Archéologique, and the chilly relics of prehistoric man assort ill with the grace and gorgeous frivolity of ghostly ballets and court festivities. The dauphin's own room houses Roman glass whose beauty is in better accord though the orderly

ranks of glass-cases are disturbing to the imagination
which strives to conjure back the crowded noisy nursery.

A modern person, unacquainted with old houses,
would be struck by the absence of passages in the
castle. Every room opens from another; nowhere is
there any privacy; a screen, a curtained bed, a portion
of a room reserved for special use by a balustrade or
dais, an ingle nook, these were all that the age could
give or indeed all that it desired. The old castle of
St Germain is in no way peculiar in this respect and
kings, perhaps less than all others, had little privacy
in their lives. Héroard, as we may infer from his
journal, could sit in solitude in his study but the life
of every one else he writes about seems to have always
been lived in a crowd. The dauphin's own personal
attendants were marvellously numerous for one small
boy; his *gouvernante*, his doctor, his foster mother and
his dresser, several ladies of his chamber and several
more women of lower rank ; his usher, his cradle
rocker and his two musicians to play him to sleep,
Indret on the lute and Boileau on the viol; these we
know of, most of them by name, on Héroard's authority.
But fresh people come and go through his pages,
servants of the dauphin's servants, captains and soldiers
of the guard, visitors of every sort from the Pope's
nuncio to a woman peddling cosmetics or a gipsy
flageolet-player. The king and the queen came
frequently to the new castle, the queen riding in her
coach and often accompanied by the king's mistress,
Mme de Verneuil. What more natural since each
lady wished to visit her own son. And now and then,
most important visitor of all, the great Duc de Sully
came riding, sending a twitter through the whole
household in hope of largesse from the superb keeper
of the king's treasure.

But it is time to turn back to the autumn of 1601 and bring the baby to his home above the Seine. On the 25th October the month-old dauphin left Fontainebleau for St Germain-en-Laye. The account of the journey is an amusing contrast to Louise Boursier's description of the queen's journey to Fontainebleau in the previous August. The baby and his *gouvernante* travelled in the queen's litter. L'Estoile, the Parisian diarist, says the child lay in the magnificent cradle sent from Florence by his great-aunt, the Duchess. It would certainly have been regal but it would have left scant room for Mme de Monglat. Héroard, on the other hand, says he was placed in a wicker basket, woven on purpose to carry him, and Héroard was himself in close attendance throughout the anxious journey. The doctor gives a fine description of what was in reality a triumphant progress, highly gratifying to all concerned except the slumbering object of it. " He left at two o'clock and slept as far as Melun. On reaching Melun at five o'clock the lieutenant-general and six town councillors met him with offers of service; the four *échevins*, bearing a canopy of white taffetas, did likewise and then, placing Monseigneur under the canopy, conducted him into the town to the house of M. le Grange." This was the same house which Louise says was so ill-prepared for the queen's reception, and where the rolling of the great log out of the fire nearly brought on a catastrophe. The curious familiarity in which the royal family lived with their subjects before the days of Louis XIV is shown on this journey; perhaps it excuses, as it must surely have influenced, the growth of the oppressive etiquette of the later French courts. While the baby was being re-swaddled, a ceremony constantly watched by a crowd of visitors of all ranks and sorts, " a woman of very middling quality among the crowd standing around, flung herself on her knees, quite overcome by her feelings. 'Heavens, would there be any harm in just kissing him,' she said, and she would have done it too had not I, Dr Héroard, held her back."

After a second night spent on the way the child reached the outskirts of Paris. Here all the high city officials, "dressed in their robes of state and accompanied by the city archers, met him a thousand paces outside the city gate. When they reached the litter they dismounted and the *prévôt des marchands* addressed Mme de Monglat as she sat in the litter holding the sleeping dauphin in her arms. The conversation between them lasted half an hour and then the procession started again. Monsieur de Monglat walked on one side of the litter and I on the other, the archers supporting us, to keep off the vast crowd of all ages and both sexes, on foot, on horseback and in coaches from storming the litter in their ardent desire to see the dauphin. At the *Porte St Antoine* he was received with the sound of hautbois, trumpets and cornets from the bastion on the right. Thence he was taken to the house of Sieur Sabastien Zamet, where he was lodged in the king's room."

It seems at first sight odd that the child was not taken to the Louvre, but the truth is that the house of Zamet, the Italian financier, was far more comfortable than the king's palace. Zamet had brought his knowledge of luxury with him from his native country, where the art of furnishing was in advance of France. Moreover, his house in Paris was a permanent home, always ready not only for himself, but for the king and certain of the courtiers who used it sometimes as a lodging when they were passing through Paris, often as a rendezvous in their love-affairs. The stories about Zamet and his house were not reputable but the rooms were comfortable and the precious dauphin would be far safer there, in the room always kept for the king, than in the Louvre. During the long absence of the court at Fontainebleau it is probable that much of the most necessary furniture was still absent making its slow way back in the wake of the king and queen. It is not, therefore, really a matter of surprise that the rich Italian's house was frequently made use of. For immensely rich Zamet was. In his early manhood he had come to France, as many Italians did, to seek a fortune. He had been fortunate enough to secure a post in Henri III's wardrobe, where he had ample opportunity to utilise his Italian dexterity in business, both on his own behalf and on his master's. Contracts and purchases for the king's needs could easily be made to yield a profit to the clerk in charge; money so gained, in the hands of a clever Italian, could again be made to yield more money, and so little by little Zamet, who began life as a *valet de la garde robe* grew into a wealthy and important financier. When, at the end of the civil wars, Henri IV allowed himself to drift more and more deeply into the many entanglements of his love-affairs, Zamet was not only a useful agent in finance but also the King's complaisant minister of his pleasures. But this did not disqualify him from receiving the queen's son and housing him comfortably for two days. The child, however, was taken to the Louvre where all those who had not already seen him at Fontainebleau crowded to see him in Paris. The king exhibited him to an extent which annoyed Héroard, who thought the baby was better kept quietly with his women, but Henri's view was that a dauphin was *enfant de France*, everybody's child and that all had a right to see him.

At last, however, on the 27th October, Mme de Montglat and her precious charge once more set out in the queen's litter, for the last short stage of the journey. Héroard, after describing the white taffetas canopy at Melun, trumpets and crowds at the gate of Paris and courtiers thronging the Louvre, ends his story of the journey with the following remarks : " The rain began just after we got in. He was put into the queen's room, in the old castle, until his own could be prepared for him. The care taken of such a precious treasure was such that nothing whatever was found ready. It is to be presumed that the fault lies with those who have charge of such matters. The nurse was short of milk."

The journey, no doubt, with all its bustle had been a trying ordeal for the doctor, more so than to the baby who was too young, at any rate, to notice its surroundings. The rooms, whose unpreparedness Héroard clearly believed was due to dishonesty in the responsible officials, the dismal autumn weather, and finally the lack of sufficient nourishment for the infant deepened the general discomfort of settling into a new home. And so began the dauphin's childish years at St Germain-en-Laye.

CHAPTER III

BABY DAYS AT ST GERMAIN-EN-LAYE

WE have seen how large the number of children living in the old castle eventually became, and naturally the greater the number of children the more swollen was the number of people of all sorts to look after them. The castle was certainly a vast nursery, but this was complicated by the fact that it was also a court, with all the hierarchy and much of the ceremonial etiquette of court life. Nor was this any the less true because, as it seems to us, of the crowded discomfort in which every one lived. Large as the building was it is still a wonder how every one was housed; king's children, *enfants d'honneur*, children of those of the household who were married, whether of the *gouvernante*, of the ladies-in-waiting, of the nurses or of the chamber-women, and in addition the whole vast crowd of attendants of every rank and occupation. However, when the dauphin first arrived the problem of housing cannot have been acute, for only his two half-brothers and their sister were so far living at St Germain-en-Laye. No court ceremonial was observed for them nor any unusual number of attendants appointed to look after them. The elder boy, Cæsar, was indeed often absent in Paris with the King. For the dauphin, on the other hand, court life began when he was as yet a new-born infant.

One of the most strictly-observed ceremonies at the French court was the handing of the shirt at the rising and going to bed of a royal personage. The right to hand it belonged to the person of highest rank present, and since royal toilets were important court functions there was sure to be claimants for the honour. Sometimes, just as the person of highest rank had hold of the king's shirt or the queen's shift, someone of yet higher rank might come in. King or queen or dauphin might grow chilly with waiting but the ceremony must be begun over again. Héroard very frequently mentions who was present at the baby dauphin's dressing and undressing. The first occasion recorded was when he was a fortnight old. A little crowd had gathered as usual and the lady of highest rank among it was the king's sister, the Duchesse de Bar. Mme Catherine, as she was still often called after her marriage late in life, had kept to her huguenot faith in a court where it was the fashion to yield to the quiet pressure of the now catholic king. Henri had tricked his sister out of a marriage on which she had set her heart with her cousin, the Comte de Soissons, but he could neither threaten nor cajole her out of her protestantism. On this particular morning she was given the tiny shirt to hand to the dresser. "The dresser told her she must make the sign of the cross over it. 'Do it for me then for I don't know how,' said Mme Catherine, but she handed it all the same." No doubt the dresser crossed it herself for luck's sake, more especially as it was the first shirt the baby had worn above his swaddling-bands. Some of the later scenes Héroard describes over this handing of the shirt are amusing. "One day little Alexandre Monsieur, as the younger of Gabrielle's sons was then called, handed the shirt and as soon as ever it was on the dauphin flung out his hand to hit him. He cannot bear him." On another day Mlle de Vendôme, aged seven, and the eight-year-old Duc de Longueville "squabbled as to which should hand M. le Dauphin's shirt. His dresser asked him 'Which shall hand it Monsieur?' He replied in his baby language 'Mamanga.' M. de Longueville snatched it from Mlle de Vendôme, while little M. de Montmorenci handed one swaddling-band and M. de Longueville the other." Presumably Mlle de Vendôme had retired in dudgeon. She may have thought that the reigning king's acknowledged daughter was of higher rank than one whose claim to the blood royal came from the famous Dunois, the Bastard of Orléans. These subtle distinctions of rank were annoying even to a lady of seven years old.

So soon as the dauphin was old enough he was taught to wait on his father and mother as others waited on him. "He was carried to the queen's *lever*. He kissed the queen's shift and gave it to her. Was next taken to the Duchesse de Bar and did the same for her; chased Alexandre Monsieur and Mlle de Vendôme all round the table." It is clear that a baby wore a shirt as well as his swaddling-clothes, so that the latter must have left the shoulders and arms bare. The dauphin's shirt was changed night and morning but the swaddling-clothes much more frequently. It would seem to have been the proper thing to watch the *remueuse* re-dressing the infant prince, since Héroard records almost daily the presence of soldiers and statesmen, great churchmen, city magistrates, ambassadors from foreign lands and deputies from provincial *parlements*, as well as ladies of all degrees. Mayenne, the defeated leader of the League, looked on "but would not sit down or say a word"; Montmorenci, Constable of France, who had held Languedoc throughout the civil wars almost as an independent principality; Villeroi, secretary to three kings in succession; and

Rosny, later Duc de Sully, who so long as Henri IV lived, controlled almost undisputed the royal finances, all these and many others visited St Germain-en-Laye and watched the dresser swaddle the infant. It was not long before other little garments were added to the shirt though the child was certainly swaddled for the first nine months of its life. On 23rd December " a satin cap was put on him and sleeves of the same stuff," probably in honour of a visit from " the illustrious Monseigneur del Buffalo, bishop of Cammerino and nuncio in ordinary, accompanied by the most illustrious and reverend Monseigneur Barberino, clerk of the chamber of his Holiness the Pope."

Among the prints in the Pepys library in Magdalene College, there is a portrait of the dauphin in a cap and an embroidered jacket worn over swaddling-clothes, and a droll little picture it is. The first portrait Héroard mentions was drawn in chalk by the court painter, de Court, in the January following the nuncio's visit. There was a second taken in March of the same year when a Flemish painter " painted his portrait in oils and he behaved very prettily for two hours, which was as long as the painter wanted." Later in the same month the ambassador from Mantua brought " the painter du Quesnel with him to St Germain-en-Laye who painted the dauphin full length. He was two and a half feet tall." So the world did not lack for portraits of the child. It would appear, therefore, that a cap, a shirt and a jacket, over swaddling-clothes was the regular dress until the child was nine months old. Then, on a certain memorable day in June, " Champagne, the court shoemaker took his measure for a pair of shoes, which was a great event." A few days later " the Baron de Treslon brought Monseigneur's shoes home. At five o'clock he was dressed in a

HENRI IV, MARIE DE MEDICI, THE DAUPHIN AND CÆSAR DE VENDÔME

[face p. 48

boddice and a petticoat of silk and over these a frock of white satin striped with silver. Mlle de Vendôme handed the shirt. His clothes became him so well that he looked quite two years old." On 4th July his hair was "combed for the first time. He liked it and turned his head round as each side was done." It was "a bright chestnut and in length quite the width of three fingers," and his dark complexion which troubled his mother "was wonderfully cleared."

The discussion in detail of the dauphin's toilet belongs to a future chapter, for we have already wandered far enough from his first frock and pair of shoes. Soon after the arrival of the shoes a further important advance was made: leading-strings were attached to his clothing to teach him to walk. By the time he was a year old "he began to walk quite well held up by the arms." He was an active boy of three before these leading-strings were dispensed with and glad enough he must have been to be quit of them. The satin cap and silver-striped frock were not his only fineries, for in very early days a coral necklace was fastened round his neck, and a little turquoise ring put on his finger. Just before his first birthday a yet more manly advance was made. "At two o'clock the illustrious Marino Cavalli, the Venetian ambassador came within the balustrade by Mme de Montglat's permission. He bowed to the dauphin, kissed his hand, put his own hand to his lips and then put on his hat again. The dauphin wore his sword at his side and his hat on his head, which he banged in like a naughty boy. He beat loudly on his drum with both drum sticks. The ambassador kissed hands again and took his leave." Was it a hat of Tuscany straw or a hat of stiff felt with a feather such as his father wore, and was the sword such a one as Tom Thumb might have used? This sword must have been one which Mme de Guiche had sent him as a gift, she who had been famous as *la belle Corisande* twenty years before. She was no longer the pretty lady to whom Henri de Navarre wrote such charming love-letters. For many years past Gabrielle d'Estrées and later Henriette d'Entragues had had all the letters but none of them were so pretty as those early ones to Corisande. It was nice of her to send the sword. The mention of the child's hat and also of the ambassador putting his own hat on after kissing hands recalls a habit of the time much at variance with modern ways. Almost every one kept their heads covered in the house, men with their hats and women with caps and head-dresses besides the false hair they often still wore at the beginning of seventeenth century, although such fashions were already altering. Only in the presence of a person of superior rank or of a parent was it usual to take off a hat even in the house. In the king's presence, therefore, no hats were worn unless perchance with his express permission, and the same formality was observed for the dauphin. An ambassador, however, was the representative of his own sovereign and as such claimed to wear his hat. He uncovered to the dauphin as an act of courtesy, he resumed his hat in right of his high position. The child's hat may have been put on as a mark of ceremony for his little head was always close covered with his baby's cap. As the dauphin grew older he often got into trouble with his father for forgetting to take his hat off in the king's presence. It was natural forgetfulness, for unless he was with the king or queen he could always wear it if so minded.

The new shoes, the hat and the sword were all signs of progress, but none were of such importance as the cutting of the first tooth. Héroard wrote on "April 13th 1602. He waked at midnight, could not sleep. Mlle de Rumilly came to call me saying that Monseigneur the dauphin was troubled with teething. I came quickly. He hardly slept at all before five o'clock. I stayed with him, leaning over his cradle and holding his right hand in mine. April 15th. The dresser put her finger into his mouth and found a tooth. M. Guérin, his apothecary set out at once for Fontainebleau to carry the news to the king." Henri was fully alive to the greatness of the event and wrote back in answer to Mme de Montglat's letter.

"Madame de Montglat. You could not have sent me any more delightful news than the continued good health of my son, of which you inform me by the hand of M. Guérin, as well as of the cutting of his first tooth. I beg you to take every possible care of him. God be with you Madame de Montglat, written this 16th day of April at Fontainebleau. Henry." In his signature the King always spelt his name with a y and not in the modern French manner. No more is said about teething so we may hope that this stage of babyhood was got through easily. Happily the dauphin escaped the troubles the older children at St Germain were enduring. On 6th March, a few weeks before the cutting of the first tooth, "Alexandre Monsieur and Mlle de Vendôme sickened with smallpox. The dauphin was moved to the new castle by the King's command." The same precaution was taken when Cæsar and the unlucky little Alexandre not long after started measles. Whatever the king's faults, and they were many, there was no lack of affection on his part for all his children, and his letters to Mme de Montglat show how constantly he interested himself in their well-being. Among such a family, for the arrival of more than one little noble and the birth of various children among the attendants quickly swelled the number of children in the castle, the outbreak of infectious illnesses was inevitable from time to time. In 1602 after smallpox in March and measles in August, there was a second outbreak of smallpox in November. On hearing of this the king wrote to Mme de Montglat, " You did quite right to send my son to the new castle so soon as you heard the little Frontenac had smallpox. Do the same with my son Alexandre and my daughter Vendôme, both of whom I recommend to your care. I beg you to send news of my son frequently."

The king not only wrote about his children; he came often to visit them and few scenes described by Héroard are more vivid than these visits. Even in the first year of the dauphin's life they have a keen interest in the glimpses they give of the ways of the royal nursery. We read on " Jan. 12th 1602 the dauphin was taken into Mme de Montglat's room while his own room and his cradle were aired and perfumed with juniper wood. The king's *maître d'hôtel* arrived, expecting to find the king already come from Verneuil, whither he had gone to visit the Marquise de Verneuil and her baby. In the meantime the queen reached the castle. She stood a long time waiting for the king and warming herself in company with Mme de Guercheville, her lady-in-waiting, and Mme de Montglat. The king arrived half an hour late and the queen met him at the door, pouting. They went together to look at the dauphin in his cradle. The king held his feet looking at them intently." Héroard had noticed at the child's birth that his feet were shaped like his father's, " broad, with small heels and toes of almost equal length."

We need not wonder at the queen's pouts. Half an hour's wait for such a cause excuses a little jealousy and annoyance. Mme de Verneuil frequently came herself to visit the dauphin. Héroard writes in the previous December, " the Marquise de Verneuil came to see him. He stared up at her and laughed. She said she was happy in the honour he did her. He always laughs whenever she talks to him." And no doubt Henriette d'Entragues had a taking way with her. Another very early picture of Henri and his baby son makes amusing reading. " June 22nd 1602. The king came at half past ten, played with him and watched him taking his broth. His majesty drank what was left over, saying, ' If anyone asks what the king is doing you can say he is supping his broth.' He made the dauphin take hold of his beard. The dauphin pulled hard so the king made him seize M. de Martigny's beard instead. He took hold of it with both hands and raised himself quite up so that he could pull harder. Then he seized M. le Grand's moustache. Mme de Verneuil came at one o'clock, fondled the dauphin but it was noticed that she did it with little heart."

The political history of the early years of the seventeenth century is not our concern, but unless we recall some of the events taking place in the big world outside the walls of the old castle we shall miss much of the interest and some of the poignancy of Héroard's journal. For instance when we read that Mme de Verneuil showed " little heart " in the caresses she gave the dauphin, or that when M. le Comte d'Auvergne came to the castle " he stayed but a short half hour, leaning on the balustrade, his face half covered with his cloak, standing on one foot and talking with Mme de Montglat in a rambling and disjointed way," we are really catching a glimpse of a conspiracy against the legitimacy of the dauphin. The Comte d'Auvergne and Mme de Verneuil were brother and sister through their mother, Marie Touchet. Marie had been the mistress of Charles IX and Auvergne was their son. After Charles' death Marie married François de Balzac, Sieur d'Entragues, and by this marriage was mother of Henriette. Henriette's father was quite willing for his daughter to take the place of the dead Gabrielle, but not without driving a bargain with the king. In return for Mlle d'Entragues' compliancy, Henri gave her a written promise of marriage, but only on the condition that their first child should be a son. It is very doubtful whether a conditional promise could be pleaded as a valid contract of marriage, but, be that as it may, and I am not learned enough to hazard an opinion, Henriette's first child, though a boy, was still-born. The king, even if he had had the smallest intention of fulfilling his promise, certainly told her that he held himself free in consequence, and soon after he married Marie de Medici. But the promise remained in the hands of the Sieur d'Entragues, who on his part claimed that the fact that the baby was still-born did not free the king, and when soon after the birth of the dauphin Henriette's second son was born, all sorts of ambitious schemes were centred round the Verneuil baby.

The claims of the d'Entragues family made a rallying point for other ambitious or discontented schemers. The kingdom was but barely pacified after the long civil war; not all the catholic nobles thought themselves sufficiently rewarded for their services or their submission, as the case might be; not all the huguenots accepted the Edict of Nantes as a complete guarantee of their safety. On the eastern border the Duke of

Savoy was still sore at his defeat in his recent war against Henri, and on the northern Turenne, not content with the duchy of Bouillon, was, like the Duke of Savoy, not only incessantly restless himself but was also a rallying point for the restlessness of others. Out of all these elements of discontent a conspiracy arose of which the king's old comrade-in-arms, the Maréchal Biron, and the king's mistress, Henriette d'Entragues, were the most conspicuous centres. But though the conspiracy seemed to be aiming at a common end there can have been very little really in common between the various parties involved. It is impossible to believe that Biron, although ready to risk fresh civil war for his own advancement, could ever have brought himself to accept Henriette's baby as the legitimate dauphin in the place of Marie de Medici's, and yet such was undoubtedly the wild scheme of Henriette, her father and her half-brother, the Comte d'Auvergne. The king felt Biron's defection very bitterly, but he was not vindictive and would willingly have given him a chance of repentance. In the spring of 1602 Biron wrote a long letter to Mme de Montglat, which must surely have given the king a reasonable hope that the conspiracy, of which he already had some knowledge, would prove no more than an outburst of petulant discontent. This long letter brings Biron and the dauphin into momentary connection and has for us an interest on that account. It was written on the 24th April 1602. After expressing his ardent wish for news of the child he begs Mme de Montglat " to send me word and do me the honour and favour, and lay me under the very great obligation to you by giving yourself the trouble of informing me of his good health, my love for him filling me with longing for his happy growth, believing

with others, that God has given him for the maintenance
of this kingdom; for he cannot fail to be endowed
with the great-heartedness, the courage and the good
fortune of the king, his father and my master, to whom
God has given these gifts in greater measure than to
any other king who ever lived. For my part, Madame,
I picture him as the handsomest and most sweet prince
that ever has been or can be, to whom all my affection
turns. . . . I should grieve if death took me before
I could give proof of my ardent zeal in his service,
which I have vowed as the very humble and very
obedient servant of the king his father."

In spite of these fair words, not we may believe
wholly insincere for Biron's disloyalty wavered through
many phases of intensity, the conspiracy went on. In
June, Henri, reluctant up to the last minute, had
both Biron and Auvergne arrested and sent to the
Bastille. There are few more dramatic scenes in the
curious memoirs of the Duc de Sully, known as *Les
Ecconomies Royales*, than the arrest of Biron. Not all
of *Les Ecconomies* can be accepted as exact truth for,
in spite of their enormous length, they are too much of
a political pamphlet, to be wholly reliable; but for
those who have courage to endure their almost un-
endurable style they will be found to yield scenes
of extraordinary dramatic vividness. Among these
is the tragic story of Biron. He was tried by the
Parlement of Paris and condemned to death. The
Sieur d'Entragues and his stepson escaped with a
short term of imprisonment. Many of Henri's best
friends hoped that the king's infatuation for Mme de
Verneuil would be cured, but the lady was too witty,
too refreshing a contrast to the queen for him to give
her up. There were reproaches, coolnesses, but in
the end she wheedled herself back into favour and her

father and brother out of the Bastille. She did not even surrender the promise of marriage, and it was only after a fresh endeavour three years later to use it as a valid contract that the king recovered it as a condition of a fresh pardon. Biron, refusing to believe even on the very scaffold that the king would really let him die, was beheaded in the courtyard of the Bastille. Héroard's last direct reference to these events of the summer is found at the end of a little scene of childish fun. " July 31st. The dauphin was carried to see the king who was abed with a hurt from a fall while hunting. The dauphin had hold of a stick, I pulled a twig from a faggot and hit his stick as if we were fencing together. The game delighted him and he came after me all round the room. Very merry and good tempered all day. At five o'clock the Maréchal Biron's head was cut off in the Bastille." It is not surprising that during this troubled summer Mme de Verneuil should " show little heart " to the child she longed to transplant with her own son, or that Auvergne " talked confusedly to Mme de Montglat."

Besides statesmen, ambassadors and soldiers of fame there were many other visitors to St Germain-en-Laye and it is amusing to see how diverse they were. In December 1601 a lady from " the Agenois, who came to see the dauphin, asked to be allowed to hold him, so that she might boast of it afterwards, and she put down her muff to take him. The nurse drew back, saying she must ask permission of Mme de Montglat, who told her no one was allowed to hold him." There is a pretty picture of an old man of eighty who came " wearing a gown," as old men did in those days. " He knelt down and wept, watched the dauphin being swaddled and then turning to

Mme de Montglat said, ' May it please God to give
Monseigneur the good luck of his father, the valour of
Charlemagne and the piety of St Louis.' As he left
he raised his eyes to heaven saying, ' May God call
me when he will for I have seen the salvation of the
world.' " The old man used exaggerated words,
which, in our knowledge of the baby's melancholy
manhood, seem pitiful as well as exaggerated. The
truth is that after so many years of war a settled
succession to the throne did indeed seem a salvation,
and it was not only old men who wept for joy at the
sight of the dauphin. One day the child " was taken
to the window to show him to a great crowd gathered
to see him. Most knelt down and many had tears in
their eyes."

There were, however, visitors of a more merry
humour. Some of them seem a little odd as visitors
in a royal nursery. One day " an old pedlar of toilette
necessities and trinkets of all sorts came out from
Paris to see the dauphin. She cried at sight of him,
called him ' the little image of his mother ' and then
began to dance to him." Perhaps she got in because
of the paints and powders she had in her pack to
tempt the dauphin's women with, but, as we have
already seen access was not difficult. Dancing to amuse
the child was often done by women of the poor classes;
Héroard tells of one " who kicked up her heels so
high as to show her bare thighs," which made the
dauphin laugh loudly.

But although entrance to the dauphin's room was
easy, no one could really approach near to him without
permission, rarely given. More than once we have
come across the mention of a balustrade in the passages
quoted from Héroard's journal. This balustrade
divided the room into two portions; a quite usual

arrangement in the houses of people of high rank. The portion near the hearth was kept strictly for the use of the dauphin and those whose immediate attendance on him gave them the right of entry; here stood his cradle, later on his own little chair, a table for his meals, chairs for the king and queen, a stool for his nurse and such things as were wanted for his own use. The other portion of the room was more or less public. Now and then Héroard specially records that a visitor was allowed within the balustrade and sometimes we can infer that such was the case. We cannot, for instance, believe that Mme de Montglat made any difficulty over admitting the deputies from Dauphiné who came to do homage to the baby in his cradle, considering how lively a sense of gratification their visit must have left behind. For the child the afternoon must have been trying. " Oct. 12th 1602. The dauphin was asleep in his cradle at half past two when the king came in, woke him up, kissed him and left for Paris. At three o'clock he was just dropping off to sleep again when the queen woke him, and then she too went off. As he was settling off for the third time the Comte de Soissons arrived, bringing with him the *deputés generaux* from Dauphiné to do him homage. They all knelt down except the Archbishop of Vienne, who was spokesman. The dauphin was still in his cradle. He stretched out his hand to be kissed." Which makes it clear that the deputies were allowed within the balustrade. " The said deputies gave Mme de Montglat a service of silver worth three hundred *écus* ; Mlle Rolant a basin and ewer of silver worth about a hundred *écus*, a gold chain weighing eighty-four *écus* to the nurse, another weighing fifty to the dresser, and pieces of gold and silver money, struck to commemorate the dauphin's birth, to various people in the castle and to the officers of Mme de Montglat's household." Héroard makes frequent allusion to the *gouvernante's* love of money and this handsome behaviour of the deputies must have made a very pleasing impression. She would, however, have been equally gracious to the Spanish ambassador, in recognition of his high position, even though he left no gifts behind him after his visit to St Germain-en-Laye. Don Hieromino Taxis came out from Paris because " he could not leave France without seeing the dauphin. M. de Sancy, who was with him, said they must make a match of it with the baby infanta of Spain, and the ambassador replied ' that there was nothing improbable in the scheme, and as the queen of France was pregnant and so was his queen, if we had a girl and they a boy they might marry the four of them together.' "

Fourteen years later the double marriage did indeed take place, bringing but little happiness to the four unlucky children; but this event lies outside our scope. What does concern us is the birth of the expected baby, little Madame, the queen's eldest daughter. To judge by a letter from the king to Mme de Montglat the mother was but little pleased; no fuss for a girl, no cannon or fireworks or couriers ready to start at a moment's notice; nor such glory for the queen as the birth of a miraculous dauphin had been. Henri was better pleased than his wife to judge by his own words. " My wife," he wrote to Mme de Montglat, " was brought to bed yesterday according to God's will. She is more vexed than I, who do my best to console her. I wish you good day Mme de Montglat. The 23rd Nov. at Fontainebleau."

It is curious how frequently people need consolation for events which happen by God's will, but Henri,

fortunately, was charmingly philosophic over the birth
of his daughter. He told her mother, when she cried
because the baby was not a son that " if she herself
had not been a girl she could never have been queen
of France," and in the public letter published throughout the kingdom he ordered rejoicings to welcome the
baby " even if, so far as we can judge, it is not so
advantageous as if she had been a boy." So little
Madame was made welcome, up to a point. In 1606
the queen's third child was born. " Mlle de Ventelet
told the dauphin that his mother had been brought to
bed. 'Have the cannon been fired?' he asked. 'No,
Monsieur.' 'Oh! then it's a girl.'" Thirteen months
later the queen was again expecting her lying-in.
" While the dauphin was being put to bed he said if
the queen gave him a little brother he should have
his cannon fired, but if it was a sister 'I shan't bother
about her.'" This fourth baby was a boy, but a
delicate little fellow who died when he was four, and
the fifth child, Gaston, grew up to be in perpetual
disagreement with his elder brother, so that after all
Henri may have been right in his estimation of girls.

Still, in spite of the dauphin's scorn, a sister of his
very own was better than nothing. On the 30th
December 1602 " at a quarter past five the dauphin
was hurriedly taken to meet Madame who arrived at
St Germain-en-Laye in charge of Mlle Rolant, M. de
Montglat and M. de Villeserin, the queen's equerry.
Monseigneur came down by the little stair next to
Madame's room and met Madame at the door as she
was being taken out of the litter in the arms of M. de
Villeserin. He was pleased to see her for he had been
told it was his sister. On the following day Madame
was brought into his room. He kissed her gently."
Madame, who like her brother was nameless till their

public baptism in 1606, lived in the south side of the castle in the rooms always set apart for the children of the royal family; to reach her brother she would have passed through Mme de Montglat's other rooms on the eastern side. On this last day of the year the king and queen came out from Paris to see the two children, and found Dr Héroard busy with the baby. In the evening he tells us the dauphin was taken to the king's room where the king was at supper, presumably in the new castle, though it seems a late hour for the child to be out in mid-winter. " The king gave him some jelly, which he liked very much, and some wine."

And so ended the year 1602.

CHAPTER IV

HÉROARD'S *Journal* for 1603, so far as it has been printed by its learned editors, is not very full. Still we can gain from it much curious knowledge. Perhaps it's most outstanding feature, in comparison with modern life, is the extraordinary lack of decency it depicts in the habits and language of the royal nursery. Even Héroard himself, who often appears to be distinctly superior in character to others surrounding the dauphin, allowed gross and injurious habits to be indulged in unchecked. It is a mistake to transpose a standard of decency, or even of modesty, from one age or from one country to another but it is nevertheless impossible not to feel that the household at St Germain-en-Laye was unusually lacking in a sense of both. The dauphin as he grew older, with a fastidiousness which seems to have been inherent in him, protested against the language used before him. "*Fi donc,* how nasty she is," he would say of his *gouvernante* when she was more than usually coarse; and he would forbid the singing of the ribald songs his father loved. One of the curious habits of the nursery was to let the little boy get into the bed of one or other of his women and their husbands, and the play and the language on these occasions are so incredibly gross that not only they cannot be translated, but even Héroard, hardened to the ways of those about him, notes his disapprobation on the margin of his journal. When we remember that " a naked bed " was the literal truth in those days it is not difficult to believe in the worthy doctor's anger. The king, too, when he returned from hunting would send for the dauphin and little Madame and have them undressed and put into bed with him, " where they gambolled about freely." Language used to the children was on a level with the habits allowed them. Before the dauphin could speak, coarse jokes about the baby Spanish princess were constantly made before him and the same lack of decency was noticeable in the language used about the king's mistresses and their children. Nothing was concealed and the only curious thing is the dauphin's attitude towards these " bastards " as he frankly called them, as soon as he was old enough to understand the meaning of the word. It is anticipating our story by several years to give, at this point, instances of this attitude, but as it grew naturally out of his earliest experiences, it may not be amiss to do so. Someone said to the dauphin that Cæsar and Alexandre Vendôme were his brothers. " ' Oh yes, but a different breed of dogs.' ' And M. de Verneuil? ' ' Oh! a different breed again. He's his mother's. I am of quite another breed, and my brother Orleans and my brother Anjou and my sisters.' ' Which is the best breed, Monsieur? ' ' Mine, and then féfé Vendôme's and féfé Chevalier's, and then féfé Verneuil's and as for that little Moret, he's lower than dirt.' " A year later Mme des Essars, a new mistress of the king's, was the subject of conversation before the children. " ' Monsieur, Mme des Essars has a daughter and you have another soeu-soeu.' ' No! ' he said. ' Why not, Monsieur? ' ' She was not born of mamma.' ' Monsieur, your papa will have her brought here to be baptized and you are to be godfather.' ' How will they bring her.' ' They will borrow a litter to bring her in.' 'Oh well! if it's mamma's litter,' said he, laughing and nodding his head, 'I shall mount the mules and I shall make them run so fast, so fast that it will all get upset.' M. Birat said to him, 'Monsieur, she is a lady whom the king loves.' 'She is a light o' love and *I* don't love her.'" Such talk was a common occurrence among the children and it was the natural sequence to the early habits in which they were encouraged and the language of those with whom they lived. It is not, however, our purpose to dwell overmuch on this side of the nursery life although it is necessary to keep it in mind if any true mental picture is to be acquired.

Happily, Héroard has many other things to tell us in the first early years, things in themselves trivial enough but giving an insight into bygone days by reason of their very triviality. We learn that in January 1603, "the dauphin chewed some duck, the first meat he had tasted; then ate some chicken and found both good." A little later a taste for sweet things was also developing. "The queen sent for the dauphin to sit at her table while she dined. He wanted some of the sweet, which was a tart made with plums. The queen bade me give him some." On another evening, "he went to the king's supper where he found the three Vendôme children seated at table. The king gave the dauphin some cherries while he put some marchpane on a plate for M. de Vendôme, his brother and his sister. They shared it between them without giving the dauphin any. He put his hand boldly into the dish and took a piece, ate half and did not want the rest." Perhaps it was as well for the sweet almond paste might have disagreed with such a little fellow. Although the child had a taste of chicken in January he was not finally weaned till the following September after he had completed his second year. No doubt he had had a variety of food before this date; certainly in October we are told that "at half-past eleven whilst the dauphin was eating the wing of a chicken the Spanish ambassador came to visit him. Mme de Montglat wiped his hand and he held it out to be kissed. He asked for something to drink and drank to the Infanta's health."

New experiences followed one on the other throughout the year. He learnt to hand the king his wine at dinner and the queen her napkin, as his earliest courtly duties at meals. He "was made to say over different syllables so as to teach him whole words," and just before his second birthday "he began to speak in sentences." Such an advance made it possible to teach him his first daily prayer, which he repeated after the *Pater* and *Ave*, these we imagine said for him by Mme de Montglat at this early age. "God give long life to papa and mamma, to the dauphin and to my sister and my aunt. Give me His grace and His blessing, make me a good man and keep me from all my enemies, seen and unseen." Daily prayers, however, did not keep the little boy from being exceedingly naughty, and we come across an unpleasant new experience in his little life in October 1603. "Waked at eight o'clock; was naughty; whipped for the first time." We shall later come across a treatise on education written by Dr Héroard, sitting no doubt in his little study up the turret stair. One sentence only interests us at this moment, showing, as it does, a sympathy with children sadly lacking in every one else responsible for the upbringing of the king's children. "We ought," writes the wise doctor, "to lisp with little children, by which I mean we ought to accommodate ourselves to their weakness and teach them rather by the way of gentleness and patience than by harshness and hastiness for ' *Patience passe science.*' We should reward them by little gifts suitable to their right-doing and only punish them in such a way as will make them feel a little sense of shame at their naughtiness rather than by terrifying them with the fear of chastisement." Héroard might hold these enlightened views but they were shared by very few in those days. The king, certainly, was of a very different opinion. When the dauphin was six years old he wrote to Mme de Montglat: " I am vexed that you have not whipped my son. I command you to whip him every time that he is wilful or naughty, knowing by my own experience that nothing else did me so much good. At his age I was well whipt and I know I profitted. This is why I desire you to do the same to him and to make him understand this."

From the frequent mention of whippings from the age of two which occur in the journal the king's letter would appear superfluous. The dauphin had plenty of opportunity for profit, but whether he got any is more than doubtful. Partial as the doctor is he has to own that the dauphin was of a passionate temperament, and obstinate as well as passionate. Many a scene of ill-temper, wilfulness and sulkiness are described, and a few of such uncontrollable passions as to cause real disturbance to health. The method of punishment, apart from its frequency, was calculated to do real harm to the natural apprehensiveness of a child. While the dauphin, and no doubt the other children as well, was quite little a good slapping followed quickly on the fit of naughtiness, but as they grew older the punishments for any serious faults were generally deferred to the following morning. It seems a refinement of cruelty and Héroard quite frequently writes some such words as these : " The dauphin slept badly, dreamed, was afraid of being whipt in the morning." Or " waked up at eight o'clock, jumped out of bed in a great hurry and had the doors shut for fear Mme de Montglat would give him the stick for his naughtiness the day before. She came along and he ran to the door to stop her coming in. I begged her to let him off and then he opened the door." Even as late as 1611, when the child had been king for a year, we learn that " the king," a ten-year-old king, " waked at midnight in a fright because he expected to be whipt in the morning, because he had been obstinate in learning the reply he was to make to the deputies of the reformed religion sitting at Saumur. His valet assured him that M. de Souvré had forgotten all about it. ' Are you quite sure? ' ' Yes, Sire,' whereupon he went to sleep again and slept till nine o'clock."

We have seen that the first whipping occurred in October 1603. The next actually described followed a stormy scene in January 1604. " The king came to see him and played with him. Something put the dauphin into so violent a passion that he nearly burst himself with screaming and everything was in such confusion that I had not the heart to watch what he did, except that he wanted to hit everything and screamed himself silly." Of course, such behaviour received its due meed of slaps. Playing with the king not infrequently ended in trouble, for Henri loved teasing his children and when they resented it could lose his own temper as quickly as the most passionate among them. An incident in 1604, just before the dauphin's third birthday, shows how alike father and son were in quickness of temper. " The king came to the dauphin's room and wanted to make him kiss him. The dauphin was cross and the king smacked him; he struggled and scratched his Majesty and pulled his beard. Mme de Montglat whipt him, five or six strokes. The king said, showing him the rod, ' Who is this for? ' The dauphin said in a passion, ' For you.' The king had to laugh. The fuss lasted quite three-quarters of an hour. The king went away and the dauphin said, ' I want Papa.' So the king came back and he kissed him." A year later Henri's quick temper caused what Héroard calls " a little tragedy." The scene arose out of the child's unwillingness to leave off playing with a favourite toy, a small drum which, by means of a spring, was played on by the tiny figure of a woman. It is a long story but it gives us an extraordinarily vivid picture of all the people concerned and is therefore worth quoting. " Got up in a bad temper; wouldn't have his frock put on. His nurse called out ' Monsieur Tabouret, here! Monsieur Tabouret, come and put on your frock.' He burst out laughing and let it be put on. Went quite good to see the king. He wanted to go down to the wardrobe room to get his little drum which a toy woman beat by a spring; it was one of his greatest pleasures so he went against his will to the king. The king said, ' Take off your hat.' He fumbled over taking it off so the king took it off for him and this made him cross. The king took away his drum too which made him crosser than ever. ' My hat, my drum, my drumsticks! ' To tease him the king put the hat on his own head. ' I want my hat! ' The king hit him over the head with the hat and he thereupon flew into a passion and the king with him. The king seized him by the wrists and held him up in the air with his little arms stretched out like a cross. ' Hé! you hurt me. Hé! my drum! Hé! my hat.' The queen gave him back his hat and

his drumsticks. It was quite a little tragedy. Mme
de Montglat carried him away bursting with passion.
He was taken to his nurse's room where he cried ever
so long, unable to stop. He wouldn't kiss Mme de
Montglat nor say he was sorry, not even when he felt
his frock pulled up. He was whipped but not on his
bare skin. He scratched Mme de Montglat's face
and kicked her. At last he got over it when his *goûter*
was spoken of. He had some toast as usual. His
nurse took him apart and when they were alone said,
' Monsieur, you have been very naughty; you must
not behave like that. You must do what Papa tells
you.' He sobbed out, ' Kill Mamanga, she is naughty.
I'll kill every one. I'll kill God.' ' Oh! no, Monsieur,'
said his nurse, ' You drink his blood every time you
drink wine.' He stopped sobbing. ' Do I drink the
blood of the good God?' ' Yes, Monsieur.' ' Then
I mustn't kill *Him*.' He grew quiet but still sobbed
at long intervals. At supper he had bread soup, ate
but little, complained and cried contrary to his wont,
leant back in his chair and put his hand to his forehead.
They put him to sleep and carried him to his room.
At a quarter to seven he woke up, slept and woke
several times, complained of his arm, could not lift
anything with it. At last he said, ' Maman Dondon,
put me to sleep.' She sang to him and he fell asleep
at half past ten. Next morning he woke early and
lay quiet, ' played with his little earthenware toys and
his little soldiers as he called his chess men. I said,
' Monsieur, who had no supper?' ' It was I. I didn't
feel well.' ' What hurt you?' ' My arm and my
head.' He had scratches on him. Got up a little
pale but merry. After dinner the king sent for him.
He looked taken aback and very unwilling to go.
' I don't want to go and see Papa.' They told him

Papa had a sweetmeat for him. He was taken half by force and made a fuss at going into the queen's room where the king was. He went in and ran straight up to the king who gave him some rose sweetmeat and kissed and hugged him."

After these anecdotes of the dauphin and his father it is pleasant to turn to others, and there were many, where they were the best of friends. Both the following belong to very early days. "The dauphin did not want Madame to dance to the king; was cross. So the king to pacify him said, 'Kiss me, my son and I won't ask her again.' They went to the gardens together where the dauphin turned on the fountain taps and wet the king." It must have been the grotto we have heard young Thomas Platter describe, where a fine spray came up from the floor and fell again like rain from the roof. Such fountains were thought the best of fun. Some thirty years earlier Montaigne describes more than one such fountain in Italy and every one's delight when the taps were turned on and some unwary guest was caught. One cannot believe Henri let himself be seriously wetted. The next scene shows how strong the child's love for his father was. "The king came into the long gallery at five o'clock. The dauphin ran up to him with his arms outstretched and quite pale with happiness, kissed and hugged him and went along with him to his closet, now holding one hand, now the other, quite silent while M. de Villeroi discussed matters of business with his Majesty. The king was delighted with him."

We have turned aside from the method of punishment used in the nursery for these two little pictures, nor need we say more here of the frequent slappings and canings all the children endured; the subject will turn up again when their lessons are described. But there were other methods of reducing a wilful child to submission, some of which show once more how mixed was, at times, the company in the royal rooms. "Dec. 2. 1604. Got up at half past eight. Wouldn't have his frock put on. Bruneau, the laundry man, threatened to put him into his bag and then into the copper. He was frightened, let himself be dressed and played with his nurse. When he was dressed he turned to the laundry man saying, ' I'm dressed now.'" On various occasions threats of a similar nature were used, now of one sort and now of another. Héroard does not comment on them nor suggest the same disapproval which he most certainly felt for whippings. Perhaps he may have thought such threatenings were a way of inducing " a little sense of shame for naughtiness " without the use of the rod. From all we have seen of the doctor we need feel no surprise at his charge's love for him, for among all those who crowded the dauphin's home he seems to have been by far the most *understanding* of the ways of a little child. He must have been very happy when he wrote the two following entries in his journal, one in May and the other in November 1603. In later years there were many similar ones showing the kindly doctor's pleasure in the child's affection. " I got back from Paris at a quarter past three. I greeted Monseigneur le Dauphin with ' God give you good day.' He pretended not to see me and began to run about hiding behind this thing and that, glancing at me with eyes full of happiness and then, laughing as he ran by me, held out his hand to be kissed. He behaves like this to those he loves." The second entry is a very pretty picture of a tiny boy. " Whilst he was being dressed

A DOLL IN LATE SIXTEENTH CENTURY DRESS

From L'Histoire des Jouets. H. R. d'Allemagne

someone said, 'Let's make haste, Monsieur, we are
going into the garden.' 'No, no, we are going up to
see M. Hé'ou'd in his room.' I came down just as
he spoke and he began to sob, saying he was sorry
I had come down and he wanted to come up to my
room to see me. So I went back to write a letter and
he cheered up. He was asked 'Which would you
rather do, Monsieur, go into the garden or up to see
M. Héroard.' 'Hé'ou'd, Hé'ou'd.' He can't yet
pronounce the letter r. He did me the honour to
come and found me writing in my study. He came in
so happily and took my hand." There were many
delightful visits to the doctor's study, where all sorts
of picture-books lived and where sympathy was always
to be found, and with his usual fond partiality, Héroard
says, " he never upsets anything and if he sees a thing
out of place he puts it straight." Some of the most
charming entries in the journal are copies of the letters
which the doctor helped the little boy to write to his
father and mother, and these may have been written
in the seclusion of the study away from the noisy
crowd below. The earliest letters were written by
Héroard holding the child's hand in his, and give the
baby pronunciation of the words. The letter r was
long a difficulty, just as the word *Monsieur* baffled the
dauphin for years. Here is a very early letter, one of
the prettiest of them all. " 27th June 1604. Papa
I now know how to w'ite but not yet how to wead.
Moucheu de 'Osni has sent me a man in armour and
a beautiful coach with my mistress the Infanta in it,
and a lovely doll to sissy. He has p'omised me a
fine bed to sleep in; I am not a baby any longer;
I was vewy hot in my cwaddle. I dwink to your
health, papa and mamma. My pen is so heavy I
cannot w'ite any more. I humbly kiss papa's

hand and my dear mamma's too and I am, papa, your vewy humble and vewy obedient servant DAUPHIN."

The ending is a quaint contrast to the rest.

But if the doctor and Dondon, the nurse, were the most constantly kind there was no want of merry society, no lack of people ready to play with the dauphin. Ready, too, to play with each other, for grown-up folk could play puss in the corner and blind-man's-buff quite naturally, or indulge in romps not always too seemly. We catch curious glimpses of such games in which the pages and the chamber-women, the king's children and the serving people's children all took part. One such romp between M. de Montglat, *intendant* of the castle, and Mlle de Mercier, a married woman attached to the dauphin, is described by Héroard very fully. " 27th Jan. 1604. The dauphin ran after Mlle Mercier, who was shrieking because M. de Montglat tried to spank her. She shrieked and the dauphin shrieked too. She ran behind the bed and M. de Montglat after her, spanking her all the time. This made her shriek louder and so did the dauphin, jumping about, turning this way and that, pointing at her and beside himself with fun. . . . Played till nine o'clock in the evening, very merry, pretending to fire at us but especially at Mlle de Mercier, laughing whenever he saw her and trying to whip her with a twig. Mlle de Belier said, ' Monsieur, what did M. de Montglat do to Mlle de Mercier?' He began to smack his hands together with a sweet smile. He got so excited that he was quite beside himself, laughing and clapping his hands as if he understood the joke."

Nine o'clock seems a late hour for a child a little over two years old to be up, but hours at St Germain-en-Laye were strangely irregular. Perhaps the same theory was held as made a contemporary Englishman write: " I would not that you should observe a certaine houre either for dinners or suppers, lest the daily custome should be altered into nature; and after this intermission of this custome of nature hurt may follow; for custome doth imitate nature and that which is accustomable the very same thing is now become naturall." Nowadays we aim at this very thing, and make the formation of regular habits the first lesson to be taught in the nursery. Héroard, himself, had a sense of the value of fixed hours and emphasized their use in his treatise on education, but no one else attached any importance to regularity neither for getting up nor going to bed, neither for meals nor lessons nor play. Some hours were more common than others for the small events of daily life; for instance, seven o'clock was a common hour for the dauphin to wake, though he was often not dressed till much later so long as he was a baby; as he passed out of babyhood he was generally dressed by seven. Later still when he was a boy-king five was quite a usual time and if he slept much after this hour he would sometimes cry and say, " People will say I am a sluggard. You mustn't let me sleep so late." Other little boys were expected to be in school by six and so he may have thought that at least he ought to be up and dressed. But while he lived at St Germain-en-Laye he was troubled by no such scruples. For instance, a few days after the great romp between the *intendant* and Mlle de Mercier he did not wake till a quarter to ten when, writes Héroard: " He got up very merry and laughing and good tempered. Don Garcia and the Sieur Conchino arrived as he was being dressed. He was playing with a toy coach in which were four dolls; one was the queen, the others Mme and Mlle de Guise and Mme de Guercheville. His visitors made him point them out and name them. The Sieur de Conchino asked where his wife's place was. He said ' Ugh,' and pointed to a shelf at the back of the coach. He refused a fennel comfit which Mme de Montglat gave to the Sieur Conchino to pass on to him. He drew back and looked quite affronted." We meet with Concini in the journal now and then and almost always with some expression of dislike on the part of the dauphin; the dislike, indeed, grew to such a passion of hatred as the boy grew older that years later Concini was assassinated on the drawbridge of the Louvre with the young king's consenting knowledge. The whole story does not concern us but some slight acquaintance with Concini and the lady whose proper place was on the shelf of the toy coach, makes the story of the dauphin more interesting. It is, of course, a very well-known tale and only needs recalling to mind in its main features. Concini, or as he was called in France the Sieur Conchino, came to France from Florence as a member of the newly-wedded queen's suite. Marie was not fortunate in the Italians she brought with her. Perhaps queens never are, perhaps they never could be fortunate in those who accompany them to the country of their adoption. A foreigner in an often critical and even hostile court, she has a difficult position to fill. Her new country wishes her adoption to be as quick and as complete as possible, whereas the queen, a newly-wedded stranger, looks back with longing eyes to her home where her own language, often the only one she knows, was spoken; where her daily habits, her tastes in dress and food were not only understood but were a mirror of fashion for others. In her new home all is strange, language, food and fashions, and the difference was much greater three hundred years ago than it is in these days of constant international intercourse. Marie knew very little French when she arrived in France; her tastes and habits were those of a mature woman, not easily changed to fit a new environment, and it was natural that she should cling to the little group of Italians who had accompanied her. The preference which she showed for them accentuated the isolation in which they lived in a court full of jealousy and intrigue but only two of these Italians occupied a prominent place in the court's unfavourable opinion; the queen's foster-sister Leonora Galagai and Concini. Leonora, small, dark and so thin as to be terrifying, if we may trust Tallemant de Réaux, was counted a witch by the French ladies. She, herself, was a profound believer in sorcery, and in especial, so great was her terror of the evil eye that she was rarely seen unveiled. The intimacy arising from a childhood spent together gave her strong will an immense dominance over her royal mistress in all matters where she chose to exert it. Soon after the queen's arrival in France Leonora chose to marry Concini, and both the queen and Concini yielded to her determination. Concini was not thought to be a willing suitor but the marriage made his fortune. During Henri's lifetime neither husband nor wife were permitted to occupy more than a very subordinate position, but after the King's death their influence and their wealth grew to a monstrous height. Concini bought estates and the title that went with them, became a Maréchal de France and the queen-regent's all-powerful minister, and the more his fortunes grew the more he was hated by the French. The boy-king shared to the full in the general feeling. He hated the Italian's arrogance, he hated his coarse language, he hated his influence over his mother. We have seen how early his childish dislike began; the following extract from Héroard in the year 1616 makes us see very clearly the changed position in which Louis, then king, and Concini, Maréchal d'Ancre, stood to each other. It is a curious contrast to the scene with the toy coach at St Germain-en-Laye in 1604. " Nov. 1616. The king went into the long gallery of the Louvre accompanied by three gentlemen, and stood by one of the windows looking on the river." The long gallery and the deep-set windows built by Henri IV to connect the Louvre and the Tuileries were pulled down by a later generation and we can only now imagine them; but to continue. " The Maréchal d'Ancre came in followed by more than a hundred gentlemen and stood by one of the other windows, without going near the king; he stood there bareheaded, while the crowd around paid him court. The king went off to the Tuileries with his heart full of anger." Héroard makes one last mention of Concini. " June 24. 1617. This morning the Maréchal d'Ancre was killed on the bridge of the Louvre between ten and eleven o'clock." He makes no comment although a blank sheet in the journal at this point has its own eloquence. The unfortunate Leonora was judged as a witch and all that the queen-mother could do for her lifelong companion was to win the concession that she should be beheaded before her body was burnt. And so did the dauphin's childish hatred work to its end.

No doubt his early dislike was aroused by an arrogance in Concini which clashed with his own arrogance. Héroard does not conceal that this was a marked trait in the child; nor could it well be otherwise when the position which he occupied at St Germain

78

is remembered. He might be spanked and whipped but none the less his extreme importance was recognized by all. He was " Monsieur " to every one about him except to his own family. To them he was "*papa petit*" to his own brothers and sisters, "*mon maître*" to the king's other children. Only the king and the queen were above him and even this he was sometimes loth to admit. Héroard gives some queer little stories of his sense of his supreme importance when he was a very little boy. One day when he was but three years old " he went into the chapel and saw Alexandre Monsieur and Mlle de Vendôme kneeling on stools. He ran up to them, saying ' Get up, get up. Say your prayers on the floor.' They were obliged to obey." Another day he came into his room and found the ten-year-old " M. de Valette, without his cloak, warming himself on the balustrade, his hands behind his back. ' Ho! ho! Valette, you are warming yourself as if you were me. Get off there, go away.' " Once one of his women asked him, " ' Monsieur who is Papa's master?' ' God,' he said. ' And who is yours?' ' I don't want to say.' No one can ever get him to admit that he has any master."

Arrogance was certainly a marked characteristic of the dauphin, but there was another one equally pronounced, which clung to him all his life. His father had many friends, boon companions, mistresses, but he had no favourites; his mother, on the contrary, let herself be ruled by favourites but it is doubtful whether she had any friends. The dauphin followed his mother in this respect and from very early days we find him lavishing his affection now on this one, now on that, a page, a soldier, a gardener's son, a keeper of his falcons, never on one who could naturally have been a real and equal friend. The earliest of these favourites

was a small page of Mme de Montglat's, Labarge by
name, who is often mentioned. " Waked up at seven;
took his shirt from Labarge instead of from Alexandre
Monsieur, just from spite." " Cross with Mme de
Montglat and Conchino but recovered his temper by
means of a present of a little carriage for himself and
a cart for Labarge." We hear from time to time of a
go-cart with which the children played in the garden.
Perhaps the " cart for Labarge " was this same favourite
plaything and the page did the pulling. After Labarge
more than one soldier of the castle guard became a
favourite at different times, from whom the dauphin
learnt his drill and played at sentry duty. One of
these, by name Descluseau, was much beloved for a
long time. But when the dauphin was moved to
Paris, in 1609, a new favourite who profoundly influenced his life came on the scene. This was de
Luynes, a young man attached to the king's hawking
establishment. He was a handsome fellow, of noble
birth but of a family of no great importance and less
wealth. However, he pleased the little dauphin, taught
him falconry, played with him at the childish games
the child still loved in spite of his governor's rebukes,
and little by little gained a complete ascendancy over
his young master. Héroard tells us that one day he
found the twelve-year-old king positively ill with the
violence of the passion he had flown into, on hearing
that Luynes was forbidden the entry into his room.
M. de Souvré may have been right but he certainly
failed to keep the boy-king and his favourite apart.
Luynes made good his position, gained undisputed
control over Louis, and finally freed him from Concini
and his mother the queen-regent.

We have wandered an overlong way from the little
boy's earliest years and must retrace our steps and

A traiſner le chariot, & autres ieux.

Autres auſſi iouent à blanle moyne,
Autres au ieu, qui plus leur ſemble idoine,
Qu'il eſt dehors ou dedans arreſté.

Le plus petit d'entr'eux exprés ſe meine
Dedans vn char, qu'vn barbet puiſſant traine,
L'autre à cheual ſur vn chien eſt monté:

A GO-CART

[face p. 80

once again pick up the dropped threads. Naturally, as the child grew out of babyhood his intercourse with other children became more marked a feature of his daily life. It is interesting to see his response to this intercourse. In April 1603 he was taken into Alexandre Monsieur's room to see the Marquise de Verneuil and her son, his little half-brother born a month later than himself. " As soon as he saw all the company he turned round, ran to the door crying and would not turn back. Generally, he was pleased when he was taken to this room. He went off to Madame la Marquise's room and played with her there, hiding and laughing. Taken back to Alexandre Monsieur's room, where all the children were, he seized Alexandre's *poule*, ran about like a mad thing, throwing it in front of him and running after it without paying the least attention to any of the other children. Mme de Verneuil touched his hair; he hit her and cried. Then M. de Verneuil was brought in but he pretended not to see him. One of M. de Verneuil's women asked her little master ' Where is Monseigneur le Dauphin ? ' M. de Verneuil hit himself on the chest but when he was scolded he pointed to M. le Dauphin." We have here an odd little insight into Mme de Verneuil's ambitions for her son. The dauphin, on the other hand, could not be brought to admit that the king was the child's father. " Someone asked him, ' Monsieur, who is M. de Verneuil's father ? ' He replied with a gibberish word of his own invention which he uses when he does not choose to answer a question. ' Monsieur, he is the king's son.' He answered quickly ' *I* am the king's son.' " The de Verneuil children were at first only visitors at St Germain-en-Laye. Later on, after the birth of both the queen's and the marquise's daughters the king decided that they should all be brought up together. With a lady so given to awkward intrigues it was safer to take her son out of her control and in June 1604, we are told that " At half past six whilst the dauphin was eating his supper he was told that ' another féfé is coming to see you.' " Féfé and soeu-soeu were what he called his half-brothers and sisters; the queen's children were *mon frère*, *ma sœur*. " ' What another féfé! ' M. and Mlle de Verneuil arrived at a quarter past seven. He was lifted down from the table at which he was sitting and went coldly to greet them. M. de Verneuil shrank behind his attendant muttering, and would not come near M. le Dauphin. The dauphin followed him about in the same cold manner to kiss him but as M. de Verneuil resisted he kissed Mlle de Verneuil instead. Seeing that M. de Verneuil would not let himself be approached the dauphin ran back to finish his supper. Taken down to the king in the court-yard whence they went to the gardens where all the children were gathered." They made quite a large family by this time. The dauphin and little Madame, Cæsar, Alexandre and Catherine de Vendôme and now the two Verneuil children; the king liked nothing better than to have them all about him.

Although the dauphin never forgot the immeasurable difference between the son of the queen and the child of one of his father's mistresses he often liked them well enough as playmates. Soon after the little de Verneuil boy's arrival at the castle the dauphin was out in the garden playing with his cart. " M. de Verneuil asked him, ' Mon maître, would you like me to get in too ? ' ' Get in, get in here,' he said." As children de Verneuil was his favourite among them all, and naturally enough as the two little boys were of the same age. The de Vendôme children suffered from being older. He was jealous of them and resented the king's affection for them. The younger boy Alexandre, at the age of six was made a Knight of Malta, a comfortable provision for a younger son, and he is always spoken of as M. le Chevalier after this date. So we hear that "The king arrived. The dauphin was very good and kissed him, but flew into a passion when the king hugged M. le Chevalier. The queen came in and Mlle de Vendôme kissed her hand. He ran at her and hit her." Another day Cæsar "on his own accord kissed the dauphin on the back of his hand and he got angry. 'Ha! you kissed me,' and he rubbed his hand on his frock." But he did not keep all his ill-temper for his half-brothers and their sister. "Dined at eleven o'clock. Did not want Madame to have anything to eat. I said 'When you are big you'll give everything to Madame.' He said 'No, I'll give her bread to eat and water to drink.'" A day or two later Héroard tells us that the two children were again dining together. "I asked Madame if she were pretty. 'Yes,' she said. The dauphin heard her and shook his head. I said again, 'Madame, are you good?' 'Yes,' she said. He shook his head and said 'She's just as good as brother Jean.' He meant *Maître Jean*, the monkey. He asked Madame to pass the jelly and she pushed it towards him saying, 'Here it is *papa petit*.' She is always so happy when she can please him." His naughty ways with his sister were by no means approved by the other children. One morning when he teased Madame and she cried Mlle de Vendôme, who was six years his senior, said, "'Monsieur I am going to tell Mme de Montglat that you have made Madame cry.' Mme de Montglat came and he said he was sorry. When she had gone again he quite suddenly and silently seized Mlle de Vendôme's right hand and gave it a good hard bite." This time we may hope, though we are not told, that Mme de Montglat did give him a slapping. Although he does not seem to have shown his best side to his brothers and sisters the dauphin was quite open to feelings of pity and kindliness both to people and animals. Pity for animals we shall come across again though the sentiment was mostly restricted to dogs, of whom he was very fond; but there is one very curious entry in the journal, which since it belongs to very early days may find its place here. Just before the celebration of St John's Eve in 1604, "The king took him to see the queen. He begged her to save the cats who were to be thrown on the bonfire." Héroard does not comment on this and we can only suppose it was some normal part of the old pagan worship of Midsummer Day. The child repeated his request the following day as a matter he had really at heart. He could be pitiful of people as well as of animals but those he was sorry for were in a position which could not arouse his easily-fired jealousy. A poor woman whose husband had been drowned, a long line of convicts marching to the galleys, a soldier punished for neglect of duty, these easily excited his compassion, and sometimes secured his help. But compassion could not overcome his natural fastidiousness, a quality which remained a perpetual matter of surprise to those around him. "At two o'clock he ate his *goûter*, and then went to the king's hall. He ordered a cripple, who was playing a flageolet there, to be put outside the door, saying 'He may go on playing but I don't want to see him.' He will not look at Olyvette, the Duchesse de Bar's fool, nor at Maître Guilleaume, the king's fool nor any fool at all for he dislikes them."

Deformity of any sort repelled him, as it does most children, but he also sent poor people from his presence because they were "dirty and smelt," a reason which Mme de Montglat obviously thought fussy.

One little boy, about whose fate the dauphin was greatly concerned, brings us for a moment into a wholly new world. In the year 1604 the French court was full of talk of voyages and discoveries, and especially of Champlain's new land of Canada. Champlain, with his fur-traders, settlers and missionaries came into very close intercourse with the Indian tribes round the Great Lakes. Champlain himself spent a whole winter with one tribe of the Hurons, whose name indeed was given them by Frenchmen from their own term *hure*, a head with bristled hair, like a boar. On one of his homeward voyages Champlain brought some of the Indians back to France and among them a little boy of whom the court made a pet. The dauphin took the keenest interest in this lad. Perhaps Héroard told him stories of the great ocean and its perilous storms and the ice-floes, in which Champlain's ship was once caught and drifted for weeks, or of the rich kingdom of the Saguenay seen by the earlier French discoverer Cartier, but which Champlain sought in vain. All through June 1604 we come across this Indian boy, a very sick little boy who filled the dauphin's heart with pity. "The dauphin watched little Canada go by, ill. Sent him his soup." "At half past eleven had his dinner. He gave a bowl of cherries a push saying, 'That's for Canada.'" Soup and jelly and cherries could do nothing for the stranger, who indeed had gone to the happy hunting-ground of his far-away tribe before the cherries reached him. In the following year the dauphin's interest in the new land beyond the great ocean received a fresh stimulus.

A large boat came up the Seine one day as far as the ferry of Pecq, just below the new *château*. In it was " a great animal as big as an eland which had been brought from Canada by M. de Monts. There was also a small boat made of woven rushes in the fashion of that country and covered with the bark of trees. Three sailors made it go through the water at an incredible speed." We can imagine the excitement of all the children at these strange sights. Was the great animal a moose? and was the birch-bark canoe really made of woven rushes within the outer covering of bark? However these things may have been, a fresh breath from the western world blew through the stuffy air of court and nursery.

CHAPTER V

GAMES AND TOYS

In an age when every man of noble birth was inevitably a soldier, unless destined for the Church, we should expect to find warlike games the most popular among all the boys living at St Germain-en-Laye. The dauphin and his brothers, the little nobles brought up with them, the pages who served them, one and all looked forward to a military life. All but the king's sons would almost as inevitably be duellists as well as soldiers; and not only duellists but as likely as not find themselves involved in the street encounters and brutal assassinations which were a disgrace to Paris until Richelieu had a few of the worst offenders beheaded to teach the others reason. These things being so we should expect to find, as indeed was the case, the art of fencing the most important lesson for a young nobleman, and one which he never thought of shirking. The natural occupation of a noble's manhood was inevitably reflected in the games of little boys. In the year 1604 we already find the dauphin " playing at soldiers with his little lords." He even possessed a complete suit of armour of his own, " with which he was enchanted, knew the names and uses of all sorts of arms and gave his orders to his soldiers as if he were an old general." So far as this last remark goes we must remember that the kindly doctor was a very partial observer. He gives us a long story of the child and his armour in this summer of 1604. " Waked at a quarter to eight; he amused himself with softly beating the drum tap of the lansquenets on himself, using his chest for the drum and his fists for drumsticks. 'Come on, soldiers! March! On guard!' He asked for his corselet and was very impatient to have it. He let himself be dressed and had his hair combed without making a fuss in the expectation of getting a casque in front of him. He tried it on but it was too small. M. de Belmont put on his gorget and M. de Ventelet handed the corselet for M. de Belmont to put on. The dauphin buckled it himself as if he were quite accustomed to wearing a cuirass. He was very patient and, so soon as he was armed, asked for his pike. He marched about the room so gaily that one might have thought he had no weight on his shoulders. No one ever saw such a sight at such an age! He began to shoot and to bang his pike against Labarge and the balustrade, marching up and down, quite silent and beside himself with happiness. Some one brought a big mirror. He caught sight of himself and immediately had all his armour taken off." Foolish someone to break into the child's magic world with the reality of a mirror.

Toy armour did not complete the dauphin's warlike toys. A few days later than the scene described above the doctor writes: " Had his boots and spurs put on and his frock and petticoat tucked up high. He put on his sword and sword-belt which M. de Lorraine had given him and seized his trumpet." The child's pleasure must have been all the greater from the fact that his frocks almost touched the ground; nor did he get free of them till he was seven years old. He wore pinafores as well as petticoats and frocks, which he wished could be plain like the white one féfé Verneuil wore, and not trimmed with embroidery like his own. We can picture the little boys, playing in

the garden in their pinafores, when we read that " the
dauphin tied his garter to his silver cannon and fastened
it to the belt of his pinafore, and walked about pulling
the cannon after him. He went as far as the tennis
court and was vexed because the wheels and the cannon's
mouth got clogged with mud. Took a great deal of
trouble cleaning them." Did he do it with his pinafore?
Probably not, because he would have been smacked
and Héroard would have mentioned it. The pike
with which he banged Labarge was a toy affair, not
likely to hurt in the hands of a three-year-old boy, but
a little later he was not content with anything so
harmless. Early in 1606 " a man gave the king four
Biscay pikes, unshod with iron. The king gave three
of them to the dauphin saying, ' One is for you and
you must give one to féfé Chevalier and one to féfé
Verneuil.' When the dauphin got back to his room
M. de Souvré said to him, ' Monsieur, I am going to
Paris. Can I do anything there for you?' ' Get my
pike mended.' ' What, Monsieur, do you want it to
prick and scratch and kill?' ' I don't want my pike
to kill, but I want it to prick; and I don't want féfé
Chevalier's or féfé Verneuil's to kill or to prick or to
scratch. Put a nail in mine.' " The number of toy
arms the dauphin had is too great to enumerate, but
among them were bows and arrows, several small
arquebuses with which he learnt to shoot sparrows
when he was old enough; swords; cannon in silver
and cardboard; toy soldiers in lead, pewter, cardboard,
wood, and earthenware; a black horse with a soldier
on it; a Turkish trumpeter a-horseback, besides
trumpets and drums in great plenty.

There is a glass-case in the Musée de Cluny, in
Paris, full of tiny pewter toys dredged out of the
Seine. Among them are a few toy soldiers, some an

inch, some two inches high, clad in doublet and hose, armed with cuirass and casque on head, arquebus in hand and sword on thigh, very complete military gentlemen of the days of Henri IV. More than three hundred years ago some small boy played with them and treasured them till one day they got swept up as rubbish and were thrown into the Seine. They have come to their own again, and once more as treasures, live in safety in their glass-case. They make the dauphin's toys feel very real to us. A tiny cannon on wheels has also found a safe haven in the same glass-case, perhaps too small to be dragged along by a garter tied to a pinafore belt, but certainly of a similar character. Such cannons, generally made of silver, were given to the dauphin on more than one occasion by Rosny, afterwards Duc de Sully, who was keeper of the Arsenal as well as *surintendant des finances*. If Sully hoped to win the child's affection by his gifts he must have been woefully disappointed, for at a very early age the dauphin conceived a dislike of the great minister, and unfortunately this dislike only increased as time went on. Sully was not popular, nor was it likely he should be. Henri had inherited a ruined kingdom and it was more owing to Sully's financial administration than to anyone else that France was comparatively rich and the King's treasury full by the time the dauphin was born. Sully was harsh and he was arrogant but it was the crowd of courtiers to whom he showed these qualities, while the bourgeois and the peasant were saved from extortion and injustice. It is difficult to read the curious memoirs, known as *Les economies royales*, which Sully, in his long years of enforced retirement, made his secretaries compile from the masses of memoranda kept throughout the years of his administration. Their style is exasperating and their bias pronounced, so pronounced indeed that the nine long volumes have often been called a political pamphlet; nevertheless, there are many brilliantly-dramatic scenes described in them and they are unquestionably an invaluable source of information. But one thing does stand out very clearly in their pages; Sully's enormous belief in himself, a belief justified both by what he did and by the king's trust in him. This attitude of Henri towards the great *surintendant des finances* had the natural result of making the court regard Sully as the source of all favour so far as money was concerned. No doubt Henri felt that this was better so, for Sully had no difficulty in refusing, seemed to enjoy it rather than otherwise, and could be not only rightly careful but even at times harshly stingy and yet be counted only the more faithful a servant. The dauphin heard complaints among his attendants from his earliest baby days, and certainly saw constant attempts on the part of one or another to beg or cajole money out of the *surintendant*. The most usual method was to entice the dauphin to beg for them, and this was another source of his dislike of Sully, for the child was never willing to ask for favours nor to beg for money which he bluntly said was " Papa's money " and not Sully's to give or withhold. Not only did he dislike asking, but he also hated to be refused so much that he never asked for anything for himself. Héroard noticed and resented the way in which all the household pestered the child to do their begging for them. Sully was well aware of this and when he thought proper would refuse the reluctant request, but the refusal was none the less galling to the dauphin's pride. We can see the relation between the minister and the little boy very vividly in the pages of the journal. One day Héroard tells us that " M. de

Rosny—he was not yet Duc de Sully—came to see the dauphin, and said to him ' Monsieur, is there anything you want. You've only to ask me.' He shook his head and replied, ' Nothing.' Soon after his nurse said to him, ' Monsieur, why didn't you ask him to give me a bed?' ' Oh! Dondon, I've asked him so many times for things and he never gives them.' " Two days later Sully again came to St Germain and the dauphin was " persuaded to ask him for various things for other people, but it was only on compulsion. He begged for a bed for his nurse, and Mme de Montglat asked him to say a word for Indret, his lutist and for M. Birat, his usher. M. de Sully said, ' Monsieur, don't worry yourself about them.' ' Yes, I shall,' he said quickly. M. de Sully asked him which of his household he liked best. He replied at once ' Indret and Birat ' just to enforce his request." Héroard often remarks that the dauphin did not care for money and more than one entry in the journal shows this indifference. At times M. de Rosny was more success-ful, but it would always be with the gift of a toy which caught the boy's fancy. The following letter was dictated to Héroard when Henri had gone north to bring the always troublesome Duc de Bouillon to reason. The dauphin was staying in Paris with the queen.

" Monday 20th April 1606 at the Louvre. Papa, since you went I have been making mamma happy. I went to the war in her room. I went to spy out the enemies. They were all asleep in a heap in the *ruelle* of mamma's bed. I waked them up with my drum. I have been to the Arsenal Papa. M. de Rosny showed it to me full of beautiful arms and so many, many great cannon, and he gave me some sweetmeats and a little silver cannon. I only want a little horse to draw it now. Mamma is sending me back to St

Germain to-morrow and there I shall pray to God for
you, Papa, to keep you from danger and to make me
good and give me grace to be able soon to do you my
humble service. I do so want to go to sleep, Papa.
Féfé Vendôme will tell you the rest, and I will only
tell you I am your very humble and very obedient son
and servant.   DAUPHIN."
When money was offered by Sully the indifference
amounted to a real dislike, probably because the boy,
young as he was, felt that the gift was not Sully's own
but came from "Papa's money," and he resented the
magnificent presumption of the *surintendant*. But it
is also clear that Sully was incapable of understanding
a child and childish tastes and pleasures, and often
gave offence in a way which must have seemed to the
poor man purely perverse. On 25th June 1606, for
instance, we read that "M. de Rosny came in with a
purse full of money to give to the dauphin. 'I don't
want it. It isn't pretty.' 'But Monsieur, there are
lovely *dauphins* in it.' 'No, its ugly. If you give it
to me I shall throw it into the moat.' 'But do look,
Monsieur, at the lovely *demi écus* in it.' The money
was emptied out on to an apron. He put it all back
and threw the purse away saying, 'Get away you ugly
thing.' 'Monsieur,' said M. de Rosny, 'what would
you like me to give you?' 'A little carriage.'" We
see the same error, the same sort of sumptuous vulgarity
in Sully, in a scene which Héroard describes just
before the king's assassination, which is worth entering
here. It shows how persistent the attitude of the child
was and how equally persistent the great man's failure
to please him. It was an unhappy error, for Sully fell
from power at his master's death and the new king,
even when he was old enough to set his mother aside,
made no effort to recall his father's most trusted servant.

93

In May 1610 the court was full of festivities to celebrate
the queen's somewhat retarded coronation, and Sully
received a great deal of fine company at the Arsenal
where he lived in close proximity to the Bastille. The
dauphin one day was driven to the Arsenal to visit
Sully, and see his pleasant garden by the river.
"'Monsieur,' said Sully to him, 'shall I give you
some money?' 'No,' said he disdainfully. 'You've
only got to ask, Monsieur,' repeated his host, several
times over. 'If you want to give money, take it to
M. de Souvré.' He had picked some sprays of blossom
from a little tree which pleased him. M. de Sully
said to him, 'Monsieur, when you next come here
you will find a hundred purses full of *écus* hanging on
this tree, which you will think lovely.' 'It'll be a fine
tree won't it?' he answered carelessly." There was no
"next time," for five days later Henri was struck
down and the great days of Sully, *le glorieux* as the
new little king called him, were over.

Sometimes, however, the dauphin would accept
money from Sully, though on these occasions it might
have been regarded as a payment rather than a gift.
If we return to earlier years we see an amusing instance
of this. "20th July 1606. At noon M. de Sully
arrived from Rosny to see the dauphin. Mme de
Montglat took the dauphin down to the courtyard to
meet M. le Duc and told him to run and kiss him as
if he were the king. The dauphin put on his armour,
took his pike, made all his company arm, placed them
on guard, made them charge and put them through
their drill. M. de Sully gave him fifty *écus* which his
soldiers snatched out of his hands before he had time
so much as to feel them. At last he had only one
piece left which he struggled to keep from Mme de
Montglat's tailor. 'Hé! Mamanga, Montailler is

snatching my money.' Mme de Montglat came up, took the piece of money from him, made all the others give up the rest and kept them. The dauphin said nothing, did not complain, but was heard to say to himself, ' But I was a soldier and I got no pay.' M. de Sully gave him a *doublon* and went away."

To judge by other entries in the journal we may feel tolerably sure that Mme de Montglat kept the money for herself. The whole household lived *en pension* with her and her husband and whether the allowance made to them was insufficient, or whether, as Héroard plainly thought, they were both stingy and grasping is difficult to decide. The dauphin was clearly of the doctor's opinion. Three months before the scene in the courtyard with Sully he had " complained to Mme de Montglat that his maman Dondon was not given any candles," and Héroard adds that M. de Montglat had refused to allow any to the household just from stinginess, although he took money from the king for the purpose. No doubt the dauphin heard many similar complaints, and at times made his own on his own account. One day " he was taken to see M. de Montglat who had the gout. He found him with his foot resting on a green velvet cushion. The dauphin drew back angrily muttering between his teeth, ' Oh! he has put his foot on my cushion and then they'll put my face on it.' Mme de Montglat could not pacify him and he went away. M. Guerin said, ' Monsieur, you have two cushions. You ought to give him one.' ' Ho! he's a fine sort of person to give it to.' Indret, the lutist, said, ' Monsieur, you ought to give him both yours.' ' I shouldn't think of such a thing. If it were you I would give them because you are poor, but he is rich and he can buy one for himself.' " Poor M. de Montglat died three months later and the dauphin cried, but Héroard implies that it was rather because Mme de Montglat's tears affected him than for any sorrow of his own. After all he was not quite six years old. Another story illustrating the child's curious resentment at his *gouvernante's* greediness belongs to a later year, but since it may not find a place elsewhere may be told now. On the last day of 1608 the New Year's presents were filling all the children's minds and the doctor's not less than theirs. The dauphin got up with a grievance on that day. " He complained that someone had taken seven *sous* from the pocket of his breeches which he had meant to give in alms to the poor. He cried about it. He came to see what my wife had brought for his New Year's gift. It was a box of very fine apricots. Mme de Montglat said, ' They are for you Monsieur. I will lock them up safe.' ' There now! I shall never see them again. She locks up everything that is given me.' She took out an apricot, bit a piece off and gave him what was left. ' Look at her! She has opened the box to eat one and then she locks it up. She says it's all mine and I never see a thing.' " The dauphin was in a mood to find fault with his *gouvernante*. The time was close at hand when he was to be moved from her care at St Germain-en-Laye, to M. de Souvré's in Paris. The day before the trouble over the apricots he had whispered to his half-sister, " ' Soeu-soeu Vendôme I am going to get a hollow stick, fill it with gunpowder, and I shall light it with a hot coal and blow up Mamanga.' M. de Guerin said to him, ' Monsieur, don't you know that papa says you won't be long with her. You shouldn't vex her.' ' Oh! its because she wants to keep all my silver dinner-service.' This was true." The dinner-service was no doubt a perquisite of the *gouvernante's* when the child left, but he was always extraordinarily tenacious of his own possessions, and perhaps, like most children, had an affection for things familiar with daily use. One day, after he had gone to live in Paris, Mme de Montglat came to see him while he was going to bed. She and M. de Souvré disputed together as to which had the better claim to the dauphin. " Mme de Montglat said, ' At his birth the king said to me, " this is my son whom I give to you. Take him." ' ' Yes,' replied M. de Souvré, ' he was yours for a time, but now he is mine.' The dauphin, who was playing in bed with his toys said, without raising his voice or turning round, ' I hope some day I shall belong to myself.' "

If the dauphin was tenacious of what he considered his own, and if, as was true, he was often greedy towards his brothers and sisters and never lavish with his gifts, he had certainly good qualities which we could hardly have expected to find. Héroard quite often remarks that he " was marvellously careful to pay for what he bought." This was the more creditable because pedlars of all sorts constantly haunted the castle and the people about him often enticed him to buy their wares. But when he paid he liked to pay in accordance, whether for real purchases or in play, with his sense of his own importance.

Here is a last picture of both Sully and of playing at soldiers, which will bring us back to the real subject of this chapter. The children were all at Fontainebleau with the king and the queen in June 1608. " The dauphin asked for his arms, his musket, bandolier and the whole set out; armed his company, added some more pages attached to the stable establishment, marched them all to the terrace and thence up into the ball-room. The drummer belonged to the company of the guard. They fell into rank, marched and then charged. The king and queen came to watch them, bringing with them M. de Sully and M. de Villeroi. After several evolutions and much pretend firing the dauphin asked M. de Sully for money to pay his soldiers. The Duke gave him a *sol*. The dauphin took it, but when he saw it was a *sol* and not a *doublon* as he had expected he flung it away in a temper. ' I wanted to pay like a prince,' he said."

Though playing at soldiers was the most common pastime there were many other games and amusements which had nothing to do with warfare. We have already heard of the little coach with the four dolls in it and the go-cart with which the children played in the garden. There was also a fine coach painted red and big enough for the six-year-old dauphin to sit on the box and be dragged about the room by the pages. We hear of a great number of presents of toys and a list of some of them, gathered at haphazard from the pages of the journal, gives much insight into the play-things of bygone days. They sound amusingly like the toys of the twentieth century but they were, of course, totally different in superficial appearance. For instance, a "little gentleman doll was very well dressed with a scented ruff embroidered with gold thread, and trunk-hose of the same stuff," which the dauphin said he should marry to Madame's doll. The toy coach, if it resembled the queen's, was gaily painted and gilt and devoid of springs. But the green earthen pots and pans with which the four-year-old little brothers, the dauphin and féfé Verneuil, played at being cooks may have varied little from the *casseroles* and *accuelles* of a French kitchen of to-day, for one of the most intimate charms about earthenware utensils is the singular continuity of their shapes throughout long

ages. Battledores and shuttlecocks, balls and racquets
must have been essentially the same, except that there
would have been no india-rubber balls. We know the
children had a see-saw in the garden " about three ells
and a foot long," but we do not hear of a swing. The
little girls had several little rooms furnished with doll's-
house furniture; one of these had a bed with mamma
and the baby in it while the midwife stood by in
attendance; another room also had a bed on which lay
Holofernes with Judith in the act of slaying him,
which seems an odd subject for a little girl's doll's-
house room. In the same glass-case in which the toy
soldiers are treasured in the Musée Cluny there are
some delightful pewter plates and dishes, ewers and
goblets, spoons with round bowls and spoons with
long bowls, all of a size to play at doll's dinner-parties.
Dear little toys of long ago children! Such dinner-
sets we know were common in the dauphin's nursery,
in silver, in pewter and in earthenware. " *Un petit
ménage* " was a frequent present, tiny toys packed in
a box which the children would have the delight of
unpacking and peeping in to see what sort of a *ménage*
it was. Héroard uses the term for all sorts of small
objects; a chalice and a censer, a cock and a woman
all made of pewter and packed up together in a box;
two little glass dogs made in the glass-works of Nevers;
a dinner-set; pots and pans to cook with, and once
" two tall candlesticks with white tapers such as are
used in church. My wife lit the tapers. The dauphin
blew them out saying, ' they'll get used up,' just as he
is always seeing and hearing from the people about
him." This is one of the doctor's gibes at Mme de
Montglat's stinginess.

Some of the presents called toys were too valuable
to be played with. Such was a cupid seated on a

99

dolphin, studded with diamonds and set with a big emerald, or a little scimitar covered with diamonds, both presents from Queen Marguerite, Henri's first wife. Such too was a gift from the Princess of Orange of a lacquered cabinet, painted with flowers and fruits and birds, brought by Dutch traders from far-away China. These and similar gifts were probably, and quite properly, locked up safe by Mme de Montglat. When the dauphin was old enough to go to the great fair of St Germain held in Paris every year he paid a number of visits to the stall of a merchant from China, but we do not know what purchases he made there, nor whether the merchant was himself a China-man. If he were he would have been as strange as the Canadian Indians and their birch-bark canoe. The world was already a big world to Paris in the early years of the seventeenth century.

The dauphin loved his toys, especially those that excited his ingenuity and gave scope to the mechanical turn Héroard says was a marked trait of his character. He went on playing when his governor M. de Souvré thought he was getting too old and scolded the poor little king. He still, at ten years old, loved his lead soldiers, his little cart to which he harnessed his dogs, his " contrivances " that he made out of cardboard. " ' Sire,' said M. de Souvré, ' when are you going to leave off these childish games ? ' ' Monsieur de Souvré, I am quite ready to, only I must do something. Tell me what to do and I'll do it.' He was taken to the tennis court." It is pleasant to know that he went on playing and that he and his favourite Luynes made quite a good toy fort in the Tuileries gardens a good deal later than this.

But besides games with toys there were many others, merry romping games in which pages, nurses, ladies in

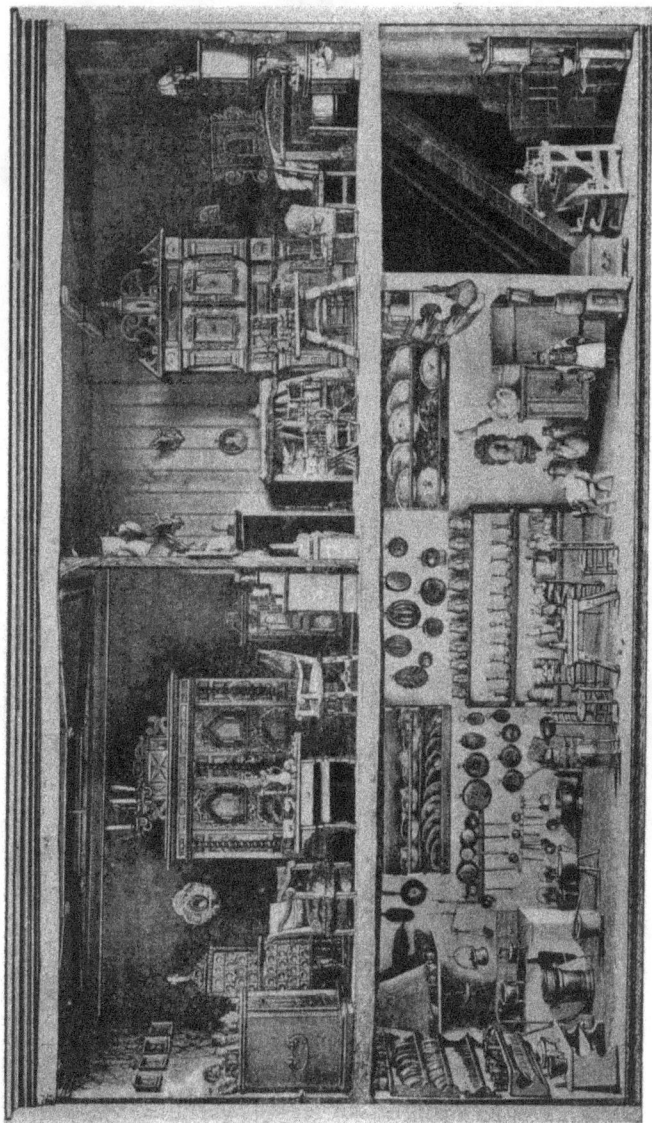

A SEVENTEENTH CENTURY DOLLS' HOUSE

From L'Histoire des Jouets.   H. R. d'Allemagne

[*face p.* 100

attendance and sometimes even gentlemen of the guard joined with the children. These games cannot be described but their names sometimes give a clue to them. The following are a few of the favourites : *La compagnie vous plaît elle ?* ; *Bis cum bis* ; *Votre place me plaît*, and *Frappemain*, do not suggest the game but when the pages played *St Jean des choux* and the dauphin joined in, kicking up like the rest at the page in front of him we can imagine the sort of rough romp it was, with laughter and shouts as Héroard says. And again when every one played at *Je vous eveille* and the dauphin would only wake up for the king, the queen and Mme de Montglat we see something gentler and more courtly. There were yet other games requiring ingenuity of language. One called *Que met on au corbillon ?* seems to have demanded quickly-made rhyming jingles from the players for the dauphin was proud of inventing " *dauphillon* " and " *demoisillon* " ; and of course his readiness was admired and recorded by the doctor. Then there were games special to certain festival days, such as the bonfires of St John's Eve and the Twelfth Night cake. A discussion over this last is curious on 6th January 1609. " They were talking about Twelfth Night and the dauphin said, ' I don't want to be king.' His nurse asked why. ' I don't want to be,' he replied. ' If you were king would you pay something for it, and if Madame or if Mlle Vendôme were chosen would they pay ? ' said his nurse. He called M. de Ventelet and whispered in his ear, ' Tell them not to put in the bean.' ' Monsieur,' said his nurse again, ' if God is king you will have to take His place.' ' I don't want it to be me,' he said. ' What, Monsieur,' they all said, ' would you refuse to take the place of God.' He looked frightened. ' Papa ought to do

that,' he said. ' But Monsieur, it is your place to take
it here.' ' Oh! very well. I will.' " A light on the
above discussion is thrown from a previous celebration
of Twelfth Night. On the 5th of January 1607, the
eve of the Epiphany, " he cut a cake of marchpane
made for him and Madame and Madame Christienne;
he was king for the first time. He wanted to eat his
piece of cake and God's also. Mme de Montglat said
to him, ' If you want to eat God's portion you must
pay money for it.' ' Very well, let somebody pay then,'
he said promptly; ' Tétai (pet-name for M. de
Ventelet), give some money.' ' How much, Monsieur.'
He thought and then said, ' Five écus.' Five quarter-
écus were given to the almoner, which were afterwards
given back." The following day another cake was cut
and he was again king, but we gather this was the
proper big cake to be shared by all. Obviously one
portion was set aside nominally " for God " and since
money had to be paid by anyone who ate this slice
in reality for God's poor. Somehow, the giving back
of those five quarter-écus seems an error. Perhaps
they were M. de Ventelet's own and he had not eaten
the cake.

These and other games no doubt filled up the
winter hours happily enough but I think we may be
sure that the best-loved games were the fanciful games
little children make up for themselves, and the con-
structive games that call for skill and invention. Of
these we hear often. The king had given the dauphin
a little page, Bompar by name. The dauphin, Madame
and Bompar " played together. Bompar took Madame
prisoner. The dauphin said Bompar was the dragon
who had seized Andromeda and he was Perseus who
killed the dragon." Bompar could not have been very
old when he came to serve the dauphin for there is

an allusion to his emergence from the age of page-
hood some four or five years later; at any rate he was
young enough to join in very childish games. Cooking
with toy pots and pans seems to have been popular
especially with M. de Verneuil. Sometimes they made
sweetmeats with one or other of their ladies in attendance, once they helped Mme de Montglat to preserve
quinces, but I fancy most often the dauphin and féfé
Verneuil contented themselves with pretend cooking
to serve on their tiny plates and dishes. Of course
there was plenty to do in the gardens, in the old
garden by the old castle as well as in the grand new
gardens with their fountains and grottos and gay
flower plots below the new *château*. Héroard describes
a very happy morning when the dauphin built a tower
with some bricks which the builders had left lying
about. " He found a bit of a plank and said he would
make a drawbridge. He told someone to go to the
carpenter, who was at work in the kitchens, and fetch
a gimlet to make holes in the plank for the drawbridge ropes. A gimlet was got and he worked it
himself but did not make much progress because he
could not hold the plank steady enough. So someone
held it and he amused himself turning the gimlet."

The dauphin loved using his hands in many ways
but probably his greatest pleasure was found in drawing
and painting. Drawing was done with chalks but
painting could only be done with a palette and oil-
paints put up into small bladders. It must have been
delightful fun to squeeze out the colours. Court
painters and sculptors were many and the children
were painted in oils, drawn in chalks, carved in stone,
modelled in wax, and moulded in pottery more times
than it is easy to reckon. The first portrait of the
dauphin was painted when he was seven months, and

interested others more than himself, but as he grew older he took the greatest interest in the various artists. He watched them attentively, asked questions, begged to handle the palette and brushes, or to have a piece of modelling wax to play with. When he was four a " portrait in wax a foot and a half high was made of him. He played with his little silver *ménage* and told M. de Verneuil to ' get away.' Mme de Montglat scolded him for being cross and he said, ' It wasn't me, it was my little wax brother who said it.' " But this anecdote, though a nice one, does not show the child's own love of artistic handicraft. The next story of an incident when he was five years old shows how far he had progressed in his ambitions. It begins with a fit of jealous bad temper with his sister, the queen's second daughter. " Mme de Montglat came into the room carrying little Madame." None of the queen's children had names as yet but this baby was called Christienne at her public baptism a year later. " The dauphin shouted, ' Put her down.' Mme de Montglat did put her down and the dauphin said, ' Wash your hands.' She washed them and he poured the water over them. ' Now wash your arms too.' But Mme de Montglat threatened to whip him so he grew quiet. The next day he stayed in bed very late, not speaking although he was awake. He was afraid of being whipped for his naughtiness of the day before. He begged Mme de Montglat to let him off and promised that for the whole day ' I'll be good, and I'll say my prayers and I'll repeat my verses, and I'll do my lessons and I'll paint. I'll paint you a very lovely cherub.' ' Oh! you are a fine painter. You couldn't paint a fine day.' ' Yes, I could.' ' How would you do it? ' ' I should take some white and then some flesh colour and blue.' ' But you couldn't

paint the sun or the moon.' 'Yes, I could.' 'How
would you make the sun?' 'I should take some
yellow and some red and I should mix them.' 'And
the moon?' 'I should take white and yellow and mix
them and then I should make a face and that would be
the moon.' To please Mme de Montglat still more
he said, 'I want to get into bed with you.' She let
him get into bed between her and M. de Montglat.
After chapel he went into his room to paint, sent for
the painter to teach him, listened to what he said,
held the brush dextrously and the palette on his thumb
just like the painter who was painting his portrait."
The dauphin no doubt must have been bored by the
number of sittings he had to give as a child so that it
was fortunate he could find pleasure in learning from
various artists. A year later than the portrait in wax,
" Master Martin, his painter, came to paint him. He
painted him wearing his corselet under his crimson
gown embroidered in gold thread, a sword at his side
and a pike in his right hand, which he held upright.
His head was covered with a white satin cap with a
feather in it. He asked for some colours and a brush
and watched what the painter did. He took his dog
Isabelle in his arms, hugged and kissed her, calling
her his little darling, for he is very fond of dogs. He
told his painter to paint his dog too. Mlle Mercier
said, ' Monsieur, soldiers oughtn't to have dogs with
them.' He answered quickly, ' But it would be to
seize the enemy by the legs.' "
      The dauphin spent many hours with paints and
crayons, and if we may trust Héroard the results were
astonishing. Many of the little scribbles and smudges
were treasured by the doctor and can still be seen
among the manuscript sheets of the journal. We can
learn some of the subjects from the following entry.

"He counted up the pictures he had painted of a wood and a hill and the sky. He said he had no colours to paint the shadows of the sun and the moon but to-morrow he should finish his pictures, and then he should paint a boar hunt and give it to Papa. So the next day he sat down and stretched a little square canvas and nailed it on a little board ready for painting. The grandson of one of the gardeners, who knew how to paint, was with him. He copied all the boy did attentively and dextrously with a great wish to learn." The dauphin had other teachers than the gardener's grandson, for Boileau, his musician, could paint as well as play the viol. The two spent many hours together while Boileau drew fancy portraits of all sorts of dead celebrities, kings, queens, and famous soldiers for the most part. While Boileau drew the dauphin drew too, and when his pictures were finished he fastened them on to the tapestry of his room. He took them hastily down again, however, hearing that the Duke of Savoy was coming to see him. "They are only to show to Papa," he said. Painting was among the amusements which M. de Souvré thought too childish for the little king.

Héroard often mentions the dauphin's pleasure in mechanical toys. We have heard of the drum played by a spring. There was a toy fountain of glass which would pump up water. Later on we shall come to a wonderful marionette peep-show which was worked with sand instead of the more ordinary water contrivance. For a boy with a taste for mechanics we can easily imagine how happy he must have been one New Year's day when "the queen sent him a watch and a pair of little knives. He wrote to thank her for her present and said he looked very often at his watch to see whether it were time to place the sentinels, and

that he meant to watch them to see if they went to
sleep, and if they did he should prick them with the
knives." He was a very little boy for such a gift,
young even in these days of cheap watches. Three
hundred years ago there can have been no cheap
watches, nothing but the exquisite work of skilled
craftsmen, as exquisite in their cases as in their works.
Anyone who wants to know the fascination of these
old watches can spend a very happy hour in South
Kensington or the Edward VII Gallery of the British
Museum studying the delicate chasing and enamelling,
the jewels set in them, the quaint shapes the cases
sometimes took. The dauphin's pleasure in his first
watch was a child's pleasure in a game which brought
him into relation with the castle guard whom he so
much admired. Some of its members were his particular friends; sometimes he played at being a sentinel
himself and knew the enormity of falling asleep on
duty. But he also, like most little boys, liked " to see
the wheels go round." Héroard had a striking-watch
and this he often looked at. The doctor says one day,
" He told me to show him my watch, made me wind
up the striking, asked all about the works, wanted to
know everything." A little later the dauphin had an
alarum-clock and found it a delightful game to set it
going. We can only hope those around him enjoyed
it as much. He had to wait till he was nine years old
before he had a striking-watch of his own. Héroard
does not tell us the precise date but he does describe
a scene in which the dauphin used the watch to outwit
his governor. M. de Souvré had one of the dauphin's
lacqueys arrested for fighting in the Fair of St Germain.
This was a serious offence for the fair was a most
important yearly event in the life of Paris and rigorous
care was taken to preserve order among the throngs

who frequented it and to safeguard the costly wares exposed. " The dauphin was asked to intercede for him. I said in a whisper to M. de Souvré that it would not be long before Monseigneur asked pardon for the man. M. de Souvré replied, ' He can ask if he likes after twenty-four hours have struck.' The dauphin heard what was said and with a sly look said under his breath, ' I'll soon make twenty-four hours strike.' So soon as he had finished dinner he bade someone bring him his striking-watch. When it came he made it strike all the hours, one after the other, and then turning to M. de Souvré said, ' Twenty-four o'clock has struck. Will you please let my lacquey out of prison.' "

One very favourite pastime was constantly indulged in which was not considered too childish for any age, that of dressing up and dancing ballets. No amusement was more popular among the courtiers, men and women alike, so that what the children did in a childish way they could still do with ever-increasing elaboration of steps, costumes and setting as they grow older. But a fuller account of the children's ballets must wait for another chapter.

CHAPTER VI

SOME of the happiest hours that the king's children passed were spent at Fontainebleau, where they lived for some of the summer months every year after the year 1604. Héroard gives us in great detail the first journey from St Germain-en-Laye to the palace in the forest in the August of that year. Packing up for a change of residence was a very serious labour, for not only personal belongings had to be moved but bedding, services for the table, and probably kitchen utensils had to go too. It would, perhaps, be more accurate to consider these household things as much personal belongings as were clothes. In the queen's journey to Fontainebleau before the dauphin's birth, we have already seen how she took her bedding with her; the following extract from later pages of the journal show how much a matter of course it was for the rich, at any rate, to travel so encumbered. The story belongs to the year 1609 and the children were returning to St Germain after an unusually short summer stay at Fontainebleau. On the first day a halt was made at Brie Comte Robert for the night. " After supper the dauphin went for a walk to Panfou, the chancellor's house, where he played on a big haycock, attacked it and defended it in turns, rolled down it from top to bottom, got drenched with perspiration and changed his shirt. Went back to Brie where his luggage had not yet arrived as the coach had broken down twice. Was put to bed in one of M. Gobelin's beds and with his sheets. He asked if the king had ever slept in it. They said ' Yes ' because he made a fuss about using the bed." On the morning of a journey the little boy loved to help pack his own bedding much as a child of to-day will pop in a favourite toy when summer holiday trunks are being filled. In 1604, however, he was too young to take any active part in the move. It must have been a great scene on that hot August morning as the cavalcade set out from the old castle. The younger children went in litters, the dauphin with Mme de Montglat and Madame with her nurse, the older children in coaches with their attendant ladies, servants a-horseback and mules and carts to bring the heavy luggage. " M. de Rosny, not yet Duc de Sully, accompanied by sixty horse went on ahead as far as Chaillot. On reaching the *faubourg* St Honoré, the dauphin complained of the stench of the gutters. ' Mamanga, there's a bad smell.' He was given a handkerchief soaked in vinegar to smell. He reached the Porte St Honoré at 11.30 and was met between the two gates by the *prévôt des marchands* the *échevins* and other town officials. The *prévôt des marchands* made a speech and a joyous song was sung accompanied by music. The litter was opened before crossing the drawbridge. The dauphin turned his face this way and that with a sweet gravity, so that all the people could see him. He went along the Rue St Honoré and down the Rue St Denis to the Porte de Paris, by the Pont Notre Dame. Just by the little stall, which stands before St Denis de la Chartre, the front mule of the litter fell down and tried to get up three times; got up at the fourth attempt with help. Throughout the journey the dauphin behaved very well but said, ' Mamanga, it is so hot. Let's go to my room.' At his entrance into Paris the crowds

shouted ' Long live the king and the dauphin,' so he
shouted too. Mme de Montglat said that it was not
proper for him to shout and told him that the people
were asking God to bless his papa and mamma and
himself. He was silent after that. They left Paris by
the Porte St Victor, and at half past one reached
Villejuif where he stopped at the house of an apothecary
of Paris for dinner. At half past five they set out again
and reached Savigny at a quarter to eight." The
following day they travelled as far as Villeroi which
they reached at half-past six, and at noon on the third
day they arrived at Fleuri, where the king met them.
" At two o'clock the dauphin asked for his *goûter*.
The king said, ' Give me some of your *goûter*.' ' No,
give me some of yours.' The queen said, ' Give me
some of your *soucre*, my son.' He corrected her with
a smile, saying ' *Soucre* for *sucre*.' " At Fleuri yet
another night was spent and Fontainebleau was not
reached till eleven o'clock on 1st September.

Fontainebleau must have been a delightful place in
which to spend the summer months. The great
palace, the gardens with their fountains and pools,
the little town beyond the *château* walls, the forest
engulfing town and palace alike, all possess an exquisite
loveliness of their own. So many centuries have gone
to the making of the *château ;* to its making, un-making
and re-making. All have left their mark but none
have robbed it of its peculiar charm; its sense of
intimacy; its warm and lovely colour; its fanciful and
yet dignified form; its infinite memories. It stands
there seemingly empty and asleep but with a sleep
full of dreams of a great and busy life. Much has
been altered and much added since the days of Henri IV
and his court, but happily much can still be seen not
greatly changed since the little dauphin was lifted out

of his litter in the court of the *Cheval blanc*. The white horse, a plaster replica of the famous statue on the Capitol of Rome, has long vanished, though its name lingers on; and the wonderfully curved double flights of steps which lead into the palace were built by Louis XIII himself many years later, to replace those up which he was carried as a little boy to revisit the place of his birth. Within the *château* the keep of St Louis, deep-buried in rooms of later date, and portions of the still earlier chapel of St Saturnin still remain; the chapel is so old that the restored building is said to have been re-dedicated by Thomas à Becket. All through the Middle Ages Fontainebleau and its forest were loved by the kings of France, but it was François I and not any of these earlier kings who was the real creator of the Fontainebleau we love. Henri II embellished it magnificently and Henri IV added greatly to it, but what they did was in harmony with the main structure. Louis XIV altered much and Louis XV added still more. Napoleon lived in this palace of many kings and left a mark which, to the modern custodian, seems the biggest mark of all. The restoration, the second Empire, followed in their turn and now the Republic is its guardian and it has become a *monument national*. But the real Fontainebleau eludes all these, republic, citizen king, emperor, *grand monarque* himself. The spirit is of the Renaissance, its mellow beauty, its stately homeliness are its own, neither a fortress like St Germain-en-Laye nor a monstrous monument to a king's pride like Versailles.

The palace in places has been much restored with that patience which is so characteristic of French work of restoration. No doubt there are many who cry out against those who repaint almost obliterated frescoes and renew worm-eaten wood. The touch of the old craftsmen cannot be restored but portions of the interior of the *château* would be but a shadow of its past splendour had not these later guardians lavished their labour on them. We may flick aside Louis Philippe, Napoleon III and the Republic as out of harmony with the ancient spirit of Fontainebleau, but without them there might have been little left of gallery and chapel and stately room for us to linger over with our minds full of old memories, our eyes seeing vanished scenes and our ears catching the lost echoes of long-silent voices and laughter. The spirit of the past is but waiting for our answering spirit to leap again into life, and once more fill the empty spaces with those whom our own mood summons; Napoleon in his throne room, Marie Antoinette in her boudoir, Maintenon looking from her window down the long avenue, or a little boy dauphin drilling his soldiers in Diane de Poitier's Gallery and angry because he cannot pay them " like a prince." For each of us there is a Fontainebleau, and what we bring with us of knowledge and of memory that will Fontainebleau give back a hundredfold.

No king loved Fontainebleau more than Henri IV. The dauphin loved it too, though one whole year which the children passed there seemed to him too long, and he wearied to return to his own special home. Héroard tells us that after this long absence, " So soon as he caught sight of St Germain he cried, ' Ah! there is St Germain, my darling St Germain. I'll call to you and you'll come to me.' " But though he might love St Germain there were many delights to be found at Fontainebleau. The king took the little boy after his arrival on that September day, 1604, to see " the gardens and the canal, gave the carp some bread, looked at the ducks and swans, the pheasants and the ostrich." The canal is there, a long stretch of still water mirroring the flickering silver of poplar and willow. It was newly made when the dauphin went to see it with his father more than three hundred years ago. Indeed it had only recently been filled with the overflow of all the many pools and fountains scattered about among the gardens. Henri had had a wager with Bassompierre, gayest of courtiers and most reckless of gamblers, that it would fill in two days. It took eight and Bassompierre won a thousand *écus* from the disappointed king. It was this same Bassompierre who, one summer when the dauphin was at Fontainebleau, taught the little boy to play at dice, but his pupil was not very apt and Louis XIII never gambled as Henri had gambled with dice and cards, with fortune and with life itself.

The canal is brimming now; carp still swim in the pool beyond the Fountain Court and swans dispute with them the food thrown by the idle onlookers by the balustrade; little boys may still gaze deep into the still reflections and say, as the dauphin said, " ' Look, there are the antipodes! ' " But the great aviary, where the ostrich and other strange birds lived, vanished long ago. We hear of a vulture with a black tuft on its head which had possibly come by way of Spain, from the southern continent of the New World. It was as big and strong as an eagle and the dauphin said, " ' It has got a head just like little de Lisle,' who has a big square head and a long nose. The dauphin is clever at seeing resemblances." Of pet animals there were many and various at Fontainebleau, especially monkeys, and awkward moments arose from this habit of the dauphin's for pointing out likenesses. Little Mlle de Vendôme had a marmoset whose resemblance to M. de Guise was commonly acknowledged. One

BOY WITH PUPPIES

From La Céramique Française. M. J. Ballot
By permission of Les Editions Albert Morancé

day when the king and the children were playing with the little creature, " The duke came in and asked the dauphin who the monkey was like. 'It's your likeness,' he answered. 'How do you know that?' 'Papa said so.'" He was not always so indiscreet in his remarks, happily for the peace of the court. Two ladies came to see him while he ate his supper, "He stared at Mme de Peschier so hard that she said, 'I can see that Monseigneur does me the honour to like me because he stares so.' The dauphin whispered into his nurse's ear, 'It's because she is so like Papa's monkey, Robert.'" Wild animals were sometimes brought in from the surrounding forest to make pets for the children, a rabbit, a squirrel or little wild birds. There is a charming story of the dauphin's own little aviary, which, although it properly belongs to St Germain and not to Fontainebleau, may find a place here while we are talking of the children's pets. The winter of 1607-8 was exceptionally severe. The Seine froze so that for weeks people crossed it on foot and on horseback; the snow lay in great heaps round the castle and Dr Héroard was kept busy with chapped skins and colds among the children. " The dauphin never complained of the cold and no one could keep him near the fire. He was always by the window which overlooks the meadows." Perhaps it was outside this window that the aviary stood on the balcony. During the frost more than one half-frozen bird had been brought to the dauphin and placed in this aviary and one day the little boy told Héroard all about his birds. " 'I have a company of little birds in my aviary where they have been ever since the frost began. I have an Ardenne finch who is the captain and another who is the lieutenant, and another who is the ensign. There is a lark who is the drummer and a gold-

finch is the piper. Every day, every single day, I have a
pan of hot ashes put into the aviary and they march round
it two and by two and warm themselves, and they sing.
Then I have some wine put into their water for them
to drink, and do you know the drummer got drunk.'"
This was a memorable frost which lasted from early
December to well into March. Héroard says the
dauphin dashed like "an escaped horse" when he
got out into the snow after five weeks in the castle.

Besides monkeys and birds the children possessed
many dogs. The dauphin seems always to have been
fond of them, except perhaps of Lion, the king's big
dog, who frightened him. Once when the king scolded
him for crying at Lion he said, "It was because I
hadn't time to think," but thinking or not thinking
Lion remained a terror. Pataut was his own pet. He
belonged to early days at St Germain and went with
him wherever he went, whether to Fontainebleau or
to Paris. In 1609 M. de Souvré vexed him by telling
him that he had too many dogs. "'Monsieur, you
must get rid of some of those of no value or who are
too old like Pataut.' 'Pataut! Oh! no. I want to
take care of the old ones, M. de Souvré.'" Dogs
were not only pets, however, for the dauphin lived in
an atmosphere of hunting, and at St Germain and at
Fontainebleau there was much interesting lore to
be learnt on their management. We hear one night
how "he talked all through his supper with the King's
huntsman, Maître Martin, about his dogs; knew their
names, what they could do, how the puppies were
trained, talking like a well-informed grown-up man
and using all the proper terms." Dogs to play with
and dogs to hunt with were a joy, but the dauphin
resented their use in bear-baiting and similar sports.
The sentiment of pity was kept strictly for dogs. He

could watch fox-cubs and little boars, trapped in the
forest, being chased round the courtyard quite happily
for in this sport the dogs could come to no hurt;
a bear or a bullfight was another matter. Watching
these entertainments was done from the long gallery
now called La Galerie de Diane, whose windows over-
look the Cour Ovale of the Palace. In Henri IV's
day it was known as the ball-room. The mistress of a
former king, however celebrated in her day, was of
little interest to the new generation. Henri II and
Diane had been dead many years, it is true, but not
long enough for Time to weave romance about their
names in its magic loom. Their daughter, the Duchesse
d'Angoulême, had her place in Henri IV's court and
the gallery, with Diane's emblems interwoven with her
lover's, was just the ball-room, whose deep embrasured
windows were excellently placed to watch any sport
going on in the courtyard below, whether tilting at
the ring, baiting bears or chasing fox-cubs.

One day Henri sent for the children to see a fight
between a bull, bears and dogs. The dauphin watched
with the rest till one of the bears got the better of a
dog, " when he shouted ' Kill the bears, kill all the
bears.' " The killing of the bears would not have
upset him any more than the killing of little foxes and
boars. It is true he ran away one day when he was
taken to see a pig cut up in the courtyard, but his
real sensitiveness was kept for dogs. On one occasion
a strolling Englishman brought a bear to be baited
at Fontainebleau, and the dauphin overheard a discussion as to whether it and the dogs should fight
à l'outrance. " ' No, no, they shan't fight to the death.' "
This feeling for dogs was lasting. Some years later
than the Englishman's bear-baiting, the boy, a newly-
made king, " went on horseback from the Louvre to

the Tuileries where he saw a lion tied to a tree. A dog was thrown to it which the lion immediately strangled. The king flew into a passion and ordered them to punish the man who had thrown the dog."

Falconry was the dauphin's favourite sport from a very little boy, perhaps through his liking for the king's handsome young falconer, de Luynes. The first definite day's hunting which the dauphin himself organized occurred when he was six years old and falcons played their part. The children were all staying for a few weeks at Noisy, near to Versailles, then only a village, and one morning the dauphin " took it into his head to go a-hunting. He said to M. de Ventelet, ' Tetai, get my coach, I am going to hunt. Taine,' as he calls the captain of his guard, ' get the hawks ready.' He gave his orders very clearly and with great gravity. At half past four he got into his coach and went a-hunting for the first time. He was driven in the direction of the mill at Versailles, saw a hare taken by two greyhounds, five or six quails and two partridges by hawks. They saw a big fox too which got away behind the mill; returned at a quarter to seven and told all he had done over his supper." His first day's hunting was certainly varied. When he went to live in Paris he spent much of his time hunting and hawking; rabbits and hares on the south side of the Seine where a dense city has nowadays pushed back the open country many miles; wolves in the Bois de Boulogne; were they brought there to be hunted or did they really haunt the outskirts of Paris? wild fowl along the Seine beyond the Tuileries, and when all else failed there were always sparrows and crows to be shot at from the Louvre windows with a little arquebus. He learnt to do this at Fontainebleau and Héroard says he was a very good shot.

But there were many things at Fontainebleau besides pet animals, bear-baiting and the wild things of the forest. Some of the dauphin's happiest hours were spent in a pastime immemorially dear to children, the making of a pretend garden. Perhaps a small Abel had begun the play and learnt it by watching his father Adam, for a love of gardening, happily for mankind, is as old and as ineradicable as original sin. Possibly, indeed, it is sin's natural antidote and the two were born together in man's soul. Fontainebleau, at any rate, was the place to play the enchanting game. The court and the big family from St Germain-en-Laye passed a great part of 1606 and 1607 there for these were years of plague in Paris and its environs; and the dauphin had plenty of time to make his garden. One day in February Héroard noted down that the children went to play in the Jardin des Pins. There were a great number of gardens within the precincts of the palace which have since been merged together, and the *Jardin des Pins* was a wooded stretch lying on the west of the pond. The dauphin and his brothers spent many hours that winter at work at their garden. It was a four-square enclosure and ditched round. The dauphin planted it with cabbages, he said, by pulling up little seedling trees and setting them in the loose soil within the enclosure. " Next day he dug hard with a spade and made a bridge into his garden over the ditch. After supper news came that the king would arrive the following day. The dauphin flushed and jumped for joy, and also a little for fear because of the garden he had been making. ' I must go and take it away for fear Papa should be vexed.' He would have liked to have gone at once." The king seems to have taken the play in good part for when spring had fully come we still find the dauphin busily digging. "The dauphin dug himself and handed tools to the others saying, 'Dig or I'll beat you,'" and no doubt féfé Chevalier and féfé Verneuil did as they were bidden. When they were tired of digging "the dauphin was taken in to see the queen. Some of his people pressed him to ask her for money. He was very unwilling for fear of being refused. The queen asked him herself, 'Do you want some money, my son?' 'Yes, please.' The queen told someone to give him three *doublons* and then she asked him what he would do with them. 'I shall give them to my little gardener.' 'What! all three, my son.' 'Yes, mamma, because my garden wants a lock and then he has been working for me a whole year.'" This must have been the "gardener's grandson" who could help at painting as well as digging, obviously a very handy boy. Here are two letters, one from Henri and the other from his little son which show a pleasant community of taste between the two; both cared greatly for the gardens both at Fontainebleau and St Germain-en-Laye.

"Jan. 31st at Paris. My son. Together with your letter Guerin brings me news of you and tells me that in expectation of my arrival you are taking great care of my gardens and plants, which pleases me very much. I have told him when he takes back this letter to give you news of me and of your mamma, the queen; and to tell you that I am coming to see you directly after the Fair of St Germain, where I shall buy some toys for you to play with, which I shall bring with me, provided you love me very much and are a very good boy. Good night, my son. HENRY."

"Thursday September 21st 1606. Papa. I am very sorry you have been ill. I wish I could be near you to serve you and help you pass the time if you liked me to. But if I came I should want your coach and mamma's, if you please. I can make such pretty gardens and I have made one here in this lovely house, which you can see if you will come one day. I have made a pretty little fountain too, and I have begun to make a little house but the reason I cannot finish it is because my valet Birat has left my hammer and chisel behind at St Germain. I am afraid of tiring you, papa, so wish you good night and mamma too. My pen is very heavy. I am and always shall be, papa, your very humble and very obedient son and servant. LOUIS DAUPHIN."

The queen does not seem to have been a mother to play with and cuddle, and Héroard never records either the sudden manifestations of passionate affection or the too often teasing games in which the king frequently indulged. Her little son often wished that she, as well as his father, would answer the letters he wrote to them, but she never gratified his wish. " ' Why doesn't Mamma write to me? ' he once said. He was told she only wrote to the king. ' Papa says Mamma makes a great many mistakes but if she wrote to me even if there were mistakes I should keep the letter very safely.' " When Marie was first chosen to be the Queen of France she wrote several times to her future husband; beautiful letters they were and the king complimented her on her knowledge of French, but so far as the French went they were the work of a secretary. She must have been ashamed, poor lady, to let her son see how badly she wrote and spelt. No doubt court life and the birth of six children in nine years kept her occupied. But if she were not a very loving mother she was more ready than the king to gratify the children's longings when money could give them what they wanted. During the summer stay at Fontainebleau, in the year 1608, the children and their little court were fascinated with an ingenious puppet show which a poor Marseillais had brought to exhibit in the hope of selling it. It was fitted into " a small cabinet and had a number of little figures which moved about by the help of sand instead of water," as was the usual method in such contrivances. " The dauphin was much amused, learnt how to start the sand and how to stop it, using the same words as the Marseillais, saying *contrepés* instead of *contrepoids*. M. de Ventadour and M. de Montespan did all they could to persuade him to send the man to exhibit his invention to the king, and to beg his Majesty to buy it. He would not answer although he heard them say that the poor man got his living this way. The longing to possess the puppet show and the fear of vexing the king struggled together in his mind. At last M. de Montespan pressed him hard, offering to go himself to the king with the request, and at last the dauphin very reluctantly said ' Yes.' After a while M. de Montespan returned and said, ' Monsieur, the king will give you the puppet show.' ' Has the man been paid?' he asked. He played very happily with the mechanism which showed the taking of Jerusalem and the Crucifixion. He was sorry for the poor man and said ' Mamanga, do please give him half a sole and half a carp and a loaf. He has had nothing to eat all day.' It was a Friday." The truth was that the king had demurred over the price and it was the queen who had promised to pay. The king had said that the price was ridiculous and lost his temper with her, saying she always spoilt their son. The price, twenty *écus*, may well have been excessive, for the man, no doubt, counted on getting a big price at court.

The puppet show, with its curious choice of subjects

has long since vanished; while it lasted the ingenious shifting of the weight of sand and the movement of its many little figures gave much happiness to a group of children, long vanished too. A complaint that modern children have too many mechanical toys is heard as often as Christmas comes round, and a desire for good old-fashioned playthings, that will not break in careless little hands, is nearly as common. The truth is that there were mechanical toys in past days but that such toys are always soon broken, whereas simpler and stronger toys may often serve more than one generation and be produced as evidence of the superiority of old things and olden days. Toys are in this like old furniture and old buildings. Only those of solid material and sound construction can defy careless usage or the decay of time; the weak and the flimsy and the badly made are gone and we know not of them. The dauphin's little drum which occasioned the " little tragedy " between the king and his son, the toy fountain which could be made to spout water, and not a few other such contrivances, have perished like the puppet show; they would all have been dingy enough by now had they lasted for us to see.

Samples of some of the most charming, because the most simple, of the children's toys have happily lasted, on which no dingy touch of time rests. Between the latter years of the sixteenth century and the early years of the seventeenth there flourished in the neighbourhood of Fontainebleau a pottery which made and sold little figures of many shapes and colours. In the monograph introducing the exquisite book of illustrations entitled *La céramique Française*, which we owe to Mlle M. J. Ballot, she tells us all that can now be known of this pottery. It belonged to the school of Bernard Palissy, to *l'art rustique* with its dishes reproducing, as a naturalist might, all the weeds and beasts of a brook, its jugs twined in high relief with wild roses, its *plaques* with nymphs and sea-monsters, sea-weeds and shells, odd and fantastic, often lovely in colour, wonderful too in the hard brilliance of its glaze. The potters at Fontainebleau could not rival the old master, but there is often great charm about the few examples of their work which still survives. In the galleries of the Louvre there are half a dozen of these little figures, and the Cluny also possesses a few; but pottery, especially pottery that was mainly used as toys, often has a short life, and examples of only a small fraction of those played with by the children at Fontainebleau still survive. The hurdy-gurdy man and the player on the bagpipes, the boy with his shirt full of puppies, the baby on the dolphin, and the exquisite figure of the woman suckling a swaddled infant all come from the pottery at Avon, near Fontainebleau. The last of these, *La nourice*, became famous for its graceful charm and was often copied in china. There is yet another figure of our dauphin on horseback, which is very similar in character to the Avon ware, though its origin is not certain. It may have been made in 1608 to commemorate the child's first riding lesson. Héroard tells us that on "Aug. 15th of that year the dauphin sent for his boots and golden spurs, rode a-horseback on all the stools in his room and on everything else on which he could climb. At five o'clock was taken to the alley by the pool and mounted on a little nag which M. de Vitry has given him. I have never seen a grown man better seated on horseback, body upright and legs well placed as if he knew all about it. This was his first ride. He returned to his room at a quarter to nine and told us the following tale. 'The court is a funny

fellow, he agrees with everything I say. When I ask
is it nine o'clock, "Yes," he says, "it is nine." When
I get my feet wet he says, "Yes Monsieur, that's a
good thing, it will refresh you." Oh! he's a funny
fellow.'" The horse in the statuette is somewhat
clumsy and the rider, not yet seven years old if the
figure does represent the first lesson, is droll enough
in his grown-up clothes and gloves and ruff.

Héroard very often speaks of visits to Avon and also
to some place in Fontainebleau itself where the children
were frequent purchasers. There seems to have been
an unending variety. One day the dauphin bought
"dogs, lions and bulls, took them back to his room
and made them all fight on the carpet." We may be
sure that the dogs got the best of the battle. Another
day "the son of M. de Saint Luc, aged four years old,
came to say good-bye to him. I whispered in his
ear, 'Monsieur, would you like to make him a present.'
'Yes.' 'Monsieur, what shall it be?' 'A sea-horse,
but don't get a cracked one.' I brought a whole one,
and he gave it very graciously." The taste for these
toys, begun almost in the cradle, seems to have grown
with growing years. Money was never very plentiful
with any of the children, but purchases of Avon pottery
must have consumed a good deal of what they did
have. In May 1608 Héroard describes an original
feast given by the dauphin in honour of a ballet which
the Princesse de Conti and a company of young people
were to dance in the queen's room. Somebody suggested that the table should be decorated with the
dauphin's little pottery figures and the child was
delighted with the idea. "The ballet arrived and
when it was over they all danced branles. The dauphin
did not want to dance so he looked on. M. de Vendôme
led the branle. The dauphin took it into his head to

dance and jumped in above M. de Vendôme and seized Mme de Moret by the left hand. M. de Vendôme said to the dauphin, 'Monsieur, take your proper place.' 'Oh! my proper place is everywhere.' He led Mme de Guise, followed by the whole ballet, to his feast amidst laughter and exclamations. There were little dogs, foxes, boars, oxen, cows, squirrels, angels playing on the *musette* and on flutes, hurdy-gurdy men, crouching dogs, sheep, a big dog in the middle of the table, a dolphin at the top and a monk at the bottom." Presumably the sweetmeats, candied fruits and cakes which made up the feast, were placed in among the medley of little figures.

This feast brings us to another play of the children in which they did but mimic their elders. At the French court the dancing of ballets had long been a favourite amusement in which everybody took part. Elaborate scenic effects and gorgeous costumes made a great part of the show, very much as it does to-day with many of the Russian ballets. The cost, and it was often very great, was borne by the group of courtiers who got up the particular ballet for the entertainment of the king and queen and the rest of the court, and the rivalry was very keen between various groups. The children's ballets were naturally simpler, often not more than dressing up and dancing for fun. Still some, especially those prepared by the older children, were carefully arranged and rehearsed before they were danced in public. Héroard describes how the dauphin dressed up in a sailor's costume got ready for a ballet the Vendôme children were dancing. "He put on the breeches and the full muslin skirt, took his sword and his sword belt and was very much pleased with himself." This ballet was evidently being rehearsed in the dauphin's room. We are told that on another occasion when the older children were dancing that the dauphin joined in " though he had to dance by ear only for he did not know the steps. Nevertheless he acquitted himself very well." At six years old we find him working hard at a ballet to dance before his father and naturally he liked to have his efforts taken seriously. " He danced his ballet in the queen's room and did it very well. The king was delighted. The baby Duc d'Orléans' dresser came in with him in her arms and Madame Christienne's nurse carried her in too and everybody danced the branles. After two turns the dauphin said to Mme de Montglat ' Mamanga, what pleasure is there in this? dancing with children! Take them away.' " Madame and her sister Christienne learnt to dance quite as young as their brother, and indeed took regular dancing-lessons younger than he did. He could admire them too when they were old enough to dance on their own feet and not in their nurse's arms. One evening Madame dressed up in the dauphin's suit, " doublet and hose of crimson, trimmed with silver lace; she danced the branle, the gaillard and the saraband. She resembles the dauphin greatly," and while she danced her brother, who had gone to bed early thus leaving his clothes for her to dress up in, looked on with approval. Madame must have been a very happy little girl that evening for we nearly always find her playing the part of adoring younger sister. Her very subordinate position in the nursery is often funnily shown by Héroard's jottings. One day the children had been rehearsing a ballet in M. de Verneuil's room and after it was over the dauphin and Madame had supper together. " When he had eaten all the sweetbread he wanted he said ' Take the dish and give the rest to my sister.' She was so pleased and said

'Well, I did want some. I felt I could eat it but I didn't dare ask Monsieur for any.' " These ballets were often no more than games of dressing up that all the children in that queer crowded nursery joined in. Here is one such game on February 1608 when they were all at St Germain-en-Laye. " Mlle de Vendôme put on a cap such as a *bourgeoise* wears, and so did Madame and the little Frontenac girl and little de Vitry and her nurse's child, and little Marguerite who belonged to Mlle de Vendôme. Little Louise, Nurse Dondon's child, was dressed as a bride. The dauphin took a kit and placed himself between Boileau and Indret, his musicians, played with them and made all the little *bourgeoises* dance. He played cadences quite nicely and the tunes people play at weddings." The children would know all about such affairs for it was the common custom for wedding parties from the little town of St Germain-en-Laye to ask permission to dance in the castle hall. It was readily enough given, too readily the dauphin sometimes thought. The bourgeois couples and their friends could be tolerated but when it came to a gipsy wedding he objected. " Take them away. They smell! " was his comment and he was very angry when his attendants danced with them.

To return to the children's ballets. We cannot describe them all but one quite elaborate one will make a fitting end to the subject. It took place in 1608 when the dauphin was not yet seven years old. " Supper was at six. The dauphin went to Mme de Montglat's room to dress for the ballet he was to dance. He did not want anyone to see him for fear of being recognized, and all the more because he, like all those dancing with him, was dressed as a girl and masked. The company consisted of Monseigneur the

dauphin, Mlle de Vendôme, Mme and Mlle de Vitry,
M. le Chevalier and M. de Verneuil; Mme de Valon's
niece, Marguerite, and Mlle de Verneuil, Nicole, the
daughter of Madame's nurse, and Louise, Nurse Dondon's daughter. The ballet was called The Lanterns
because each dancer carried a half-hoop twined with
bay leaves, from which hung a tiny lantern with a
lighted taper in it. They were to dance three figures,
one an H, one an O, and one an L; then they passed
under the hoops and finished with a courante. They
went to the king's room at eight o'clock where the
ballet was danced before him. It was very well done
although they had not previously rehearsed it in
costume and masked. The king, who was talking to
two jesuits, was so pleased that tears came into his
eyes. The whole court admired them. They had
only taken four days learning it. When the dauphin
was in bed he saw the Piedmontese soldier who had
arranged the ballet. He pointed to him saying, 'There's
the man who made it up,' as if he wanted to give
honour where it was due.'

Now and then the children tried their hand at a
play where parts had to be learnt, although this was
by no means so popular as dancing in character. One
day in April 1609, the dauphin's "little gentlemen," as
Héroard calls the sons of nobles brought up with the
king's sons, played some scenes from "Bradamante."
The dauphin had a few lines to say as Charlemagne,
but when they came before the king to act he said
"'I've forgotten my part.'" We must suppose that he
was prompted into saying his speech, though Héroard
doesn't say. It had been an unlucky day before this,
for at five o'clock he had been taken to the garden
where the king was. "Near the sluice to the pool
there was a little water-course a foot and half wide to

carry the water to the canal. The king made him jump this water-course, which he did without running. The king told him to jump it with a run but the dauphin was afraid he might miss his jump and tumble in and make all the court laugh at him. The king jumped himself and made others jump it to encourage him. M. de Souvré threatened to whip him, and he said he'd rather be whipped than jump. This annoyed the king and he said he was to be whipped. Taken away protesting that he would jump. Was whipped three strokes with the birch-rod which was the first time with that; said "'That doesn't hurt.'" He kept up his pride but all the same it was not a good preparation for playing Charlemagne.

Acting was, however, generally left to professional players. In Paris at this date a comedy was acted every night at the Hotel de Bourgogne, to which court and bourgeois went alike. Young Thomas Platter, who described the fountains of St Germain-en-Laye for us, wrote an equally vivid account of these comedies. L'Estoile, the diarist, often mentions them but Platter's account is the most amusing. He tells us that caterers would advertise the price of a feast with so many courses, including silver, lights, flowers, and if a comedy was desired after it, so much extra for one. It was obviously the proper termination to a really fashionable dinner-party. But for those who did not care to pay for a private entertainment there was always the company at the Hotel de Bourgogne. Platter does not say what plays he saw, obviously light enough in character, but he describes " an actor called Valbran, who plays every day after dinner a comedy in French verse and after it a farce, made up of anything droll which may have happened in Paris, love-affairs and such tales. He is so clever in reciting verses, unrhymed lines or prose, and in embellishing his recitals with such amusing buffoonery that hardly anyone could help laughing, especially if they knew the tale or the people it concerned; for everything at all out of the common that happens in Paris is at once told to Valbran." When the dauphin lived in Paris the queen would often take him to see these plays. The boy was bored by them but he told Héroard that he always laughed, even if they were in Italian, because he did not like people to think him ignorant.

The love of plays was not confined to Paris however. Henri IV built a new wing in the Fountain Court at Fontainebleau with a hall to seat a large audience and leave room for the players. There is an interesting entry in the journal during the dauphin's first visit to Fontainebleau in 1604. " Sep. 18th. The dauphin went into the great new hall to hear a tragedy played by the English players. He listened very quietly until the moment when one of the players was to have his head cut off," when presumably he was frightened and was taken away. We should like to know what the play was, but there are no clues beyond what we can gather from the above entry and from a game popular among the children for a week or two after. " The dauphin," we learn from more than one similar entry, " dressed up with his pinafore tied round his head and a white scarf on, and marched about with great strides saying ' tiph-toph! milord.' " It is in vain that we turn to " The Elizabethan Stage " for even Sir Edmund Chambers can tell us nothing more. He says " that it is conceivable that the theme may have been the execution of John Tiptoft, Earl of Worcester, at the restoration of Henry VI in 1470." More he cannot say on the subject of the play, but he does tell us that a company of English players was acting in Paris early in the seventeenth century and that either this or another company of strolling players certainly spent some weeks at Fontainebleau in the year 1604, acting in the king's new " great hall."

There were many and various entertainments in this hall as the summers went by, and each entertainment found its echo in the children's games. Now it was pantaloon, now a marvellous tumbler or a child rope-dancer who excited them to emulation. Life at Fontainebleau must have been very full of interest but perhaps because of its crowded life, its constant bustle of the court, the forest palace never quite took the place of St Germain-en-Laye, their very own home. The dauphin at any rate was always happy to return there.

CHAPTER VII

It is clear how deeply interested Héroard was in the dauphin's education from the tone of many of his comments on the events he describes in his journal. Proofs of the good doctor's preoccupation with the subject occur on nearly every page. Stories from the Bible and from history which he told, the small library of illustrated books in his study always ready for the child to look at, the unpremeditated lessons over a meal or out at play in the garden, lessons all the more effective because they were not thought of as lessons at all, must have formed a most valuable part of a very imperfect education. That it was so imperfect must have been a constant source of regret and anxiety to Héroard, for we know from his own pen of what paramount importance he considered the education of a prince to be. So important did he think it that he wrote a long treatise on the subject in the form of an imaginary conversation between himself and the dauphin's governor, M. de Souvré. It would be interesting to know if this treatise, in which M. de Souvré, a nobleman of distinguished family, humbly questions and the doctor, of no nobility at all, politely but with an artless infallibility replies, was ever presented. If it were it can hardly have been accepted with the admiring docility shown by de Souvré in these imaginary talks; certainly there was nothing in his method of bringing up the dauphin, after the child came under his care at eight years old, to indicate that he agreed with the doctor's theories. They were not, indeed, in accordance with current views on education, and yet, in spite of this fact, the treatise does throw considerable light on the methods of teaching in vogue at the beginning of the seventeenth century. The conversations are six in number, the first three of which are wholly occupied with a discussion on the choice of lessons suitable to a little child, while the three later ones are almost as wholly concerned with the special studies proper for a boy destined to be a king. These last are long and prosy and not, generally speaking, applicable to most children, but the first three are full of the naïve piety, the reasonableness and the real sense of values which are characteristic of the doctor throughout the whole diary. The talks were supposed to have been held very early in the morning in the gardens or forest of St Germain-en-Laye during one hot spell of summer weather. One of them opens with the following little *mise en scène*. " At dawn of day, worn out with the extraordinary heat of the night, I arose with the intention of going into the park both to breathe the fresh morning air and to secure an hour or two for quiet thought. But on leaving the castle I met an honest fellow who told me M. de Souvré was awaiting me in the forest. Changing the direction of my steps, therefore, I came up with him and found him walking apart from his menservants in pensive mood." As M. de Souvré had already listened to three days of instruction it was good of him to await a fourth so eagerly. This fourth was a dull talk and does not concern us and we shall do better to turn back to the first morning.

M. de Souvré began the whole discussion by raising the question of the age at which a boy should be

A PORTRAIT IN EARTHENWARE

*From La Céramique Française. M. J. Ballot
By permission of Les Éditions Albert Morancé*

handed over to men for his upbringing. Héroard replied that he thought twenty months or two years long enough for a child to be suckled, as a diet of only milk for a longer period would make him soft, but that although weaned he should still be left in the charge of women till he was six years old, for women understood children better than men. It was important, however, that the woman in charge should be a person of good manners and well instructed, for a child was capable of being taught so soon as it could speak. The first lesson for it to learn was to fear and obey, the second to love right and shun evil. " Then, as it were in play, their minds should be lifted to higher things, to admiration of matters beyond their ken, speaking to them often of God, and by showing them the heavens above lead them to the knowledge that He created all things; that He is Lord and King of everything in heaven and earth; that the sun they see, the moon and the stars are His house, the palace wherein He dwells. By marvelling at all these things a certain fear will be engendered wherefrom piety will spring." Héroard also considers that it would be well to draw up a short catechism of those things necessary for faith as well as of those which long usage has elevated into laws of conduct and observance, always taking care not to make a superstitious man instead of a religious one. " For," he goes on, " the religious man is gentle, kindly, brave and charitable; loving and reverencing God and at peace in his own soul; the superstitious man is a brute beast full of guile and cruelty, cowardice and ruthlessness, who can only image to himself the judgments and divine vengeance of God." The whole passage throws a most interesting light on the mind of a man who had accepted catholicism but who, remembering his hugue-

not upbringing said in his heart, as Henri IV had said,
" but after all are not we all Christians? " In Montpellier, where in his boyhood Héroard had seen religious
warfare in its most savage form and waged with equal
cruelty by catholic and huguenot in turn, he had
learnt that " the superstitious man is a brute beast,
full of guile and cruelty, cowardice and ruthlessness."
Gladly would he have this lesson taught to a future
King of France, the pacification of whose kingdom
had been made possible by tolerance.

In the matter of reading and writing, the doctor
thought that these should be taught by a woman
who could herself speak correctly and write a good
hand. De Souvré was anxious to know what books
should be used, and here Héroard was in agreement
with the general opinion of his day. He answered
that a child should first learn by heart a selection of
the Proverbs of Solomon, from which he would learn
many good precepts all the more likely to be remembered by a pupil who was a king's son because
their author was himself a great and good king. To
the Proverbs of Solomon should be added *Les quatrains
de Pibrac*, a book very famous in an age when Solomon
and Pibrac were held to be the first sources of a sound
education for little children. We shall return to the
quatrains later on. Héroard next recommended that
" as soon as a boy can read a little he should read the
historical books of the Bible, which he would study
with both pleasure and profit, enjoying the history and
learning from it many things which a Christian child
should know." It is clear from many passages in the
journal that the Bible in French was in common use
in the children's home. Fifty years earlier the possession of a Bible in the vernacular was often a very real
danger, but in the boyhood of Louis XIII, France

was more tolerant in matters of religion than any country in Europe, while catholic reform and huguenot teaching had both brought the Bible into a wide-spread use. But Héroard would not restrict children only to the Bible, for he " was not so unmindful of these small people as to forbid other books so long as they may learn something good or something true from them." There were other writers than the Sieur de Pibrac who had written in such a way as to teach sound morals and good behaviour in a pleasant manner. " Such was the ancient Æsop whose fables, written so delightfully, have come down to our own day."

Writing should be taught along with reading so that as soon as a boy's intelligence was sufficiently developed, at six with forward children and at seven years old with more backward ones, the more serious studies could be approached. Latin came first in importance, not so much to allow the pupil to enjoy classical authors as to enable him to read the works of learned men on all subjects, since Latin was the common language of the educated throughout Europe; for this reason less time should be spent on grammar and learning by rote than on acquiring fluency in reading. Here, as in much else in the doctor's treatise, we feel the influence of Montaigne. Greek was only necessary for scholars, but, on the other hand, it was highly desirable to learn the languages of modern countries; nor should a pupil neglect to learn to speak his own tongue with correctness, " free from affectations and insincerities calculated only to hide his thoughts." Languages were, however, by no means the only subject necessary for a sound education. Nature should be studied but " without the pupil's confusing himself with contentious matters." Arithmetic and geometry also, for without a knowledge of these " a man would be ignorant of much which he ought to know in peace and in war." Music was not to be neglected for though no man need sing himself he should be able to listen with pleasure and find rest in music when troubled with affairs. Poetry and philosophy could be usefully employed; to the first he should be an attentive listener, of the second a diligent disciple so long as care was taken that the writings of both poets and philosophers were of sound morality, " for many attract by the beauty of their cadences only to poison youth by their wickedness."

Héroard next strikes a very modern note. Geography, both of the world at large and of France in particular, was to be an important lesson, especially necessary for a prince. After speaking generally on the study the doctor continues: " Taking a compass and rule in hand make him measure the whole terrestrial globe and after that let him go on to that portion of the earth which, in God's time, will fall into his hands. Teach him, by pacing his room, the roads and the routes about France first, and then the world; teach him something of the nature of foreign nations, their history, their manners and characters, their laws and customs, so that, when he is king, he may shape his enterprises and carry out his designs over the whole world." A study of the stars was to follow the study of the earth, and after this some slight knowledge of mechanics was desirable since " the dauphin had an extraordinary aptitude for such things." And so through the long course of studies, reading, writing, languages and mathematics, poetry, philosophy, music, geography, astronomy, and mechanics we reach the study of history, " the real school of princes whereby they may learn the wisdom of age while yet they be

young." Héroard has much to say on this last subject,
a favourite one with him. M. de Souvré, not un-
naturally, asked whether all these subjects, except indeed
reading and writing, could be studied in the eight
years between six and fourteen, at which age a young
noble was expected to devote his time to a serious
study of riding, fencing, courtly manners and so on in
the famous Academy of the Sieur Antoine de Pluvinel.
We shall hear more of the Academy later on and of
the great de Pluvinel too, but so far as the education
sketched out by Héroard went he replied that eight
years should be sufficient for a boy of intelligence if
he had a good teacher. If anything remained unlearnt
a part of each day might be given to study for two
years more. From the formidable list of subjects we
might imagine that a boy's whole day would be spent
in lessons, and it is therefore a relief to learn that the
doctor believed in play as well as in work. " Let him
study two hours in the morning and two hours in the
afternoon. He should be up and dressed by seven
o'clock and study till nine. Then to church, and
after mass be free till eleven, at which hour he should
dine. Lessons should begin again at one and end at
three. He should then be free till six o'clock supper
and he should go to bed at nine." Not only was
there to be time for play but its importance as a means
of happiness and health was very present in the doctor's
mind. " In their playtime, children should be free
to enjoy themselves, walking and dancing, running
and jumping, playing at tennis and pall-mall, riding,
hawking and coursing," any healthy pastime they
fancy, but keep them from the over-strenuous fatigue
of hunting till they were nearer manhood. Héroard's
excellent views on games are thus expressed: " For just
as we ought to make young people happy so we must

not neglect the care of their bodies, giving them exercise at the right time and in the right place, lest by laziness they lose their health and strength and drift downwards until they are unfit for anything. Their games should be suitable to their years, the season and the place they live in." No doubt he remembered the mad indulgence in hunting of his first royal master, Charles IX, and the effeminancy of his second, Henri III. The beloved dauphin, Louis, was to be trained to be the perfect king had Héroard had his way. And this is how he sums up his disquisition on education in words that recall Bacon's dictum that " reading maketh a full man." " Learning," says Héroard, " is useful to the formation of character and if learned men are often stupid and perverse that is not the fault of their learning but because they use and abuse it to wrong ends. Knives are to cut meat and bread, not to murder men; corrosive sublimate and arsenic are not intended to be put to a cruel use; wine should rejoice the heart of man and not destroy his reason. Learning is the key to a full life."

When the lot of a schoolboy in any country early in the seventeenth century is considered we are struck by the sanity, the kindly common sense of Héroard. He may err in thinking a child between six and fourteen can study so many subjects but he does insist on short hours, kindly methods and healthy, happy play. Montaigne had raised his voice against the stupidity and brutality of schools as he knew them, but half a century later than Montaigne a French writer still wrote of the schools in Paris as cold, dark, and evil-smelling, straw on the floor and the various classes huddled together on benches in one room. The floggings, he adds, were so severe that boys were known to have died from the cruelty of their

BOYS AT PLAY

[face p. 140

masters. In turning over the pages of a contemporary Englishman we can find an interesting parallel to Héroard's treatise, and since the education of boys in England and France did not greatly differ, we might pause just long enough to see what this Englishman thought. John Brinsley the elder's "Grammar School" was not published till 1612, but his experience was already old and he seems often to have arrived at very similar conclusions to the French doctor. The age he recommends for a boy to enter school is between seven and eight. Brinsley thinks six too young and " if any be sent so early they are rather sent to school to keep them from troubling the house at home . . . than for any great hope that they should learn anything in effect." A dame school was the proper place for little children, and Brinsley agrees with Héroard that a child was best taught to read by a woman who could speak her mother tongue properly. By six years old children should be able to read and this they could easily do if the teacher recognizes a child's love of rhyming, " for rhyming pleases children, ba, be, bi, bo, bu and so on up to more letters as land, sand and so on; and then hard syllables such as gnaw, puddle, month, weight and many others," and he adds, " the easier and more familiar the matter is to them, the faster they learn." A little further on he returns to the advantage of rhyme and metre: " Children should first learn their Abcie and primer. Secondly the psalms in metre because children wil learne that booke with most readinesse and delight through the running of the metre, as is found by experience. Thirdly if any require any other little booke meet to enter children the *School of Vertue* is one of the principall and easiest for enterers, being full of precepts of civilitie and such as children will soon learne and take delight in."

I have had the *School of Vertue* in my hand, a tiny
volume printed in now somewhat faded black-letter
type. The verses are the merest jingling couplets full
of instruction in daily habits and of rhyming graces
before and after meals. Here is a sample showing
how a boy should go to school. Other portions of the
same long set of verses will be found in a subsequent
chapter.

> " With thy cap fairly brusht thy head cover than
> Putting it off in speaking to any man.
> Cato doth counsel thee thy elders to reverence
> Declaring thereby thy duty and reverence.
> Thy shirt collar fast unto thy neck knit,
> Comely thy cloathing about thee make fit.
>
> .   .   .
>
> This done thy satchel and thy books take
> And to the school haste do thou make.
> But ere thou go with thyself forethink
> That thou take with thee pen, paper and ink.
> For these are the things for study necessary,
> Forget not thou them with thee to carry.
> The souldier preparing himself to the field
> Leaves not behind him his sword or his shield.
> No more should a scholar forget foolishly
> What at his school he must occupy."

The comparison of the schoolboy and the soldier is
positively poetical in such a " false gallop of verses."

But once a boy has entered a grammar school
Brinsley and Héroard cease to be in agreement except
in the importance of learning to use the mother tongue
correctly. Latin in the Englishman's school, just as
it was in all French schools of the date, was the principal
and almost the only subject taught. Greek and Hebrew
might perhaps be added later on but at any rate a
" knowledge of English must go along with Latin so

that reading the first is not forgotten in learning the second . . . for our chiefe endeavour should be to express our minds purely and readily in our own tongue." The school hours recommended by Brinsley were common to both countries. Six o'clock in the morning was the proper hour for boys to be in school, and school-time seems to have lasted, with breaks for meals, church and some play till half-past five. Brinsley does, however, advocate the plan for keeping " one part of an afternoon weekly for recreation as a reward for diligence, obedience, and profitting." Whether such a plan was ever observed in France I do not know. The marvel is that children ever survived the long hours and brutal punishments of a now happily past age. Héroard does indeed stand out as a " modern " in comparison with his contemporaries just as does Montaigne.

While boys of the lesser nobility and the bourgeois classes went to grammar schools the sons of the wealthier nobles either had tutors or went to such a school as the Collège de Navarre in Paris. Henri IV and his cousins, Charles and Henri de Valois, had all been to the Collège and it may have been there that Henri IV had been well whipped to his lasting good, as he told Mme de Montglat. So far as lesson-times for the children at St Germain-en-Laye went they were certainly far removed from the hardships endured by other boys, but they were not without their worries and whippings. Early hours were, of course, common to everybody and therefore seven o'clock could not be considered a hardship for school-time to begin. As a very little boy the dauphin, and no doubt the other children as well, got up when they pleased; but as they grew older these habits came to an end. Some months after Henri's death Héroard wrote in his journal: "The king waked at seven o'clock. He was so vexed that he had been left to sleep so long that he nearly cried. 'Oh, dear, they'll think I am a sluggard. I don't want to be dressed in my own room. I don't want all the people to see me. They'll only say I am a lie-a-bed.'" Unlucky little king of ten years old. His "own room" had been his father's room and the child was terrified to sleep in the bed where he had seen the murdered king lying. So he slept in a small room opening from it, his *cabinet*, and only went into the larger room for the ceremony of a king's levee. Seven o'clock might seem early enough for the court to be up and waiting but evidently it was considered a late hour. A month later on a winter's morning we learn that "The king got up at six and said his prayers. He let his hair be combed without a fuss contrary to his wont; breakfasted at half past seven having done no lessons as a reward for being quiet over his hair." It is quite clear that there was no hardship in these hours. Héroard, in his treatise on education, mentions five o'clock as the common hour for him to meet M. de Souvré, for by six the king might expect them to join him in the garden. To get up early on a cold and dark winter morning may have been disagreeable but at least it was the common habit.

In the matter of whippings over lessons these, as we might expect, were frequent though the punishments were rather for naughtiness than for ill-learnt lessons. As for instance when "Mme de Montglat said he must do his lessons. He hid his book in his hat. She saw it and asked, 'Monsieur, where is your book?' 'Little de Luz has run away with it.' 'Monsieur, look in your hat.' Was whipped for telling a lie." Mme de Montglat does not seem to have

been over-sensitive in the matter of truth-telling herself
to judge by the following. " While going to bed the
dauphin said to Mme de Montglat, ' Mamanga,
don't beat me to-morrow morning.' She replied,
' Monsieur, I promised not to.' ' Oh! I know you
did, but you'll hear me repeat my verses and then
you'll say, " and now I shall spank that boy." ' She
had twice whipped him after promising not to do so."
Perhaps breaking a promise was not quite the same as
telling a lie in her eyes. When the dauphin was six
years old the king gave orders that one of his gentlemen
was to hold him while he was whipped instead of, as
heretofore, one of his chamber-women. It may have
been promotion but we can imagine a special sting in
the following chastisement. " At two o'clock Boileau,
his viol player, came to give him a dancing lesson.
The dauphin was very rude to him and tried to kick
him. Mme de Montglat saw it and made Boileau
hold him while she caned him." And Boileau was a
favourite as well as the injured party.

But it is time to go back to the dauphin and his
earliest lessons. Héroard's naïve belief that a baby of
a few months old was not too young to profit by a
moral lesson is both funny and pathetic. In December
1601, he was already eager to train a child not yet
three months old. He tells us that the dauphin
" listened attentively while I told him that he must be
good and just, and that God had brought him into the
world with this intent, and to be a good king; and
that if he were so God would love him. He smiled
at these words." If he could smile at ten weeks old
at the little moral lesson we need not be surprised at
the following entries in the journal a few weeks later.
" Dec. 12th. He began to recognize people and to
call them in his baby way. When the dresser asked

who I was he babbled quite plainly ' E'ou'ad.' He loves to hear music. Dec. 21st. His nurse asked him ' Are you papa's darling?' He said ' *Oui*.' Messieurs de Villeroi, Alincourt, du Laurens and others were present." It is noticeable that the doctor likes to mention the witnesses of these and similar surprising manifestations of intelligence. *Oui* is a sound a child could more easily be supposed to babble than our English yes; possibly he may have made some such sound on this occasion as on another when " M. de Ventelet told him God was his only master and he answered *oui* with a smile." Héroard is on surer ground when he tells us that in the following March the child began to reach out for things which were offered him. " It was the Psalms of David in M. de Bourges' version. I had given it to Mme de Mont-glat " ; or when about the same date " he crowed and danced to the viol played by Boileau." In the previous December he had already shown a liking for music. It was a taste which grew with him and which he cultivated with success.

These anecdotes of babyhood are not really education, though it is interesting to see this early love of music. But real lessons began very early. Both Héroard, the Frenchman, and Brinsley the Englishman, recommend very much the same books for " enterers," or as we should say, beginners. For English children the Proverbs of Solomon to be learnt by heart, the Bible to learn to read in, the metrical Psalms and, if any variety were needed, the *School of Vertue* with its moral lessons in rhyme, would be sufficient. The Proverbs of Solomon and the Bible are equally to be used by French children but instead of the Psalms and the *School of Vertue* they were given *Les quatrains*; nor in Héroard's scheme were they restricted to these for were there not the fables of Æsop and other little tales " either true or teaching some sound moral." So it would seem that the dauphin was better off than the boys in Brinsley's grammar school. Perhaps these latter had to wait till they could read Æsop if not in Greek at least in a Latin translation.

Not many people nowadays read the *Quatrains de Pibrac*, which had such an immense vogue in the late sixteenth and throughout the seventeenth centuries. Their author was a man of good birth and education, a member of Henri III's *Conseil d'Etat* and more than once an envoy on diplomatic missions. In his native town of Toulouse he occupied a high position and so lived that on his death Montaigne wrote of him: " His mind was so pleasing, his opinions so wholesome, his manners so gentle that his loss was a heavy one for the kingdom of France. A rare and gentle soul whom fate had placed in a corrupt and stormy age." De Pibrac's quatrains number over a hundred and some of them seem little suitable for children, but suitable or not, every well-educated boy and girl in France learnt them as a sure source of morals and good manners. Some, however, contain lessons suitable for quite little children, as for example the following:—

> " Tu ne scaurois d'assez ample salaire
> Recompenser celuy qui t'a soigné
> En ton enfance, et qui t'a enseigné
> A bien parler, et sur tout a bien faire."

Had the dauphin heard this one day when he sat at supper kicking his shoes off while he ate? " His nurse wanted to put them on for him. 'No Maman Dondon, I won't let you put on my shoes.' ' Why not? Monsieur.' ' Because you suckled me when I was little.' " To a child of five years old a little boy of two, for he was not as we have already seen weaned until that age, seems very young. At five too, the quatrains were already a daily task. Not long after this date the dauphin gave a very characteristic lesson in manners to two of his gentlemen in which we seem to catch an echo of de Pibrac. " He was taken to hear mass, carried by M. Birat who was bareheaded, and M. de Belmont followed with his hat on his head. He said to M. Birat, ' Put on your hat.' ' Monsieur, I do very well as I am.' ' No, no, put it on, you are old. Belmont, take yours off.' " Perhaps the following quatrain, on consideration for the aged, had entered into his lessons that week.

> " Es jeux public, au theatre, à la table
> Cède ta place au veillard chenu.
> Quand tu sera à son age venu
> Tu trouveras qui fera la semblable."

These verses, if not very interesting, are reasonable enough for a child to learn but the following seem less applicable to a little boy " who feels its life in every limb "; and yet, since they come early in the book and we know the dauphin could repeat the first fifty verses before he was seven years old, he must have learnt them along with the rest.

> " Ce que tu vois de l'homme n'est pas l'homme
> C'est le prison ou il est enserré,
> C'est le tombeau ou il est enterré
> Le lit branlant ou il dort un court somme.
>
> Ce corps mortel, ou l'oeil ravi contemple
> Muscles et nerfs, la chair, le sang, la peau
> Ce n'est pas l'homme ; il est beaucoup plus beau.
> Aussi Dieu l'a reservé pour son temple.
>
> A bien parler ce que l'homme on appelle
> C'est un rayon de la divinité
> C'est un atome esclos de l'unité
> C'est un degout de la source eternelle."

The verses which Brinsley the elder would have English children taught compare sadly enough with the Sieur de Pibrac's quatrains; it may well be that the dauphin, with his sensitive ear, liked them best when he least understood their import. It is a common enough trait in children. Pibrac's teaching was broader in feeling as well as written in better verse than the vast majority of moral lessons in rhyme, and not only was this so but he was possibly one of the very first to launch upon the world a conscious sentiment which has grown to such power and such universality that few would readily believe how modern it is.

> " Ayme l'honneur plus que ta propre vie.
> J'entens l'honneur qui consiste au devoir
> Que rendre on doit, selon l'humain pouvoir
> A Dieu, au Roy, aux lois, à sa Patrie."

" *Sa Patrie*," a new word, almost a new sentiment in 1576, a sign that the mediæval ages were indeed gone, a forecast of fresh troubles for humanity when the sentiment outgrew control.

We learn from chance remarks from Héroard that the children often did their lessons together. On " June 18th, 1606, M. le Dauphin repeated the first four verses of Pibrac as if they had been part of a play, and M. le Chevalier followed him and then M. de Verneuil." Sometimes they showed off their proficiency to the king, and at such times the dauphin's intense jealousy of his brothers made him almost painfully anxious to excel. If it was only Madame who competed with him there was no such feeling, for of course he was older and a boy. When the two children were five and four years old, Héroard tells us that " The king arrived from Paris. The dauphin hung round his neck and took him to the large study.

Madame said her verses to the king and Monseigneur repeated his proverbs. M. and Mlle de Verneuil were there too and they all amused the king by scrambling for small coins which he threw them. M. le Dauphin took all he picked up back to the king. He does not care for money." The dauphin seems to have had a ready power of learning by heart, although we have to remember, as he himself said, "What a funny fellow the court is," and how it always admired him. But he certainly enjoyed learning songs and verses. One day "He asked little Ventelet to teach him a song she knew. He learnt some of it and she said, ' Heavens! Monsieur. What a quick mind you have.' ' My mind is like Papa's monkey Robert's cheeks. He stuffs and stuffs everything in them.' " He could think over what he learnt for Héroard says of him at five years old " he repeated fifteen quatrains and then said over his proverbs. One of these ran thus, ' He who holds his tongue is wise,' and he added out of his own head, ' He who let's it wag is a fool.' " He had his preferences among the Proverbs of Solomon, one of which he made Mme de Montglat repeat over and over again, " *l'homme est heureux qui a trouvé une femme heureuse.*" We may suspect here some jingle in the words which pleased him. But that he could think out the meaning of words at a very early age is clear enough. " April 5th 1605. Mme de Montglat taught him to say ' I believe in God the Father, etc.' He learnt it very well. Then she taught him to say ' God is a spirit.' He repeated this too and added out of his own head, ' I'll wager He isn't the one who haunts the red gallery.' " Prayers and creeds were obviously taught in two languages for sometimes he would say when being put to bed, " Mamanga, don't say ' Pater,' say ' Our Father.' " Here is a prayer

" of which the dauphin was very fond. He taught it
to Madame while they were at Mass. ' Lord God and
Father, I beseech Thee to help me, through Thy holy
Spirit, so to rule and govern myself that all I do, say
or think will be to Thy honour and glory, to the salvation
of my soul and to the edification of Thy people.' "

The Bible in French was certainly a much-used
book. Out of it he learnt his letters when he was
four years old. " March 14th 1605. He amused
himself with a Bible full of pictures. His nurse named
the different figures and pointed out the letters. He
knew them all and repeated them over." Héroard had
too a book of engravings with biblical scenes among
them, which was one of the first books which the
dauphin went to see in the little study up the turret
stairs. The doctor was always ready to tell stories
about the pictures. " Jan. 5th 1605. I showed him
the picture of David and Goliath in my book of
engravings. I pointed out Goliath's head on the spear.
He looked at David on horseback and said ' there is
the little dauphin on his big horse.' " The next
time we hear of this picture-book he wanted to know
much more about David and Goliath; he was two
years older and no longer saw himself in every picture
of a boy. " Sep. 18th 1607. At a quarter to four
was undressed and put to bed for a rest. His women
told him stories about the Fairy Melusine. I said to
him ' they were only fairy tales and not true.' Mme
de Montglat then told him about Daniel in the lions'
den which pleased him very much. I went on with
the Tower of Babel and the confusion of tongues,
' Were there any Frenchmen there? ' ' Yes, Monsieur.
The Frenchmen made the mortar and they got the
stones.' Then I told him about David slaying Goliath.
He made me repeat it and asked whether David was

as big as M. le Chevalier, who was ten years old, if his sling was made of cord, if the stone was a piece of slate. He remembered the word slate because he had seen, on his walk in the garden, a big table made of slate and had heard them say that slate was a very hard stone. He then asked if Goliath was very tall, as tall as his room, if his horse was very big and could carry six men; and if Goliath was very heavy and could he mount his horse alone. At each of the tales I told him he asked ' Is it true? ' ' Yes, Monsieur,' said I, ' they are all in the Bible.' ' I want to learn them myself,' he said, ' and then I can tell them to Papa because they are true and are in Mamanga's Bible. My sister can tell stories of the wasp who stung the goat's back which isn't true but I shall only tell true stories. Mamanga, have you your Bible here? ' ' No, Monsieur.' ' We must get it then and when we go driving you can read to me.' "

Héroard could tell stories which were not true if there was " something good or useful " to be learnt from them, as we know. One night " while the dauphin was being put to bed he began to talk about the figure of Orpheus on one of the fountains at St Germain, which played on a lyre by means of the water. I asked him what the strings were made of. He said copper which was quite correct. I began to tell him the story of Orpheus and how he played the lyre and taught men to play too. I showed him a picture of Orpheus and told him that after his death his lyre was set in the sky with all the other stars. He asked ' Aren't there any viols there too? ' " We cannot but feel that the good doctor is here more willing to give a lesson on the stars than to tell of an Orpheus who could play

" Such strains as would have quite set free
His half regained Eurydice."

Perhaps this was too near a fairy-tale. But we must not carp at a man who could amuse a tiny boy so charmingly as in the following long extract from the journal. "The dauphin waked at seven o'clock and turned himself round and round saying he was going to the fountains to turn on the taps, swish, swish, 'Say thank you M. Francino.' I answered 'Many thanks M. Francino. Do you want to be paid?' 'Yes.' I put a *quart d'écu* into his hand. 'Ho! ho! is it for me really?' I said 'I gave it to M. Francino, not to M. le Dauphin because princes are not paid wages.' He listened to me and hid it in his bed. 'Monsieur, where is the *écu* I gave you?' He gave it back to me and at once began to talk of something else. We talked of going a-hunting and of the boar and the stag the dauphin would kill and send to the king. 'The king will give you a hug and take you into his beautiful gallery in the Louvre!' 'The Louvre? where is it?' 'In Paris. It is Papa's house. In his gallery he has beautiful armour of gold and silver, and he will say, my son, take whatever you like and here is the key of my gallery because you are a good boy and not wilful, and you have killed a boar and a stag.' We talked a long time very happily. Then he said 'When I go to Paris I shall run an Irishman through with my sword.' 'But, Monsieur, princes must not hurt people and never hit them. If you meet a naughty Irishman you must tell someone to send him to one of Papa's judges.' "

The reference to the Irishmen is curious but the point is made clear by an entry in the journal of L'Estoile written a month later than the above talk between Héroard and the little dauphin. He says: "All the Irish in Paris who were very numerous were sent out of the town, being fellows very expert in all sorts of knavery beyond any others whose profession it is to do nothing and live at the expense of other people. . . . They were put into boats in the charge of archers to be sent back over the sea to the country whence they came." No doubt that, previous to this drastic measure, there was much talk over these unlucky and undesirable Irish and the dauphin was quick at hearing the chatter that went on around him.

All this story-telling, however, is scarcely lessons though it would certainly have helped " to stretch and stimulate a child's little mind." But Héroard very early began intentional instruction although not in the form of set lessons. For instance, while the dauphin was at dinner one day he " arranged his cherry stones on his plate and told me they made a windmill. I taught him the names of the winds; he thought them over awhile and then repeated them to himself, ' *est, ouest, north, sud.*' After supper he again arranged his cherry stones along the edge of his plate and named them ' *est, ouest, north, sud.*' Then he called to me, ' Moucha Hé'ou'ad these are the four winds. What is their name in French?' I told him ' *Levant, ponant, tramontane, midi.*' " We have here an interesting example of the popular contrasted with the more correct names. *Tramontane*, however, seems like a memory of Héroard's southern home, for in northern France there are no mountains to give to the north wind a name so fitting to it in the south. It is curious to notice that Héroard calls it *north* and not *nord* as in modern usage.

We know that the doctor took a lively interest in the earth around and the skies above him and we may therefore suppose that it was he who interested the dauphin in an eclipse of the sun which occurred in

1608. The dauphin, and perhaps the other children too, though Héroard rarely mentions them unless the anecdote requires it, had *goûter* at three o'clock out of doors. " It was just the hour for the eclipse. He had had a pan of water brought out which he could watch the reflection of the sun." Another time it was a map of France which amused the two good friends, the elderly doctor and the little boy. Héroard fastened the map on to the tapestry. " Someone pointed out the town of Provins. He at once stretched out his hand saying, ' Let's eat some rose sweetmeat.' " Provins, no great way east of Paris, was famous for its roses and still more famous for its rose sweetmeat, of which the dauphin had a piece at bedtime every night. Here is one of his earliest letters written on the subject. Had someone been joking with the little boy or were there really not enough roses for all?

" Monday 17 October 1605. Papa. All the apothecaries of Provins have come to beseech me to beg you very humbly, as I am doing now, to send my company to a different garrison, because my soldiers love rose conserve very much, and I am afraid that they will eat it all up and leave none for me. I have some every night when I go to bed, and I pray God to send you to see me very soon and to give me grace to serve you humbly.

I am Papa your very humble and very obedient servant. DAUPHIN."

The old sweet-scented Provence roses were really named from Provins, but the English gardeners had no map pinned on to tapestry to correct their confusion between the little town in northern France and the big province in the south. Hanging maps and pictures on to tapestry was an easy way of exhibition. We may

recall that Boileau hung his portraits of famous historical
men and women round the dauphin's room. The
child tried to copy some of them but since nothing is
said of the results we may conclude his attempts were
not over-successful. He did better with a " bird from
China. ' Look, Mosseu Hé'ou'ad, I've done it without
looking. I had it in my head.' I told him it was
very well done but that the bird lacked its crest.
' Yes, but the crest wasn't in my head. I'll put it
there and then I'll draw it.' "

But of all the sources of the dauphin's early education
the doctor's small store of books must have been the
best. We hear of perhaps a dozen with illustrations.
After the Bible came the animal book, Gesner's *Icones
Animalium*. There never was, nor has been since, a
more delightful book of beasts and birds and fishes.
The Latin descriptions may be beyond the reach of
most but none could fail to enjoy the woodcuts, so
vigorous and, wherever the artist had actually seen the
animal, so faithful. Farmyard and barn-door animals
and birds, beasts of the chase, hawks and dogs, all
these are excellent. Where the picture is drawn from
description only or copied from other artists' works
there is still a realistic charm about them more delightful
than the truth. The porcupine's bristles, the camel of
extraordinary length, the rhinoceros with scales like a
delicate pattern in an eastern fabric, who could desire
them otherwise. But Gesner was a great observer,
anxious always for the truth. He gives a picture of
a hyena and contrasts it with one in a Greek manuscript
simply to emphasize the creature's correct form. Nay,
so anxious is he to be exact that on learning that his
picture " of a giraffo or cameleopardis " was inaccurate
he inserts another, and better one, in an appendix.
The first drawing, from hearsay, was of a deer with

A GIRAFFE

From The Icones Animalium, Gesner

an elongated neck, but later through a friend he received from Constantinople " a more accurate picture of this rare and marvellous animal." The giraffe had been presented to the " Emperor of the Turks " and a picture was drawn and sent to Gesner in Geneva in 1559. It is a delightful picture, the most *giraffest* giraffe that ever was drawn and the description of it is as delightful. Gesner's books of animals and birds were a never-ending source of pleasure and unobtrusive instruction to the children at St Germain-en-Laye, though oddly enough there is no mention of his book on fishes.

Next in affection to " the lion book " came " the book with the buildings." Here we are met with a difficulty. Héroard undoubtedly possessed a copy of the *De Architectura* of Vitruvius, the diagrams of which would seem to have had a curious fascination for the dauphin. But there is also a reference to a book on the antiquities of Rome in which the child found pictures, as he thought, of familiar places. " ' See,' he said, ' there's Fontainebleau and there's my room, and that's the door to go in by and there's the white horse and there's Mercury and there's the garden and the pool.' " From the child's naïve chatter we seem to be looking at a picture of the Capitol although the garden and the pool present a difficulty. Probably a page was turned while he talked and a fresh picture had come into view. Was this one of several sixteenth century publications on the antiquities of Rome? Or again it may have been a copy of Vitruvius' work containing, in addition to the classical plates, pictures of Rome as it was in the sixteenth century. We are the more tempted to believe this because it was Vitruvius that the dauphin eagerly asked to see after a long absence from St Germain-en-Laye, where the book was always kept. There were many editions of *De Architectura* printed before 1600 and although some have pictures much more modern than the date of the book none that I have seen have any illustrations to fit in with the child's ideas about them. So it must be left to conjecture.

There was a highly interesting book on the siege of Ostend with pictures of soldiers and cannon, and yet another generally called " the hunting-book," from which the dauphin learnt much on the kingly craft of the chase. A big book of engravings, which was the dauphin's own, illustrated all sorts of trades. " He opened his book of engravings. ' Moucha Hé'ou'ad show me the people with spectacles.' After these we looked at the clock-makers and the distillers while he asked questions about everything. I showed him a picture of silkworms and another of the Emperor Justinian sitting on a chair." Just what Justinian was doing in the book is not said. The silkworms would have possessed a special interest, for Henri IV was at the moment vigorously pushing the planting of mulberry-trees in France and this despite the obstinate opposition of Sully, who maintained that if Providence had intended that silk should be made in France mulberry-trees would have been indigenous to the soil. There were other books than these illustrated ones; for instance, the historian Matthieu presented a copy of his history to the dauphin, " to which Monseigneur listened very attentively while sitting in Madame's room, bidding those who made a noise to keep quiet."

After picture-books, story-telling and impromptu instruction on the winds of heaven or the countries of the world we come to actual lessons. These had, of course, their place, at first very irregularly and later on as a daily task. Lessons in writing followed the

A LION

From The Icones Animalium, Gesner

[face p. 158

early ones in reading. They were not popular and
there are not a few entries in the journal which describe
the dauphin's evasions of this task. Naturally the
first lesson was interesting. "June 18th 1606. He
brought his little desk in which was his paper, his pen
and his ink pot into the dining hall, saying, ' I've
brought my copy book. I am going to school.' He
made a round O very well." But sometimes he was
rebellious. "At three o'clock did his lessons against
his will. He lifted up his legs and put them on his
copy-book, leaving his thighs bare. Mme de Montglat
gave him a good whack with the cane on them." And
sometimes, again, he was coaxed into doing them.
"Aug. 1608. He said he would do his writing; sent
for Beaugrand, the scribe. He sat in the study and
the Messieurs de Mortemart with him but while they
wrote he would not set to work at his copy. Stayed a
quarter of an hour and then left. He came to my
room, went to the gallery and then into the chapel all
to escape lessons. Mounted his horse by the pool,
bold and well seated as the day before. Played at
building a fort with four bastions with the sand of the
path." Presently having played truant long enough
he went back to the Palace where he met " Beaugrand,
his writing-master. ' Go away, I'm not going to
write this morning.' ' Monsieur,' I said, ' here is a
little book belonging to a German gentleman and he
begs you to write something in it. It will be seen all
over Germany.' ' I'll do it. Is there an Emperor in
Germany?' The desire for glory made him write
the words I set before him, taken from the poet
Manilius: ' *Lancibus ut gentes tollatque prematque. Louis.*'
The German's name was Guillaume Friderich. The
Prince of Wales had written: ' *Fax mentis honeste
gloria, Henricus P.*' Count Maurice of Nassau had

written: '*Je maintiendrai.*' The Earl of Essex, whose head was cut off in England: '*Virtutis comes invidiae. Robertus comes Essexiae,*' and on the following page his enemy, Cecil, had written: '*Vana sine viribus ira. Guilielmus Cecilius.*'" What has become of the German traveller's little book with its singular collection of autographs? A little later the writing lessons were made more attractive by allowing the child to write a letter instead of tracing over a copy-book maxim or, as he grew older, writing entirely with his own hand. Here are three such letters written one at the beginning and the other two at the end of 1607. The effort of writing them himself robs them of the charm of those earlier letters which he dictated.

"Wednesday. January 24th 1607. He wrote to the king very cheerfully, wanted to be quick. Dumont, clerk to his chapel, traced the letters for him; he followed the tracing quite dextrously, correcting anything he had not done quite right. 'Papa. I do so want to see you, but any how I can tell you a great many trees have been planted. I am, Papa, your very humble and very obedient son and servant. DAUPHIN.'"

It is interesting to see how often the child's letters report the progress of the king's gardens and plantations at St Germain and Fontainebleau.

The other two were both written in the autumn.

"November 22nd 1607. The dauphin repeated his verses and sentences, asked to do his lessons and did more than he was wanted to; spelt whole words without a mistake. He wrote without any tracing or any help, 'Papa and mamma, I love you very much and I do so want to see you.   Loys.'"

"November 26th 1607. The dauphin wrote a letter to the king without having the letters first traced, but only dictated to him. 'Papa, this is just to show you I can write without a copy and that I am not naughty any more. I am, papa, your very humble and very obedient son and servant. LOYS.'"

Lessons were certainly very irregular for all the children, but sometimes a fit of virtue came over the dauphin who, feeling very virtuous himself demanded an equal virtue from the others. "He took it into his head to do his lessons, asked for his book and called Madame to come and say her lesson too. She came very unwillingly and repeated it between her sobs. Not being able to hear her the dauphin said, 'I think she talks Swiss.'" Henri often complained of his son's obstinacy and here is a comic example of this trait in the dauphin's character. "Jan. 1. 1608. Woke at seven and got up to get his New Year's gifts. He wrote a letter to the queen in which he would not write the word *bien*, he would write it *bian*, saying it looked better like that. He was so obstinate over it that a fresh letter had to be written in which the word did not occur."

After reading, writing and spelling came Latin and theology. Latin the dauphin began at six with the kind doctor for his teacher. A few months later M. de Souvré superseded Héroard and in 1609 a regular tutor was appointed. The journal supplies us with a resumé of this tutor's first lesson. "After breakfast M. des Yveteaux gave him his first lesson. He began with a little discourse setting forth that he must remember that God had caused him to be born a Christian in the Apostolic Church, the son of a great king and that he must for that reason love and honour the king and queen as his superiors and also as his father and mother; and he told him that virtue could be learnt from books. He then began with making him read the beginning of the story of Joseph and he then set him the following written question to answer: Should churchmen be called to the counsel of princes, and what was his opinion. ' I don't know,' said the dauphin."

Poor little boy of eight years old. He must have learnt far more from his picture-books and Héroard's stories than he could learn from des Yveteaux.

CHAPTER VIII

So far, except for casual references, very little has been
said on the music and the musical instruments which
played so important a part in the life of Louis XIII as
dauphin and as king.   It is always a dangerous thing
for those who are not musicians to write about music;
nor is the age an easy one even for those who are
musicians, for the period covering the end of the
sixteenth and the beginning of the seventeenth centuries
was essentially one of change, an age in which music,
as we know it to-day in all its marvellous complexity
was in its infancy.   Moreover this new music-sense,
dimly felt in its slow approach, was co-incident with
the evolution of an instrument capable of both creating
and interpreting it.   The famous instrument makers
of Brescia and Cremona may not yet have produced
the finished marvel of the violin but at least they had
come very near to it.   Like all transitional periods the
age gives rise to many contradictions and interpretations
among modern writers and these variances of opinion
do not make it easier for those who can make no claim
to musical knowledge.   Music however was far too
intimately interwoven with the dauphin's life to be
here passed over.   Most people who care for old
music know the little airs with their soft melody and
plaintive cadence which are attributed to Louis XIII,
nor is there anything improbable in the attribution.
Music was a subject to which he had given careful
and intelligent attention from a very early age;   it

163

was probably his earliest and his most lasting pleasure.

No one who has studied his reign can think of him as a happy man. Fate had denied him the vitality which made his father so intensely alive, whether in peace or in war, whether in poverty as King of Navarre or in luxury as King of France. Louis began his reign with tears for his father's death and his own kingship, and what glory it brought was not given to him but to his great minister, Richelieu. His marriage, thrust on him when he was scarce out of childhood, brought him no happiness nor any children till within a few years of his death; his intercourse with his mother, his brother and his half-brothers was an almost unbroken series of quarrels. His later favourites among men were disloyal to him and to France and he let them die miserably; he bored the two or three women for whom he showed a certain cold friendship. And thus it seems probable that music remained his keenest delight in manhood as it had been in nursery days. The *vingt quatre violons*, the " four and twenty fidlers all in a row," whom he established in his court must have given him many happy hours. We can feel sure that Louis XIII was keenly alive to the quickening development of music, the final emergence of the violin able to express " depths of pain and heights of passion " and to set the pulses throbbing with a sense of life never attained by the music of the older viols. It is true that Héroard invariably speaks of the stringed instruments in use in his day as *violons*, but in France the word was in common use before the term violin was adopted in England; moreover by *violon* he seems generally to mean a tenor and not a treble viol. Certainly before the advent of the seventeenth century the old French word *vielle* had become restricted to the quaint stringed instrument, in England called a hurdy-gurdy, in which the turning of a wheel produced the sound on the strings; just such an instrument as the little earthenware figure of the hurdy-gurdy man, made in the pottery at Avon, played. In England, viol was still the name of the soft-toned instruments with five, six or even more strings which were tuned either in fourths or thirds. Spenser does indeed write in the *Shepherd's Calendar* :—

> " I see Calliope speede her to the place
> Where my goddess shines
> And after her the other muses trace
> With their violines."

But Spenser was a great borrower of words at all times. Of these viols there were treble, tenor, bass and double bass; there was also a very small treble viol, small enough to go into a pocket and known as a *pochette*. Dancing-masters used to use a similar tiny violin, a kit, which they played as they showed off their steps in waltz or quadrille. Such a kit I remember as I and my cousin, both of us small children, watched a dancing master fiddling and dancing in perfect solemnity before a whole school of young ladies. " Hey diddle, diddle, the cat and the fiddle " shouted my companion and even the politest pupil, well trained as they all were in decorum, tried in vain to smother a giggle.

The music played on these viols was song and dance music, or music for viol and lute, and sometimes for a number of viols playing together, but it was never solo music. The dauphin as we know had Indret his lutist as well as Boileau his viol player. Lutes and viols, however, were by no means the only instruments from which the children at St Germain-en-Laye derived pleasure. In the journal, of a medical student, Felix

Platter, already referred to in previous chapters, there is an interesting list of instruments which were used in playing an aubade to a young lady in Montpellier, and since it is a comprehensive list it is worth our while to glance at it. The aubade began at midnight, an hour which might be more proper for a serenade had the music not been such as to banish any possibility of sleep. It was indeed a complete concert beginning with "*roulements de tambourin* enough to waken the whole street." After this came trumpets followed by hautbois. These were replaced by cymbals, fifes and drums and they in their turn by viols, and the aubade finished with a trio on lutes in which young Felix Platter played his part. He tells us " the aubade lasted an hour and a half and as soon as it was over we were taken to a pastry cook's where we were royally feasted. We sat drinking muscat and hippocras all the rest of the night." A great occasion for a poor student, but one would like to know what the street thought of the disturbance to their sleep.

The instruments mentioned by Platter all occur at different times in the pages of Héroard's journal, some for courtly and some for military use, some for church and ceremonial occasions, and some played by the strolling mountebanks or gypsies who showed off their tricks or dances at St Germain or Fontainebleau. But to these must be added yet others before the list of all the sources of music within the dauphin's reach are exhausted; organs in the chapels, tiny spinets, which were carried from room to room as the listeners found most convenient; nor were flageolets and mandoras absent. Finally there were human voices, choir men, children of the chapel, carol singers and all the song music sung by each and all for amusement. There was no lack of music in the dauphin's life.

Drums were the first thing to interest him as he emerged from babyhood, and before he could speak Héroard relates how the child picked up the various drum taps. "October 26th 1603. Taken to see the king and queen. At the king's table he beat on the dinner-service the French and the Swiss drum taps. Found his drum and began over again. The king was charmed." He was not always content with only two varieties of drum taps, for two years later we learn that " whilst standing at the window he amused himself with making the captain of the guard order all the drum taps beaten by the company's drummers, Spanish, English, Walloon, Italian, Piedmontese, Moorish, Scotch, Lombard, German, Turk and last of all the French. Then they beat a *chamade* and an assault. At last he said, ' That will do. But beat the march to battle as you go.' " If we return to his third year we find a sense of melody growing alongside of his pleasure in the rhythm of the drums. " Coming out from Mass he made two little choir boys march in front of him, singing as they marched. He was so entranced with the music that he never took any notice of the fountain as he passed it although he generally takes the greatest pleasure in it." Soon after this, when he was only a month over three years old, " M. de St Geran told him about a spinet. He would not rest till one had been brought to his room for him to see. M. de Geran made his page play on it while Hauteville played the lute and Boileau the viol. He listened entranced. At a quarter to eight I said, ' Monsieur, here comes the little sand man.' ' Put me to bed,' he replied."

This love of music grew as his age increased. At four years old the doctor wrote of him, " All dinner-time he was in a transport of joy with the music of the

king's viol players. There were fifteen of them. At
the end of dinner he asked them to play ' *la guerre.*'
It was the first word he had spoken all through dinner.
They did not know it." In the next anecdote two
pronounced sentiments clashed in the child's mind, his
love of music and his fastidious sense of what was
fitting. "August 5th 1605. Sat silent at dinner
because he was so happy listening to a crippled flageolet
player, who after playing a long time accompanied by
two viols said in a gruff voice, ' Monsieur, drink to
us.' The dauphin grew very red and said crossly,
' Send them away. I want them sent away.' I said,
' Monsieur, he is a poor man. You mustn't send poor
people away.' ' Poor people mustn't come here.'
' Monsieur, not all poor people but those who play as
he does may.' ' Let him go and play downstairs.
Mamanga, he has all upset me. I only drink to Papa
and Mamma.' "

Boileau and Indret must have talked and played
music to the little boy a great deal in this summer of
1605. Héroard, as usual, is full of naïve surprise at
the child's quickness in picking up what was said to
him. "The dauphin whistled on the ends of his
fingers against his lips saying ' this is the bass,' then
whistling a higher note, ' that is the *chanterelle,* and
this one is the tenor.' He was quite right. He must
have learnt the notes and their names from Boileau
and Indret." In the summer of the following year
the dauphin began meddling with the instruments
themselves though Héroard does not venture to say he
could really play on them. "June 4th 1606. The
dauphin called Indret his lutist and Boileau the viol
players and a soldier who played on a mandora and
then taking a lute himself said, ' Let's make music.'
He placed them round the head of his bed." A

month later " he took a little *violon*, a kit that is, and played with Indret and made us sing *Hau ! Guilleaume, Guilleaume* and *Maître Amboise, ho ! ho ! d'ou venez-vous ?* Then he danced the Frog ballet very prettily and in good time without ever having been taught."

Strolling players on musette and bagpipes pleased him although sometimes, as with the flageolet player, their persons and manners spoilt his pleasure and he sent them away. Once when Indret played the bagpipes to his dog, Pataut, the dauphin got beside himself with laughing. "He is not generally a great laugher." This last phrase occurs quite often showing him as a child who rarely laughed, who did not readily see life humorously but who on occasion could " get beside himself " with mirth. It is a characteristic worth noting. Now and then we hear of a lesson from one or other of his musicians. " M. le dauphin took a big lute and made Indret put his fingers on the keys while he twanged the chords. They began with cadences and then played and sang *Ils sont à St John d'Anjou, les gens, les gens, les gensdarmes.* After that they played *a bergamasque, saraband* and the bells; when he had finished he rolled on the floor pretending it was the sea, and M. le Chevalier copied him." Singing was a great pastime with all the children and their house-hold, especially in winter-time. Some of these songs accompanied games, some were old ditties popular among the women in charge of the children, some Héroard says it was a shame to hear them sung at all by innocent little voices. Carols were sung at Christmas time and the dauphin delighted in them. "He made his usher sing carols which the man had himself written and above all the one where the words " crown of laurels " occurs. His usher gave it to him in writing and he was so impatient to read and learn

it by heart that he left off eating his meal." Another
time " The dauphin sang carols and made others sing
them. Mlle de Ventelet told him how poor the new-
born Christ was with no sheets and laid in a manger.
He sprang up and said eagerly, ' If I had been there
I should have given Him my bed and my sheets.'
This was a wonderful favour on his part for he never
lets anyone, not even the king, sit on his bed." There
was, however, one style of singing in which the dauphin
took no delight. On 22nd November 1610, Héroard
says of him, he was then no longer the dauphin,
" The king was very cross because M. de Souvré
wanted to take him to Notre Dame. He did not want
to go, he said, because there would be High Mass,
' Yes, Sire, but there will be music and you are so
fond of music.' ' Yes, but there are two sorts of
music and one sort I don't like.' This was plain-song."

Dance music was as common as song music but still
since the dauphin often objected to dancing lessons
less is said about dance than song music. His sisters
and half-brothers were keen dancers and Madame and
little Madame Christienne welcomed the visits of the
dancing-master. Here is a list of dances other than
ballets which occur in the pages of the journal.
*Corrante, gaillard, bourrée, vielle bourrée, branle, saraband,
saugrenée, combat* and a comic dance called " as the
monk trots."

Music and singing might be enjoyed and even
studied " as a relief from affairs of importance," as
Héroard wrote in his treatise on education; but a
proficiency in dancing, even for little princes unwilling
to learn, must be acquired by all who lived in court
circles. It undoubtedly came under the heading of
serious study, a negligence of which was corrected by
the use of the birch-rod. Indeed as a boy of noble

THE BAGPIPER AND HURDY-GURDY MAN

From La Céramique Française.   M. J. Ballot
By permission of Les Éditions Albert Morancé

[face p. 170

birth, unless destined for the church, grew out of childhood the importance of his physical training became more and more pronounced, till by the time he was fourteen he was ready to abandon all other lessons for the exclusive study of fencing, riding and manners. To meet the demand for a fine training in these things, so essential for a *gentilhomme*, a school known throughout France as the Academy had been started in Paris towards the end of the sixteenth century. Its founder, the Sieur Antoine de Pluvinel, was so famous for his teaching that no young noble could afford to endanger his career by neglecting a course under him. Pluvinel's riding-school had its home in the vast establishment of the royal stables just outside the Louvre, and it was here his pupils learnt to ride, to joust, to tilt at the ring, how to break and train horses, how to treat their ailments, the proper dress to wear for riding and the best kinds of spurs and stirrups to use, in short a very complete education in horsemanship. Other things were also taught in the Academy but in separate establishments; such as fencing, good manners, the many and complicated duties of a page. The dauphin was certainly taught to shoot with an arquebus for when he was taken to live in Paris Héroard often makes a brief entry, "studied, wrote, shot, danced." It seems probable therefore that the use of arquebus and pistol was part of the course at the Academy; possibly dancing and ballets may have had their instructors too, for certainly a knowledge of all these things was essential for a young courtier. Pupils of the Academy could be either day pupils or, if their homes were in the provinces, could be lodged by the Sieur de Pluvinel at a high cost and in the charge of their own servants. Such was the case with Armand du Plessis de Richelieu who had a brief but merry time at the Academy before he was entered at the Sorbonne as his first step towards the cardinalate and the supreme control of France. The exquisite art of fencing, on a knowledge of which in an age of savage duelling and still more savage assassinations, a man's life depended was taught by masters as well as all these other accomplishments, but de Pluvinel kept the riding-school in his own hands. He would also seem to have been the supreme authority on dress.

A delightful book, *Le Maneige Royale*, was published after his death in 1623, in which all his profound knowledge of horses was set down in the form of imaginary conversations between Henri IV, M. de Bellegarde and de Pluvinel. One edition was adorned with many fine engravings in some of which Louis XIII shows off his own horsemanship and at the same time illustrates the famous master's lessons. The boy king, rather plump and dark in colouring, swarth as his discontented mother said when he was a baby, rides, jumps, tilts, and carricoles in innumerable positions, while the court stands round admiring and learning from de Pluvinel's instruction. The old governor, M. de Souvré, is generally among the bystanders, as well as the king's brothers and *enfants d'honneur* now grown to young manhood. The greater part of the book is taken up with a discussion on the horse, his breaking-in, harness, ailments and so on all of which was knowledge essential to a cavalier if he aspired to be a *bon homme à cheval* as well as a *bel homme à cheval*. A *bel homme*, says de Pluvinel, knows how to sit; to hold the reins; to look serenely and cheerfully straight between his horse's ears; to keep his shoulders straight and his stomach well out, leaving a hollow in the back; his knees well in and firmly held and his feet no less

firm in his stirrups; heels down and turned out lest
the spur should inadvertently touch the horse; finally
know how to keep his seat whatever pranks the animal
might play; these things if a cavalier be well and
suitably dressed made him a *bel homme à cheval*. Not
many, to Pluvinel's regret, ever aspired to more. In
answer to a question on what makes a *bon homme à
cheval* he answered, " To make a *bon homme* you must
have judgement, a drug sold very dear at the apothecary's and very little of it for much silver. You must
understand a horse and its needs, its training and
everything in short about it. But when all this is
learnt you will not be a *bon homme* unless you are also
a *bel homme*, for if a man has not a perfect seat he
cannot ride a horse with fine judgment." Henri IV,
who is supposed to have visited the riding-school to
discuss equitation with the Sieur Antoine, asks what
he first taught a new pupil. The great master of the
Academy showed no hesitation in his reply, " I teach
them first to dress with propriety and comfort." Hats
must not be too high, six inches is ample and three
and a half for the brim's width to keep the sun out of
the eyes, and it must fit well so that it cannot fall off;
the hat riband or cord must be of silk or of gold or
silver thread. A ruff is better than a falling collar.
It is well for the doublet to be white, in winter of wool
and in summer of linen and it must always be hand-
somely embroidered. In winter a tunic with loose
sleeves can be worn over it. Gloves should be long,
fringed and embroidered to match the hat and belt.
Trunk hose must be wide and not lower than the
middle of the thigh so that the shapeliness of the leg
may be seen, and they must be wide enough to make
the waist look slim. Boots, of cowhide or wild boar,
must be higher at the back than at the front so as to

make the leg look longer; their toes must be square and the spurs *à la Damville*, an invention of the late Constable Montmorenci. " In short, Sire, I want my pupils to be dressed exactly like M. de Bellegarde." Exquisite M. le Grand, as Bellegarde was mostly known. He had out-lived Henri and most of Henri's court but he was still the best-dressed man of his day when the book was published. Although the permanent home of the Academy was in Paris, on occasions when the court made a prolonged stay at Fontainebleau de Pluvinel came with it and carried on his instruction to the young nobles there. Héroard speaks of some of these lessons and describes the dauphin's delight when some of his *petits gentilhommes* met with a tumble.

In addition to the lessons learnt by other boys the dauphin had others special to his position. As a king's son destined to be a king himself a high importance was attached to the behaviour proper to a prince; etiquettes to be observed at court ceremonies, festivities and at church functions; manners to relatives, a troublesome matter this in so complicated a family; reception of ambassadors and of princes from foreign countries who from time to time visited France; all these things had to be carefully taught and studied. Some of the events and difficulties in connection with this side of his education are worth noting. One of the most complicated bits of court etiquette arose out of the return of Marguerite, Queen of Navarre, to the court. It was undoubtedly a somewhat difficult position to manage with due attention to the dignity of all parties. Her title of queen had been conceded to her after the dissolution of her marriage with Henri IV, and both as queen and daughter of the House of Valois she was entitled to every respect possible to her anomalous position. The king had shown the greatest reluctance to allow her appearance in his new court but Marguerite, wearied with life in remote Usson, had made permission to live in Paris one of the immutable conditions of her consent to the petition to the court of Rome. Even after Henri's marriage to Marie di Medici she could not return until her very entangled financial affairs had been straightened out, and the dauphin was four years old when at last she re-entered the city she had not seen for more than thirty years. It must have been a strange return to a world once so well known and now so changed. Marguerite seems to have genuinely welcomed the birth of an heir to the throne of France and expressed the keenest wish to see the child. This Henri was quite willing she should do but it was of the utmost importance that the proper etiquette should first be discovered. How was the dauphin to address the lady? *Maman* was a title which he gave to certain people with a qualifying word after it. Thus his mother was just maman, Mme de Montglat, by a childish contraction was Mamanga, his nurse was Maman Dondon. If to show respect and affection, Marguerite was also to be a maman what was the correct word to add? In July 1605 the discussion was in full swing at St Germain-en-Laye. " Queen Marguerite was mentioned and somebody asked what Monsieur was to call her. Someone else said he was to call her ' aunt.' ' No,' said the dauphin, ' I shall call her " sister " and Madame can call her " aunt." ' " A day or so later he was told that his mother wished him to address the Queen of Navarre as " Maman " and had written to say so. It may have been an unwelcome command to the proud little boy, but in the end a happy compromise was arrived at, pleasing we may hope to every one. " Aug. 6th. At half past

four the dauphin got into the queen's coach and drove
to meet Queen Marguerite. He was accompanied by
Madame, M. de Vendôme, M. le Chevalier and M. de
Souvré. When they met the queen's litter they alighted
and approached her on foot. Ten paces off the dauphin
took off his hat. He was then lifted up to kiss her,
saying, 'You are very welcome *Maman ma fille.*'
'Many thanks, Monsieur,' she replied, 'I have been
wanting to see you for a long time.' She kissed him
again and he grew shy and hid his face in his hat.
'Heavens!' said the queen, 'what a lovely boy you
are. You look every inch a king born to rule.' She
kissed Madame and the other children. The dauphin
then got into his coach and she into her litter. He
went to sleep on the way back and was still asleep
when he was carried into his room at half past eight.'
It was a curious little group that thus met on the road
to Paris; Marguerite, the unwilling bride of the
St Bartholomew Massacre, the dauphin, Marie di
Medici's son, and the children of Gabrielle d'Estrées,
the king's mistress, whom Marguerite had utterly
refused to allow to supplant her as his wife. The day
following the meeting the king and queen were at
St Germain with Marguerite as their guest. The
two ladies got along quite well together. Marguerite's
position in Paris depended largely on a good understanding with her younger cousin and the Queen of
France was often glad to avail herself of the Queen of
Navarre's consummate knowledge of dress and court
life under the Valois kings. We may wonder what
Henri and Marguerite talked about; they had done
little but quarrel in old days but Marguerite had wit
and charm and may well have been a welcome change
from the heavy-witted queen who never learnt to speak
French properly. Héroard tells us that they did talk

together and for a long time. " Aug. 7th. At ten
o'clock the dauphin went to the long gallery where
Queen Marguerite and the king had been quite an
hour talking together. Queen Marguerite gave the
dauphin a cupid set with diamonds and a big emerald
on which a dolphin was engraved; the cupid seated
too on a dolphin. She gave Madame a circlet of
diamonds for her hair and a basin and ewer of gold to
the dauphin's nurse. He said ' Maman ma fille I
thank you for Maman Dondon.' " Although in Usson
Marguerite had been poor enough she now seems to
have become wealthy, with debts paid and her estates
restored. She often made costly gifts to the dauphin
and made him her heir at her death, but he never
seems to have cared for either her or her gifts. Diamond
studded cupids pleased him no more than the Duc de
Sully's tree laden with purses, and no doubt such
valuable presents were locked up by Mme de Montglat
as soon as given. But he was quite ready to ask for
a gift he could really value, as we see from the following
letter. " Taine " was always a great favourite and he
was glad to please him. " Mme de Montglat asked
him to write to *Maman sa fille*, Queen Marguerite, on
behalf of Captain Mansan. ' Yes, Mamanga, let's
write. Come along Taine, Moucheu Hé'oa'd, come
and write.' Taine is his pet name for *Capitaine*. He
sat in the turret and had the patience to write the
following letter while I guided his hand." He could
not yet pronounce the letter r.

" Tuesday August 16th 1605 at St Germain. *Maman
ma fille*. I want you vewy much indeed to give Taine,
whom papa gave me to guard me, the lordship of
Morcourt. I ask you vewy humbly and I will do you
vewy humble service and give thwee little jumps for

pleasure if you'll do it, because it the first thing I
have asked you to do for me. And so I am, *Maman
ma fille*, Your vewy humble servant. Dauphin."

The Queen of Navarre is not often mentioned in
Héroard's journal but here is one very characteristic
scene. " May 9th 1607. Taken to see Queen
Marguerite. He had to be forced to pay her his
compliments. Ran away and sent for the little fox
cubs recently given him and set his dog Pataut to
hunt them down the gallery. May 10th. He had
scarcely opened his eyes before he was whipped for
not behaving properly the day before to Queen
Marguerite."

The proper way to receive ambassadors and other
people of importance was taught while the child was
still in his cradle, as we have seen in earlier chapters.
Ambassadors from many countries, envoys from
Switzerland, deputies from Dauphiné, magistrates from
the great cities of France and the Papal Nuncio all
were received in turn. The most original of these
visits was that of the ambassador of the Grand Turk
in 1607. " The dauphin watched the arrival of the
Turkish ambassador, Mustapha Aga. He was mounted
on a bay horse and alighted at the foot of the steps in
the Fountain Court, attended by M. de Brèves, a
janissary, two other Turks and two slaves. He had
come to ask the King to deliver up the Turkish slaves
freed from the Spanish galleys at the capture of Sluys
and afterwards sent to the galleys of Marseilles. The
king granted his request. M. le dauphin took it into
his head to go to the king's room to see the Turk.
He got as far as the gallery and they had to pretend
that the king had sent a valet to tell him to go back
to his own room. He went without a word. M. de

Souvré arrived saying that the ambassador was on his way to visit him. So he began to help spread the carpet for his reception, stretched it himself and picked up a wisp of straw that he heard M. de Souvré order someone to remove. His chair was sent for. 'They must bring the big one,' he said. Several false alarms of the ambassador's approach were given while he was playing with his little gentlemen. 'Set me in my chair, quick, quick,' he said. When seated he scolded this one and that for the way they wore their hats. The ambassador came and the dauphin put on a look calm, grave and yet sweet, drew himself up in his chair and looked steadily at the Turk as he reached the edge of the carpet. They gazed at each other silently. Then the ambassador took a piece of green damask woven with many colours and advanced to offer it for the dauphin's acceptance ; he next un-wrapped a small Turkish shirt embroidered with bunches of flowers which he also offered him. The dauphin took them both quietly. The ambassador said in his own tongue, translated by M. de Brèves for many years the French ambassador to Constantinople, that those who were poor could not make handsome gifts but these were offered with affection and his was asked for in return. He then craved leave to kiss his hand. He kissed the dauphin's left hand and prayed God to give him long life and the desire to continue the friendship which his father and his predecessors had always shown to the Grand Turk. This done the ambassador left by way of the gardens. That evening while the dauphin was playing on Mme de Montglat's bed I began to talk with him about this Turk and I said to him, 'Monsieur, one day you must go to Constantinople and five hundred thousand men with you.' 'Yes, I'll kill all the Turks and this one too.'

'Monsieur, you mustn't kill this Turk because he
came to see you and gave you a present.' 'But Turks
don't believe in God.' 'Excuse me, Monsieur, they
do believe in God but not in Christ Jesus, who is the
son of God.' 'Who do they believe in then?' 'In
Mahomet.' 'And who is Mahomet?' 'Monsieur,
he was a bad man who deceived them and made them
believe he was sent by God to teach them to believe
differently to the teaching of Jesus Christ.' He thought
for a little while and then said suddenly, 'Ho! ho!
I'll kill them all but I'll have a mass said before this
one and then I'll have him baptized.' 'That would
be quite a good thing to do but you must have him
baptized first and then say the mass before him.'
'Why?' 'Because he cannot be a Christian until he
is baptized nor hear mass before he is a Christian.'
'I see.' And then we were interrupted."

The dauphin would not have forgotten his own
baptism in the preceding September and this may
have made him more anxious to confer a similar
blessing on Mustapha Aga. Of all the great court
ceremonies in which the little boy had taken a part
none had exceeded the magnificence of this public
christening of the three eldest children of the king and
queen; nor had any demanded a more careful inquiry
into the minute etiquette proper to each participator
in the ceremony or more careful instruction of the
dauphin and his sisters. As usual Héroard ignores
the little girls, who were in a sense merely included
in the function for convenience sake. In accordance
with the custom of the French royal family all three
children had been baptized on the day following their
birth but this private baptism did not complete the
full ceremony of admission into the Catholic Church.
It did not even include the giving of a name so that

until their public christening Monsieur le Dauphin, Madame and the *petite Madame* were all the names the children had. The queen's fourth child, the Duc d'Orléans, was a delicate little boy who died at four years old before he was deemed fit for the completion of his baptism, and he never had any name in consequence, only a title. The Vendôme children had not been accorded the dignity of *enfants de France* so that the full ceremony of baptism had been carried out at birth, but Henri had given way in the case of the Marquise de Verneuil's son and daughter. These two were not fully christened until December 1607 when " on the eighth day of that month was baptized by the reverend Father in God, Messire Henry de Gondy, bishop of Paris, the high and mighty prince Henry, the king's natural son and not legitimate, named by the very mighty prince Loys de Bourbon, dauphin of France and Madame Elizabeth his sister; at the same time was conferred on the said Lord Henry, with the permission of the curé of the place, the sacrament of confirmation and the clerk's tonsure." Thus runs the public announcement of the event. Héroard rather curiously says that the christening took place on the 9th and not the 8th of December. It was a Sunday and he tells us that at half past three the dauphin and his sister Elizabeth were taken to the chapel " to present Monsieur and Mademoiselle de Verneuil for baptism, accompanied by M. de Vendôme, M. le Chevalier and several lords." M. de Verneuil was named Henri and his sister Gabrielle. They all supped in the king's hall at a feast given by his command and there was dancing after it but only one viol, played by Boileau.

And now we will see how the dauphin and his two little sisters fared in comparison with this sorry show.

The christening took place at Fontainebleau and probably the palace had never seen a more gorgeous spectacle. The chapel would have been scarcely large enough to hold the actual actors in the pageant and would have been wholly inadequate for the crowd of courtiers who were only onlookers. To meet the difficulty the gathering was held in the Cour Ovale and the actual ceremony took place under the gateway, known ever since as the *Porte du Baptistère*. Here under a canopy was placed the ancient copper font in which the *enfants de France* were always baptized, and both gateway and courtyard were " decorated with an unheard of magnificence." Both the official and Héroard's accounts of the great day exist and it is amusing to place them side by side. By combining them we can reconstruct the whole scene both on its ceremonial and on its human side. From the doctor's journal we learn that on " September 14th 1606 the dauphin got up at eight o'clock and was dressed in his white satin dress ready for his christening. He breakfasted at half past nine and was taken first to the king and queen and afterwards to the chapel of St Saturnin." This was the old chapel in the Cour Ovale and not the more modern one of the Holy Trinity in the Cour du Cheval Blanc. " At eleven o'clock he dined went to see his state apartment, was very fidgetty and afraid that water would be thrown over him. The king had frightened him but they reassured him. At four o'clock he left his room with the following ceremonial." Héroard left a space here but he never filled it in and we must go elsewhere to learn the order of the procession to the improvised baptistry. This the Mercure Français informs us " consisted of the Prince de Vaudemont with the taper, the Chevalier de Vendôme with the chrism, the Duc de Vendôme with the salt, the

Duc de Montpensier with the ewer, the Comte de
Soissons with the basin, the Prince de Conti with the
cushion, M. de Souvré carrying the child and the
Duc de Guise bearing the train of the ermine cloak
hung from the dauphin's shoulders." Eighty nobles
followed preceding the godparents, the Cardinal de
Joyeuse as proxy for the Pope and the Duchess of
Mantua, the queen's aunt, who was there in person.
Nobody mentions the little girls in the procession so
perhaps they and their godparents came in by a side
door. They can be seen, however, in a picture of the
scene. "The weather," we further learn, "was
extremely fine and bright but the cloaks, the caps,
the buttons and the swords of the noblemen covered
with precious stones out shone the sun. The luxury
and magnificence of the princesses and ladies were so
great that the spectators could hardly bear the glitter
of the gold, the pure whiteness of the silver and the
brilliance of the pearls and jewels which covered their
dresses. But the queen outshone them all for she had
two thousand pearls and three thousand diamonds
sewn on to her robe." Such was the official account
of the cortége and every one felt how entirely suitable
it was to a prince's baptism. The questions and
answers were in Latin and the dauphin repeated the
Pater, the *Ave Maria* and *Credo* " with such grace that
not one of the spectators on beholding behaviour at
once so Christian and so royal could restrain their
tears of joy nor who were not seized with a profound
delight, admiration and affection at the sight of one,
of so tender an age as Monseigneur le Dauphin, who
combined a cheerfulness and a sweetness so elevated
and so serene." This was all very well for the official
news to be read in Paris but Héroard gives us the
little natural touches in which he excels. From him

183

we learn that " the dauphin arrived under the canopy placed over the font and at half past five he was baptized with the completion of the ceremony by the Cardinal de Gondi. The dauphin was questioned and gave the proper answers and then himself laid bare his chest to receive the oil while M. de Montbazon turned down his collar for the anointing of his shoulders. He said with a smile, ' Oh! it is cold!' At the salt he said, ' I've swallowed it. It was nice.' The ceremony lasted an hour and he was then taken back through the king's and the queen's rooms to his own. As they went along the terrace he saw Descluseaux on guard in the courtyard with his regiment. He shouted to him, ' Ho! ho! my darling! There he is my darling.' " It was a long and tiring day for a little boy scarcely five years old. After this event the dauphin could sign himself Louis, or as he generally spelt it Loys, although he was still called Monsieur by every one about him. The choice of his name annoyed him greatly when he found féfé Verneuil was to be called Henri. It was all the more annoying because as godfather he would have to name his brother at his christening. " ' I won't have it. I won't name him Henri; it's papa's name, he'll be better than I because I'm only Loys.' He stuck to his decision for a long time but was at last turned from it mainly because he was told that the King wished it to be so. When he was in bed Mme de Montglat said to me that Monseigneur had consented to name M. de Verneuil Henri; I took the opportunity to tell him that his own name was much more beautiful and I talked to.him about the king, Saint Louis, of his piety and his justice, and how he had made war on the Turks, and how he had pierced the tongues of blasphemers with hot iron, and had died in Egypt

184

THE FIVE ELDEST CHILDREN OF HENRI IV AND MARIE DE MEDECI

LOYS DAVPHIN DE FRANCE. MONSEIGNEVR LE DVC D'ORLEANS. MONSEIGNEVR LE DVC D'ANIOV. MADAME CHRISTINE. MADAME ELIZABETH.

[face p. 184

fighting the Turks, and he had gone up to Heaven where he was a saint. He listened very attentively." The little sermon seems to have sunk into the child's mind for three days later he " held at the font " his half-brother and named him Henri without any fuss. The little Duke of Orléans was, as we have seen, never publicly christened and had no name; Gaston and Henriette Marie came too late in the family to have very much fuss made of them, for their father was killed while they were very young so that they were not long children of a reigning king. The children of the king's later mistresses were never on the same level as those of either the Duchesse de Beaufort or the Marquise de Verneuil.

The next court function in which the dauphin had to take a part was a terrible ordeal. Being received into the Christian faith in a white satin frock surrounded by a glittering court weeping tears of pious joy was well enough. It was quite another thing to be called upon to represent the king on Maundy Thursday. In the year 1607 Easter fell on the 15th April and on the previous Wednesday " the dauphin was taken to the king who was abed with a feverish cold. The dauphin would not let a word be said about his washing the feet of the poor on the following day. ' I don't want to. They smell.' At last he gave in a little when the king told him he could not go himself and he wanted the dauphin to take his place. On the following morning he was asked if he would wash the feet of the poor people nicely. ' Ho! no. I'll wash the girls but not the boys.' Afterwards he could not be persuaded. He breakfasted at nine o'clock and was taken to the king, who asked him to perform the ceremony in his place. He said ' Yes, Papa.' At ten o'clock he was taken to the Ball room, the Galerie de Diane that is, where he listened to a sermon by the bishop of Embrun during which he amused himself with pricking a piece of paper with a pin, making birds and animals. After the absolution he was taken by force on to the dais accompanied by the Prince de Condé, the Prince de Conti and the Comte de Soissons, who served at the ceremony as if the king himself were present. When he came near to the first poor person he saw that water was being poured into his own basin and this finally upset his temper. No one could force him to so much as kneel down for he only shrank back crying. The almoners had to take the office on themselves and do it in front of him. When it came to serving the meats he would not touch a single dish that was handed to him but the purses he gave quite cheerfully. When it was over he was very glad. Mme de Montglat asked him why he would not wash the poor people's feet when his Papa, king that he was, did it so willingly. ' Yes, but I'm not a king,' he said." On this occasion also we have an official account to compare with this deliciously natural description by Héroard. It is too long to give in full but it is amusing to read that " Monseigneur le Dauphin washed, dried and kissed the feet of the poor who, according to custom had been first examined by the king's doctor to see that they had no dangerous ailment, and whose hair had been shaved, and who moreover had been clothed in a scarlet gown with a large towel of fine linen which covered them down to their feet, according to the usual practice. At first Monseigneur had shown a little reluctance at washing and kissing the poor people's feet, he being too young to understand the meaning of this ceremony and being afraid of being laughed at; . . . but looking round him and seeing the Comte de Soissons with his staff of office followed by all the king's *maîtres d'hôtel* marching before the dishes for these poor folk he began to smile and forthwith very willingly took his part in this pious ceremony perceiving that no one was mocking him. The dishes numbered thirteen, one for each poor person and were carried in by the greatest nobles. There were thirteen *écus d'or* also and here Monseigneur showed the greatest pleasure in giving them and so this royal ceremony, never before performed by a dauphin or any *enfant de France*, came to an end."

We are glad to learn more about Maundy Thursday from this description but we may feel sure that if the dauphin had been a good boy Héroard would certainly have given him all the credit due. Instead he behaved exactly as a nervous child might be expected to behave in circumstances of unusual publicity. Perhaps it was as well that he was taught so early to take his part in court ceremonial for he was only nine when he became a king.

CHAPTER IX

In the following chapter our subject will be the meals of the children at St Germain-en-Laye, not only the food eaten, but the method of serving it and the manners observed at table. The age was one of transition when habits, thought good enough all through the Middle Ages, were yielding slowly to the greater refinements of modern life. The French court had undoubtedly progressed but we should fail to catch the significance of this progress if we remained in ignorance of the earlier, and still prevalent, customs of the nation as a whole. As in the case of education certain parallels between English and French manners will be given, partly because the rules for both have often a common origin and observance and so can supplement each other, partly because their occasional divergence helps to illustrate the standard of behaviour at table commonly accepted in France. Those readers who have already come across descriptions of banquets in the seventeenth, and even in the eighteenth, centuries must have marvelled at the number of courses and the quantity and choice of dishes served in each course. The order of serving certain kinds of food is also one which has obviously changed greatly in modern times. I can very well remember a dinner served in a town on the Rhine forty years ago where the fish course came after soup, meat and dumplings had all been eaten, so that when I meet with meals in the seventeenth century where the broth was served in the fourth

course and crabs were eaten with dessert I remember
this dinner and remind myself that the order of dishes
is not an immutable law of nature. With enormous
feasts, however, we have nothing to do. No one
thought of serving the children at St Germain-en-Laye
with six courses and twenty dishes to a course, although
now and then we do meet with a surprisingly long list
of dishes. In a footnote to the printed portion of
Héroard's journal a description of a supper eaten by
Louis in 1611 is given. This account has been taken
from that part of the journal which still remains un-
printed and from the fact that it is not incorporated
in the text we may, perhaps, infer that it is one of
many similar records written for the doctor's own
guidance in matters concerning his charge's health.
This inference is confirmed by the careful way in
which he notes the exact quantities of each dish eaten
by the king of ten years old. It began with "corinth
raisins," currants that is, "in rose water," and continued with "egg *soupe* with lemon juice, twenty
spoonsful; broth four spoonsful; cocks combs, eight;
a little boiled chicken; four mouthfuls of boiled veal;
the marrow of a bone; a wing and a half of chicken,
roasted and then fried in bread crumb; thirteen spoonsful of jelly; a sugar horn filled with apricots; half a
sugared chestnut in rose water; preserved cherries;
a little bread and some fennel comfits." These last
were for digestion's sake. After such a supper at ten
years old they may well have been needed, but the
custom of eating such lozenges, or comfits, was very
generally followed. Those flavoured with fennel had
been a favourite with Henri IV and his son was always
apt to copy his father. Many were the herbs and spices
used in making comfits; aniseed, saffron, coriander,
fennel were all home-grown and cheap; nutmeg,

cloves, pepper and cinnamon came from far away and were costly but all these, and more too, were employed by the makers of *épices* as they were called. Great care was taken in their manufacture and boxes filled with a variety of the little lozenges were deemed a suitable present for a superior whom one wished to please.

It is curious that no mention is made of vegetables in the foregoing supper, although we hear of them very often elsewhere; later on we shall come across some of those most in use. The order in which the dishes were served is quite in accordance with modern ways except that corinth raisins would seem more appropriate for dessert than as *hors d'œuvres*. The serving of both *soupe* and broth might seem superfluous to those who did not know the distinction between them. In the seventeenth century the word *soupe* retained its original meaning and was employed not for the liquid but for the sopped bread floating in it; both were eaten together but the liquid was not necessarily a broth made from meat or poultry. In this case we are told that it was a mixture of eggs and lemon juice, and probably water, whereas the broth which followed would have been made from a meat stock. Héroard tells us the number of spoonfuls of soup and broth which were eaten and this raises a somewhat interesting point. He does not say whether they were eaten with a spoon or were only ladled out with one into the dauphin's bowl. The truth is that the use of spoons for soup was only just coming into fashion and supping broth out of the bowl was still the most usual way, the sopped bread being lifted out with the fingers. Here is an extract from a Swiss student's account of a meal in his boarding-house, written late in the sixteenth century. " We eat a *soupe* with turnips and carrots in it. It was mutton broth or very rarely beef broth, and not much either. Every one ate the *soupe* with their fingers out of their bowls. At supper there was always a salad followed by a small roast; what was left wouldn't give anyone indigestion." Here we see the *soupe* eaten with the fingers but in the next account he describes how " one of us, a German," which was a common term for all Teutons, " made a most unnecessary fuss by asking our hostess for a spoon, of which there were none in the house. We had only one big knife on the table, chained to it, which every one used in turn. Our convenient custom of a separate spoon for every one is unknown here." These foreign students were all continental " Germans " but we can infer that spoons were also in use in English houses from the books on manners written for English children. There were many of such books published before and after our dauphin's date, both in French and in English and their great similarity point to a common ancestry in a distant past. Many of their rules, generally written in doggerel rhymes, continued to be printed long after changes in the art of polite behaviour had made them entirely out of date. But there are instances of a difference in the customs of the two countries and where such occur it is worth while to note; for instance, I can recall no verse in a French *Livre de Civilité* to parallel the following English rhyme, written in the fifteenth century:

> " Kutte with your knyf your bread and break it not,
> A clene trenchour before you eke ye lay,
> And whenne your potage to you shall be broughte
> Take your sponeys and soupe it in no way
> And in your dysshe leave not your spone I pray."

In a somewhat later book, wherein a page is instructed in his many duties, the directions for laying a table are as follows. " Set your salt on the right side and on the left side of your salt set your trenchour, one or two. On the left side of your trenchour lay your knife singular and plain and on the side of your knife a white bread. Your spoon upon a napkin folded fair . . . See that there be a knyfe, spoon and napkin for all diners." These are, of course, directions for a well-to-do English household, whereas the student in the boarding-house described the ways of homely French citizens. But on the other hand the French *livres de civilité*, which do not mention the use of soup spoons were certainly intended for the children of nobles as well as of citizens. We may recall a day when Henri " supped " what was left of the baby's broth out of the bowl.

We often hear of silver dinner-services but one day in the year 1607, Héroard tells us that whilst the dauphin " was taking his soup out of a porcelain bowl someone praised the use of china. I told him the Grand Turk drank out of china cups. ' Ho! then I won't have my soup out of china.' ' Monsieur, the Grand Turk does it because he is a mighty prince and only great kings and princes use china.' He considered the matter and then pulled his bowl back asking ' Does Papa use china? ' ' Yes, Monsieur.' " There is something very delightful in the knowledge that only great princes could use china brought by strange routes from far-off Cathay. It brings to mind the Elizabethan song in which the writer sings of

" The Andalusian merchant that returns
Laden with cochineal and china dishes
Reports in Spain how mighty Fogo burns
Amidst an ocean full of flying fishes."

The dauphin and his brothers and sisters had forks

for their meat as well as spoons for their soup. Their use had been long in fashion in Spain and Italy but it was a fashion very slow to spread. No doubt the queen would have introduced into the French court some of the luxuries of her Florentine home and forks may have been among them. The sight of them on Italian dinner-tables certainly came as a novelty to both English and French travellers at the end of the sixteenth, and even in the beginning of the seventeenth, centuries. Twenty years before the dauphin's birth Montaigne preferred to use his fingers when travelling in Italy but he liked to have a fresh napkin for every course to wipe his fingers clean. In the museums of South Kensington and of Cluny in Paris there are forks dating from early in the seventeenth century; one in the Cluny is made of three strands of heavy twisted wire strong enough for each strand to make a prong and the three united to make the handle, others have only two prongs and are small and dainty things of silver. Some examples in South Kensington are two-pronged with beautiful chased or enamelled handles, but these are often part of a little set of knife and fork with a case to hold them. In the present day a three-pronged fork is within the reach of the poorest house-hold; fifty years ago the iron two-pronged fork was common enough not only in cottage homes but in the kitchens of most middle-class families; readers of *Cranford* will recall how, in a still earlier generation, Miss Matty left the peas untasted because she *could* not eat them with a two-pronged fork and *would* not shovel them in with her knife. Forks, whether with two or three prongs, were rarer in the dauphin's day than even the use of spoons for soup but there were strict rules for the fingers which replaced them. For instance, not more than three might be employed to lift a portion from the dish to the plate nor should more than one hand be raised to the mouth at a time. "Do not," says one book on manners, "use both hands like a monkey nor fill your mouth too full and gobble like a pig." Others forbid the young diner to "press the cheese and butter on to your bread with your thumb. It is better to smear soft things with a knife or crust of bread. Do not dig the egg out of its shell with your fingers nor with your thumb turned down, nor lick the inside clean with your tongue. It is better to use a sippet of bread." Which of us cannot remember in our childhood the little pile of sippets set by our nurse when we had a boiled egg for breakfast, and which we dipped in and brought out all yellow. It was a very old survival of table manners, just as are the finger-bowls on our dessert-plates. Washing the hands after a meal was never omitted by any but the roughest people, and it was an almost universal custom for a basin and ewer to be brought round to each diner in turn. These were small and dainty things in rich houses, of silver or pewter; the ewers, in the dauphin's day, were sometimes of the hard glazed pottery of quaint colour and fantastic decoration made famous by Bernard Palissy, and many examples of these long-necked little jugs in metal and earthenware can be seen in museums. They were used for pouring the water into basins over the fingers of diners. The habit was long continued, for the use of forks did not banish the use of fingers, and kings and queens and their courtiers made no difficulty about picking up bones and gnawing them bare many years later than the days of Louis XIII.

These revelations into ways that seem to us somewhat barbarous must not, however, lead us astray. We should form a very mistaken conception of these

years of Louis' childhood if we imagine them lacking
in luxury, or, as then understood, in refinement. The
same student, who described the *bourgeois* meals he
himself ate, gives a delightful picture of Paris as the
wealthy then knew it. *Plus ça change plus c'est la
même chose* we could say, only the Rue St Denis is not
now the centre of fashion it was then, nor happily
are birds treated so barbarously in the belief that it
made their flesh tender. " In the long and important
Rue St Denis there are many inns, restaurants and
pastry-cooks, as well as houses where one can arrive at
any hour one pleases and find plenty of living birds,
such as pigeons, quails, hazel hens, pheasants and
other game birds. The result is that anyone, who
wants to make a banquet and can settle the price to
his liking, can have as many birds plucked alive as he
likes, and fried or roasted. There is no lack of fish
either, nor of colonial produce, nor sugared things nor
good wine. . . . If one does not wish to be troubled
by entertaining at home one can find special houses
with signboards with ' rooms for banquets ' on them.
To arrange an entertainment one is only asked to state
the day, the greater or less costly style, the number of
the guests, to what class of life they belong and the
price per head . . . the host will not regret the cost
for he will find it cheap considering what he gets for
it. These caterers know how to manage everything
so well to every one's liking, choice food, desserts,
tapestries and vases to ornament the room, furniture,
serving-maids, music and a comedy if you like, a very
paradise on earth. For in Paris you can buy or hire
everything you can desire if you have money."
  The hours at which meals were eaten at St Germain-
en-Laye were not bound by any hard-and-fast rule,
nor was the room in which they were served always

the same. The most usual hour was half-past eleven
for dinner and half-past six for supper; breakfast had
no fixed time and the informal afternoon meal, *goûter*,
was eaten when and where the whim took the children.
For the first years of his life the dauphin dined and
supped alone, his meals being brought into his own
room, but when Madame was old enough to sit at
table she generally joined him. A little later the king
had a fancy to make all his children dine together
which was a very sore point with the dauphin.
One day when he and his *féfé* Verneuil were both
four years old he overheard his father giving orders
that the little boys should dine together. " The
dauphin said, ' Oh, no, no, valets shouldn't dine with
their masters.' Once at the very height of his affection
for the young soldier, Descluseaux, Héroard suggested
that he should be asked to sup with the dauphin.
' No, I don't want him.' ' You don't love him as
much as you say you do then.' ' Yes, I do, but not
to eat with me.'" To eat and drink with an inferior
was an insult to his rank and only the queen's children
were his equals. The king thought differently and
the day following his command, " M. and Mlle de
Verneuil dined with the dauphin for the first time.
He did not like it and the king asked why he did not
want his *féfé*. ' Because he isn't Mamma's son.'"
We gather from subsequent scenes that a common
dinner-table for all the king's children was not always
the custom, for more than a year later we find little
de Verneuil asking the dauphin, " Mon maître, would
you like me to dine with you?' The dauphin said
very brusquely, ' No.' Mme de Montglat asked him
' Why not?' ' Because he'd make a habit of it and
I don't want that.' ' Monsieur, papa would like it.'
' Oh! very well then, I am quite willing.'" He

may have said he was willing, for he never opposed his father after a few sharp lessons in babyhood, but he certainly never *felt* willing. We come across more than one fit of bad temper on the subject a couple of years later than the above anecdote. In "July 1607. He did not wish his own gentleman to serve him at supper because he had touched Mlle de Vendôme while helping her to seat herself at table. He was very obstinate about it. Someone mentioned the thunderbolt which, about three o'clock on the previous day, had fallen in the room at Moret, where the Comte de Moret, two months and a half old, was in his nurse's arms close by the window, but which harmed no one. I remarked that the room we were in seemed to be full of naughty people. The dauphin did not say a word to me but immediately after he said, ' Guerin, take the napkin and serve me.' " Thunder as a judgment on " naughty people " was an old fear of the dauphin's. One day, two years before this occasion, " he was naughty. M. de la Court told him that the thunder would come and carry him off. He left off being wilful and asked ' What is thunder? ' ' Monsieur, don't you remember that you called it God's drum? ' He listened full of wonder and then said to Mme de Montglat, ' Mamanga, who is God? What does He do? ' " The baby at Moret was the child whom the dauphin contemptuously refused to call a féfé. The fear of thunder did not cure the little boy's arrogance for in the following September there was another nursery fuss. On this occasion Madame Elizabeth took it on herself to reprove her brother in language far too coarse to translate in full. " The dauphin was cross and did not want M. de Verneuil to have dinner with him. Mme de Montglat insisted that he should. Madame Elizabeth from her

end of the table scolded the dauphin. 'Ha! Jesu!
Monsieur, you mustn't behave like that. Nobody
thinks that you are the king's only son. You mustn't
have such fancies. Mamanga will purge them out of
you with smacks. She'll give you a whipping.' He
dared not say a word, listened but pretended not to
hear. Madame went on: 'Ha! Monsieur, you
mustn't talk like that to *gouvernantes;* it isn't pretty,
Monsieur.' She said this because he told Mme de
Montglat he wouldn't do what she wanted." It is a
positive pleasure to find that Madame could stand up
to her elder brother in so truly a sisterly fashion.
Mme de Montglat was never slack in the training of
her big nursery full and we can feel confident that
with or without the help of smacks they attained the
standard of table manners accepted at court. One of
her lessons recall an old dilemma which in my childhood I found peculiarly annoying. It is summed up
in the nursery saying, " Those who ask can't have and
those who don't ask don't want." One day in April
1607 the dauphin " dined with the king who was
eating a stew of venison for dinner. The dauphin
said to Mme de Montglat: 'Mamanga, I should so
like to eat some of that.' 'Monsieur,' she said,
'you must not ask for things.' When the king had
finished the dauphin said: 'Papa, please give me some
of that dish.' The king replied: ' It is all gone, why
didn't you ask me before?' The dauphin said
grumblingly: 'Papa, I wanted to ask but Mamanga
wouldn't let me.' "

There were rules for drinking as well as for eating,
but before we consider them, one curious custom of
the day should not be passed over. In all houses of
the wealthy it was thought proper to protect the wine,
set on the sideboard ready for a meal, from the risk

of poisoning the diners. Happily there was an infallible test for poison in the drink; if a piece of a unicorn's horn was kept on the sideboard, no matter how small a piece it was, it would act if not as an antidote at least as a detective of poison. Unicorns and their horns were hard to come by even in those days of easy belief in marvels; but by some happy adaptation of nature the narwhal, who did exist was able to supply the lack of the unicorn who did not. Gesner in his *Icones Animalium*, which the dauphin called the "lion book," has the following charming note on the unicorn and its miraculous powers. "I hear also that from new-found islands a horn of a beast called the unicorn is brought, recommended against poison; what it may be I have not yet got to know. Enquire, however, if it be the horn of the rhinoceros, for both old and later authorities confound this beast with the unicorn." Gesner gives a picture of a rhinoceros with a hide worked in patterns like watered silk, but a real rhinoceros notwithstanding, for Gesner's animals are very real. Rhinoceroses were but little easier to come by than unicorns but there was a good supply of narwhal tusks to be got from those who sailed the northern seas, and the rich and the great kept a bit of one of these on their sideboards and felt all the safer for it.

The rules concerning the niceties of drinking were based on the fact that separate drinking-vessels were not set on the table for each guest. A separate spoon might be allowed in England but there is no word said of a separate cup. Montaigne noticed with surprise in a Swiss inn that a cup was set at each place; he was certainly not accustomed to see them in his own country. Both drinks and drinking-vessels were placed on the sideboard and each diner, when he wanted to drink, called for wine and was served in a cup which would be used by several in turn. Neatness in drinking was, therefore, an essential piece of good manners.

> " Whanne ye shall drynke your mouthe clene with a clothe
> Your handes eke that they in no manere
> Imbrowe the cup, for thanne shall none be lothe
> With you to drink that ben with you y fere."

This English rhyme is much earlier in date than the seventeenth century though not so old as Chaucer's lines on the Prioress:—

> " Hir overlippe wyped she so clene
> That in hir coppe was no ferthing sene
> Of grece, whan she dronken hadde her draughte."

But the advice was no more out-of-date in England in 1600 than it was in France in bourgeois households, nor in noble ones either, for that matter except in the case of very special people. The student whose anecdote on the lack of spoons we read just now tells us that " we had as much wine as we liked and a great deal of water mixed with it," *bien baptisée* as Montaigne called it. " The maid poured out as much water as we wanted and then added the wine. If you did not empty the cup she threw the rest away." The cup was used in common but the drink was served fresh for each guest. It is clear, however, that the dauphin had a cup of his own. There was a silver-gilt goblet which he often used but we also find him using a glass. Here are several instances. " Whilst drinking he looked about him. M. de Souvré told him he ought to look into the glass and gave him a lesson how to do it." Another time " he danced up and down in his chair to the sound of a lute and a viol, drank as he danced waving his glass about." A few months later certain envoys from the Swiss cantons

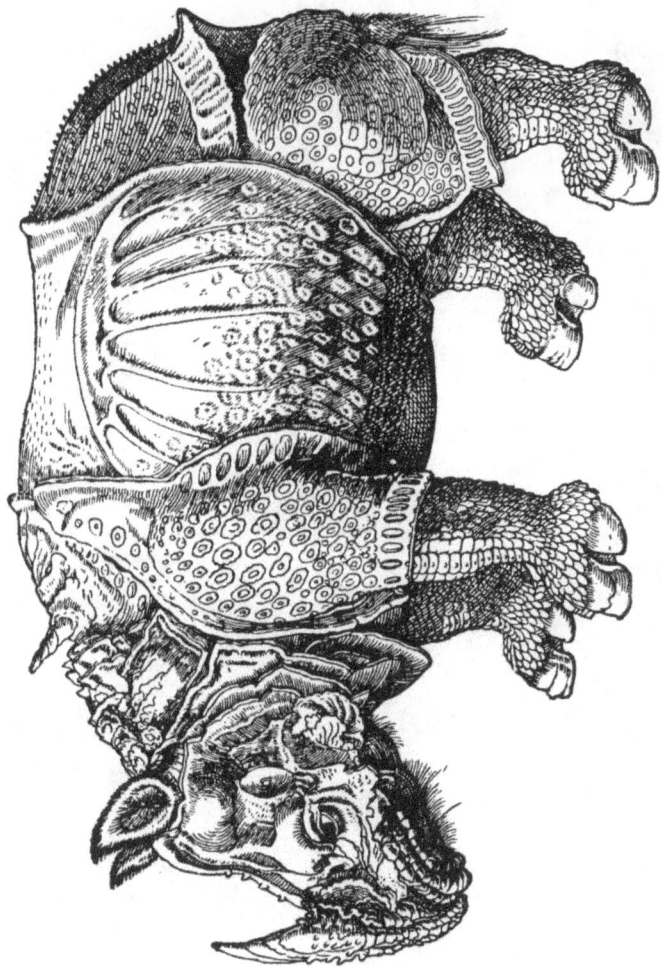

A RHINOCEROS

From The Icones Animalium, Gesner

[*face p.* 200

came to see him. " Before they left Mme de Montglat sent for wine to drink at the collation, and she whispered in Monseigneur le Dauphin's ear that it would be proper for him to drink to them. He said quickly, ' Have my glass brought.' It was fetched and a very little wine was put in with plenty of water. He drank to them, just a taste. They were greatly pleased and said his courtesy would be talked about a great way off."

We may feel sure that the dauphin's goblet and glass were kept for his own use. He was so extraordinarily tenacious of everything connected with his personal needs that it would be strange if it were otherwise; of his bed on which even the king might not sit; of his cushions which M. de Montglat had the effrontery to use for his gouty leg; of his silver dinner-service that Mme de Montglat kept as a perquisite when he left her care for M. de Souvré's. " ' Soeu-soeu Vendôme,' he whispered one day, ' I am going to get a hollow stick and fill it with gunpowder and I shall light it with a hot coal and I'll blow up Mamanga, because she means to keep my silver dinner-service.' " A little boy like this would not be likely to share a glass. Perhaps at court separate glasses were coming into fashion along with forks. It was an age when customs were slowly modernizing.

What the children habitually drank is a somewhat difficult matter to determine. Héroard strongly disapproved of wine for children and some of his entries on the subject are curious and amusing. All the children were in the habit of joining the king at his dinner when he came out to St Germain-en-Laye, and on such occasions he gave them all sorts of titbits and sips, often to the doctor's annoyance. " The dauphin drank some of the king's wine mixed with

water. He was thirsty, ate some of the king's marchpane, drank some more wine, a good draught. 'Ho!
how good it is. It would be better still if it were red,
very red indeed,' he said. I must look into this."
The doctor did his best to check a taste for wine as
the following long story shows. The scene took place
in July 1607, when the dauphin was almost six and
his half-sister eleven years old. " The dauphin dined
at eleven o'clock. He asked for some of Mlle de
Vendôme's tisane. M. Guerin said it was wine she
was drinking. 'All right, it is the same thing, give
me some.' He looked at me and told me to let them
give him wine. I replied, ' Monsieur, it will do you
harm.' ' Papa lets me.' ' Monsieur, that is when you
dine with him.' He began to get angry and said to
me, ' You are a snow man, you are an ugly thing.'
' I daresay, Monsieur, but you will not have wine to
drink, because it is bad for you.' Upon this he seized
a knife and flaring up in a passion threatened me with
it. I said ' Good-bye, Monsieur. I am going away.'
I went to my room. He sent after me several times,
and after refusing three or four times I came back.
He said he was sorry and wouldn't do it again and
then he asked for some drink. His own drink was
served him but he wouldn't have it, only tasted it on
compulsion. His mind was set on the wine. He
wanted it, I refused it. ' I don't love you. You are
a snow man.' ' Monsieur, I shall go to the king and
tell him.' ' I don't care.' ' Very well, Monsieur,
since I am no good here I will say good-bye, and go
to the king.' I went away and would not return.
Meanwhile he went on with his dinner. At two
o'clock he came to my room after asking if I had
really gone. He was told that I had gone in my coach.
' Ho! his coach is at Vaugrineuse and Mamanga's is

in Paris.' Mme de Montglat brought him to my
room. He hesitated at the door. When he came in
I bowed without speaking. At last he came up to
me. ' Please don't go away.' ' Monsieur, what good
am I here if you will not do what I think good for
your health?' ' I won't do it again.' And peace was
made." In 1609 the dauphin left St Germain for
Paris. " At a quarter to eight he got into the coach,
dry eyed, and left St Germain for the court in charge
of M. de Souvré. . . . At six in the evening his
supper was served from the queen's table. It was the
first time he began to drink wine as his usual beverage."
But the lesson taught by Héroard was not forgotten
for, when Madame Elizabeth came to pay him a
visit a few weeks later, the dauphin said at supper:
" ' Sister, you are too young to drink wine. I drink
it but I am a year older than you. Maître Giles do
not give my sister wine, she is too young.' " Sometimes the difference between eight years old and seven
is very great. This was not the only occasion when
the dauphin kept a careful eye on his butler, Maître
Giles. One day at breakfast the dauphin saw M. de
Souvré drinking wine, and he immediately wanted
some too. For dinner Héroard had had to give way
but on the prohibition of wine for breakfast he stood
firm. At last for the sake of peace M. de Souvré said
" he would not have any wine either. Monseigneur,
suspecting that he meant to drink it after breakfast
was over, told his butler to leave the room and watched
carefully to see that the wine went with him."

The exact nature of the drinks other than wine and
water is difficult to determine. *Tisane* is what Héroard
generally mentions but a *tisane* could be made of many
things. Perhaps its earliest mention is in a late fourteenth century book, *Le bon menagier,* which Dr Eileen

Power has lately brought before the English public as *The Good Man of Paris*. The recipe is two hundred years older than the dauphin's days, but it sounds a likely enough survival. Here it is : " *Tisanne Doulce*. Take water and boil it, then for each sester (here no doubt the sester of eight pints) of water put in a bowl heaped with barley, and it matters not if it be hulls and all, and two parisis (2½d.) worth of liquorice, item figs, and let it be boiled till the barley bursts; then let it be strained through two or three pieces of linen, and in each goblet put great plenty of chrystallized sugar." This is really a barley-water but there were also *tisanes* of herbs of many kinds and others made with flowers, borage, clove pinks, elder flowers, lime flowers, roses and violets; and again toast-water was also used, for we find a slice of toasted bread sopped in water, as a common *goûter*, and both bread and water were consumed. *Tisanes* of whatever nature were made by steeping the ingredients in boiling-water until the flavours were extracted; they are still in common use in France and some make pleasant drinks. The dauphin's *tisanes* are generally sweetened; we may recall how the queen once asked him for " soucre " at his *goûter* and how her little son smiled at her pronunciation. Beside *tisanes* Héroard speaks now and then of a *lait d'amandes*, which was a drink made from crushed almonds boiled in water and sweetened with plenty of sugar. Milk he never mentions but this is not sufficient evidence that it was not in use among the children; all we can say is that it is odd he does not speak of it.

Breakfast and this little afternoon meal called *goûter* were both quite slight; breakfast seems to have followed morning chapel and to have been at nine o'clock, but for special reasons we may find it served at seven or eight; *goûter* had no regular time nor any formality in serving it. The journal often speaks of it and often in the following typical way: "Eat *goûter* at a quarter to three standing up. It is to be noted that from the moment he gets up in the morning until he goes to bed at night he never sits down except for dinner and supper." Madame Elizabeth seems to have shared his restless habits and one day she even went so far as to dine standing up. "Just like a serving-man," said the dauphin scornfully. Bread was the principal food at both breakfast and *goûter*, indeed so far as breakfast goes no mention is ever made of anything else. Now and then for the afternoon snack, one can hardly call it a meal, we hear of a piece of marchpane, some dried plums or raisins and on birthdays a fruit tart, plum tarts for summer birthdays and apple tarts for autumn ones. Sometimes a *goûter* was offered in hospitality as when the dauphin "drove in his coach to the Abbey of Saint Sixte. *Goûter* at three o'clock, confiture, bread and biscuits from the Abbess' table, "but a feast of this sort was a rare treat. Considering how often bread was eaten dry, as it still is in France much more often than in England, it was natural for the children to be particular about its quality and flavour. Often they preferred the coarser bread of the servants to the white bread served to themselves. Now and then there was a special reason for this preference as when Héroard records that "the dauphin ate our brown bread because he said his own was bitter. It was quite true and it had been bad for several days. The next day bread was bought for him in the village. The flour for his own was musty." Still bad flour was not always the reason for eating the household bread for a little later, when we might suppose that fresh flour had been procured, we learn that " the dauphin breakfasted with the king at nine o'clock. Ate the bread my servants eat and the king ate it too." There were many other times when the common bread was preferred and eaten by the children with relish for their *goûter*. It would be interesting to know what this household bread was. Yeast bread was still a fairly new invention although by 1600 the bakers of Paris were already famous for their rolls made of white flour and brewers' yeast. There was a great variety of these little loaves, some made with milk and butter, some plain and crisp but all of them disapproved of by the medical profession as likely to cause indigestion. They must have been a great contrast to the old loaves of leavened bread, baked round and flat and which became hard so soon as the least bit stale. No doubt these old loaves were made of white wheat flour for the very wealthy but by far the larger part of the people eat bread of mixed flour, generally wheat and rye. Unlike the new yeast bread these brown leavened loaves were generally un-salted for the heavy salt tax made salt a luxury. Their hardness was shown by the habit of cutting them into thin rounds and laying several of these slices one above the other, on the dinner-plate. A course of meat could be served on the top of each slice which, sucking up the gravy or sauce, would be eaten with the meat, leaving a lower slice ready for the next course. These *tranchées* are sometimes confused with the trencher on which they were placed, and no doubt in poor houses they were a sufficient substitute for any other plate. Biscuits, such as we heard of at the Abbey St Sixte, were as great a novelty as the new yeast bread and were considered very suitable for the fashionable light meal known as a *collation*. These *Collations* were served after a ballet, at a wedding dance or after any ceremonious call such as we have seen the Swiss envoys making on the little dauphin. With the biscuits were served confitures, light pastries, *cornets d'oublies*, sweetmeats of many kinds, preserved fruits and candied violets and rose leaves. Wine, either plain or spiced and made sweet with sugar was served with these dainties. Are the light horned shaped wafers known as *oublies* still sold in the Paris streets to eat with ices? *Cornet d'oublies* the dauphin called them and ate all he could get.

Because our modern supply of cane-sugar comes to us mainly from the New World there is a not uncommon belief that its use, along with that of turkeys, potatoes and tobacco, coincides with the discovery of America. The truth is that sugar reached Europe both from the east and from the northern coasts of Africa centuries before the Portuguese navigators carried the sugar-cane to Madeira and later across the Atlantic to Brazil. In the sixteenth century the best sugar was grown in Madeira and its production in the western world was still small early in the seventeenth. No doubt, before the days of our immense supplies from the West Indies, sugar was a luxury for the well-to-do, but the extraordinary numbers of sweetmeats, of candied fruits and confitures sold in the shops, and the variety of recipes for making them at home printed in the old cookery-books, show how plentiful sugar must have been even three hundred years ago. A list of the fruits most often used for candying and preserving gives us a good notion of those most commonly eaten. It includes apples, apricots, quinces, pears, plums and peaches, cherries, sorbs and chestnuts. Dates and walnuts were also candied but I do not recall any mention of these two last in the pages of the doctor's journal. Most of the others were also eaten fresh and to them must be added oranges and grapes. Quinces were made into marmalade and one day the dauphin watched Mme de Montglat preserving a pan full over the fire in the Great Hall.

The candied fruits, the jams, the sugared orange and rose water were no doubt very nice and we can very well believe how welcome the *prévôt des marchands* and the *échevins de Paris* were when they came to pay their respects on New Year's Day, bringing as an offering a dozen boxes of sweetmeats and as many bottles of wine and hippocras. We can picture Mme de Montglat locking them up in her cupboard as she locked up another New Year's box of candied apricots to the dauphin's indignation. No doubt the children had a share of the sweet things but Dr Héroard would have forbidden the wine and the hippocras. There were probably as many ways of mixing this much-loved spiced drink as there were of making punch in the following centuries. Here is one method typical of them all, although many have a greater variety of spices. " Take two pints of white wine, one pound of sugar, a little mace, two corns of white pepper put in whole, a lemon cut into quarters. Leave them to infuse together and strain before stirring." Water is not mentioned but a pound of sugar to two pints of wine sounds intolerably sweet if there were no more liquid added, but I fancy water was added as desired at the time of drinking.

When we turn to the dishes served at meals we find no lack of variety of meat, or poultry or vegetables. Indeed a cookery-book of the time amazes us by its large range of materials and the infinite care and skill shown in procuring them. We read of live fish and fresh oysters brought in barrels of sea-water from the coast to Paris; of elaborate ways of fattening poultry with meal soaked in beer; of hatching eggs in ovens and rearing the chickens for early spring supplies; of veal made superlatively tender by feeding the calves on new-laid eggs; of verjuice made in the new way from grapes instead of from sorrel leaves, and of the many pickles prepared with this superior vinegar. Cucumbers, pumpkins, cauliflowers, pears and green apricots and many others. The French cooks already possessed their delicate sense of fitness. Note, for instance, the distinction of sauces served for pigs' and sheep's trotters and the feet of calves and bullocks; vinegar and chopped onions with pigs' trotters but parsley and vinegar with sheep's, both to be fried. On the other hand, calves' and bullocks' feet must be boiled and served with pepper and saffron. The use of capers with boiled mutton is still in favour and, if we tried it, we might enjoy calves' liver eaten with a black sauce of sugar, pepper and vinegar. Dishes of liver were popular. In September 1610 the little king sent the English ambassadors who were dining at court "a pasty of chickens' livers and a dish of ortolans from his own table and drank his wine to their healths. They sent back word that they did not presume to drink to him but that they would drink his health to each other." We may not share in all their tastes but we cannot deny that it was discriminating.

Héroard rarely tells us much about the food in any detail but there are many slight mentions of this dish or that from which we can learn much by collecting them together. We have already read of one very complete supper, which gave us a long list of dishes; here are others which I give without comment in the brief manner in which they are mentioned. "Supped with the king on onion soup, oysters, sole fried in batter and a spoonful of the king's digestive powder."

"At supper a mackerel was served for the first time.
'What is that?' the dauphin asked. 'Monsieur, it is
a mackerel.' He opened the fish's jaw. 'It is ugly.
Take away the ugly thing.'" These were fast-day
suppers. On meat days we read of "a large helping
of hare pie and brown bread," of minced partridge,
of sweetbreads, and "a cutlet fried in bread crumb.
The dauphin peeled off the outside to eat it alone.
I said to him, 'Monsieur, you only want to eat the
part which will make you passionate.' 'Papa does it.'
It is quite true and he imitates the king in everything."
Indeed he copied him so faithfully that one day when
Mme de Montglat scolded him at dinner for not
saying "thank you" he promptly replied, "Papa
never does." Héroard was not peculiar in his belief
that fried meat bred passionate tempers. French
doctors seemed to have regarded it with the same
disapproval with which they regarded the delicious
rolls of the Parisian bakers. The opinion must have
been widely diffused for I remember an English
warning against "fried meat, that stops and dis-
tempereth all the body, back, belly and bowels," a
very comprehensive condemnation indeed. I have not
spoken much of eggs as an article of diet but they
were cooked and eaten in many forms. The dauphin,
who was very fond of cooking, one day made a supper
for M. de Souvré of hard-boiled eggs chopped up
with bacon, poached eggs and *œufs perdus*, the recipe
for which is not given. It is to be hoped the cooking
was successful for M. de Souvré would certainly not
have been allowed to leave the dishes uneaten. Most
of the common fruits and vegetables have already
been spoken of in the lists of pickles and candied
fruits. Here are a few more gathered haphazard from
the pages of the doctor's diary. "The dauphin would

not eat beetroot after tasting it and as for the green
fennel the king gave him he said he would plant it in
his garden." "He ate everything the king gave him
except the salad. It had too much vinegar." "Tried
a piece of melon, spat it out saying 'not nice.'"
"Threw a stick of asparagus at M. d'Augé who had
helped M. le Chevalier to chicken broth before him."
And here is a vegetable served in a way unfamiliar
to us. "The king and queen were at dessert. The
king gave the dauphin some compôte of wild carrots."
Some of the king's tastes in food the boy could not
bring himself to share, however much he tried. Possibly
he may have liked melons when he was older but he
never shared Henri's passion for garlic. One spring
day, "Seeing the king eat fresh butter and garlic on
his bread the dauphin said he would eat some too.
Swallowed two little slices which the king cut for him,
making himself do it to please the king." Eating
fresh butter and garlic in the springtime was thought
good for the health but Henri needed no such induce-
ment; he was too much of a Gascon for that in spite
of his Bourbon father. His grandfather, the last of
the Albret kings of Navarre, is said to have rubbed
his grandson's lips with garlic at his birth to ensure
his being a true Gascon, but Henri neglected to do
the same for his son in turn. Perhaps from this
neglect, perhaps from his northern breeding, a taste
for garlic was beyond the dauphin's power to acquire,
even to be like his father. Héroard tells us of several
attempts on his part and here is one of them. Henri
was dead and Louis a boy-king. "The king asked
for garlic at breakfast, said it was nice, that he liked
it and then all at once remarked, 'Well, after all it's
not worth anything,' and gave the rest to M. de la
Rivière who is a Gascon." Perhaps the courtiers

were pleased at the difference of taste in their kings.
Henri had certainly been a trial, for the constant
eating of garlic is not a habit which can be concealed
from others.

Imperfect as these lists of foods and drinks are,
they are sufficient to give us some insight into the
meals of those days, and to convince us that the
household at St Germain did not lack variety. Indeed
there is no reason to doubt that they lived very well.

CHAPTER X

TOILET AND DRESS

No one can read Jean Héroard's journal without
feeling how little child-nature has changed in the three
hundred years which have elapsed since the old doctor's
death. Outward forms are different but not the
inward spirit; the small pleasures and terrors of childhood, the droll sayings, the dolls and toy soldiers,
playing at making gardens and houses, learning to
read and to write and how to behave at meals, none of
these differ in their essential qualities. The world
changes but the children are for ever the same. There
are, however, two aspects of daily life in which their
ways were profoundly different from ours; the constant
use of the rod and an indifference to soap and water.
We might add a third in the lack of decency in personal
habits but this is, in fact, only a branch of cleanliness
and can be included in the second. Whipping little
children was but a part of the general brutality of the
age in regard to punishments, and it is a side of nursery
life we have already studied in previous chapters. In
this chapter I propose to discuss the common attitude
towards washing among the people of the seventeenth
century. It is not easy to form any conclusive opinion
on the subject and I do not pretend to do more than
place certain evidence, partly contradictory in character,
before the reader. His conclusions he must draw for
himself; if he finds the evidence inadequate, as indeed it
is, he should turn over the pages of M. Al. Franklin's
La vie privée d'autre fois, and study in that storehouse

of curious knowledge the pages devoted to matters of
the toilet in the age of Henri IV. What we have now
to determine is how much washing was a part of daily
life. So far as hands go we have already seen that
good breeding required that they should be washed
before and after meals. But was washing the body
generally practised? In Héroard's journal we frequently come across an entry such as the following :
" Waked up at seven o'clock, was dressed, his hair
combed " and sometimes " said his prayers " is added.
The editors of the printed portion of the journal
append to one of these entries a footnote to point
out that " at the beginning of the day the word
washed is never used." They would have been justified
in including the end of the day in their note, were
there not at least two mentions of washing at bedtime,
as we shall presently see. The fact that the doctor
does not say that the dauphin was washed as well as
his hair combed is extremely suggestive but it is, after
all, only negative evidence. We cannot judge the
habits of one nation with any safety by those of another
but the following directions for getting up in the
morning, written by a contemporary Englishman, are
not only amusing in themselves but do agree with
what we know from French sources. The advice given
is really traditional and can be met with in many
forms. " When you arise from bed," he says, " extend
forth all your limbs for by this meanes the animal
spirits are drawne to the outward members, the braine
is made subtill and the body strengthened. Then rub
the body somewhat with the palms, the breast, back
and belly gently, but the arms and legs with the hands
either (or) with warm linen; next the head is to be
scrubbed from the forepart to the hinderpart very
lightly. Put on your clothes neat and cleane; in the

summer season first wash with cleane pure water but in the winter season sit somewhat by the fire, not made with turfe or stinking coal but with oake or other wood that burneth cleare. After the body is well clothed kembe your head well from the forehead to the back part some forty times at least; then wash all the instruments of the senses, as the eies, the ears, the nostrils, the mouth, the tongue, the teeth and all the face in cold water." The old writer goes on to recommend rose water or fennel water to cleanse the eyelids " of gummy matter," and " dentifrices or cleansers of the teeth not only to make them white but also to conserve them." In the *School of Vertue*, so highly thought of by John Brinsley, the elder, much the same routine is enjoined. This is how a good child should get up in the morning:—

> " Early in the morning thy bedding forsake
> Thy garments put on and thy selfe ready make
> Thy hands see thou wash, thy head likewise keam
> And in thy apparel see torn be no seam.
> A napkin see that thou have in readinesse
> Thy nose to cleanse from all filthiness.
> Thy nails if need be see that thou pare
> Thy ears keep thou clean, thy teeth wash them fair."

Here only the hands, ears and teeth are to be washed. Nothing is said of " cleane pure water in the summer season," nor of that rub with a linen or the hands, which with the help of the fire of oak logs would have done much to keep the skin in healthy condition. I remember once spending a night in a cottage, where I slept under the thatch in a room with three large beds in it and the merest passage-way between. The family who once filled them were all gone to other homes and the old father of them all rested in the churchyard. Only the mother was left. In the very early morning she set a red pan for me in the kitchen and I fetched water from the spring for my tub. "As for me," she said, " I'll have a dry wash in the wood'us." I think dry washing was much used in our forefathers' times and that their skins were kept cleaner by hard rubbing than we should be willing now to believe.

A few decades earlier than the dauphin's birth the richer people in Paris had indulged greatly in steam-baths, *étuves*, kept by the barber-surgeons as part of their establishments. The first street cry in the morning, in a city famous for its cries, was that of the apprentices shouting, as they ran through the streets rousing noble and well-to-do citizens from sleep, " the *étuves* are ready! " But these popular baths were too often places of ill-repute provocative of much disorder. So far as their use as a means of cleanliness went they ceased to exist before the seventeenth century, though their medicinal use continued much longer. Great houses often had their own *étuves* ; Fontainebleau certainly had in Henri IV's time, and we know from Sully's *Ecconomies Royales* that the king made use of steam-baths in more than one place as a remedy for indisposition. Movable bath-tubs were brought into bedrooms, but when we come across a mention of their use there is always a suspicion that it was for medicinal and not for cleansing purposes. It is, however, hazardous to believe that any marked degree of dirtiness was tolerated among the well-to-do. We have a proof of this from the dauphin's extreme sensitiveness to the unpleasant odour of poor people. " They are dirty, they smell," was too common an objection not to be founded on a much higher standard of cleanliness among those with whom he habitually lived. Once Héroard tells us that the dauphin "watched some gipsies dancing in his anteroom. He would not let M. Birat nor any of his household dance with the gipsy women. At a quarter past nine he went to his room, was undressed and put to bed. I asked him if he would have let me dance. 'No,' he said, 'I shouldn't like you to touch the hands of those wretched women. They are so dirty. I shall have a great bundle of juniper lighted in the ante-room.'" Nor is this an unique experience. It was customary to let wedding-guests from the little town dance in the great hall as well as gipsies; strolling players and mountebanks also showed off their drolleries and tricks, and more often than not the dauphin objected to watching them on account of their mal-odour. It is necessary to keep in mind the marked difference between the rich and the poor in this respect. This difference would partly arise from the cleaner clothes of the well-to-do, but I think we must admit that either by "dry washes" or wet ones those who had means and leisure did attain to a certain level of cleanliness. Somewhat later than Henri IV's time court ladies took to having large baths brought into their bedrooms. I fancy most of us remember the fairy-tale of the stepmother who promised to give the first wife's child milk to wash in and her own child water, but quickly reversed the rule after the manner of fairy-tale stepmothers. Milk baths were certainly not unusual in the eighteenth century and probably earlier, not because milk was a pleasant liquid to wash in, but because, at a time when there was little desire for privacy outside the drawn curtains of one's bed, a few pints of milk added to the bath-water gave a measure of opaque propriety. Were the baths of the fairy-tale really of milk or only the milk-clouded water such as fine ladies liked to shroud themselves in? It is not our business here to discuss the question, nor need we think that the ways of fine ladies are any real evidence on the ways of ordinary people. The habits of the children at St Germain-en-Laye, however, are likely to be a guide to the habits of the time, for the method of bringing up children is apt to be very much the same for all classes above the really poor. We cannot argue from the dauphin to a peasant's or a poor city workman's children, but we can assert that what Mme de Montglat thought proper for her charges was what any well-to-do mother would practise.

Unfortunately the information to be gathered from Héroard's journal is but meagre. All that he says on matters of the toilet shall be set before the reader and from these quotations he must draw his own conclusions. We know that the baby was washed in wine and oil of red roses at its birth. The use of this oil, a sovereign specific for new-born babies, was probably continued for some weeks, or even longer. In the November after the dauphin's birth " his face and head were rubbed with fresh butter and oil of sweet almonds as his skin seemed to be dirty." Thereafter there is complete silence on the subject of keeping the child clean until the 9th September 1604, when we read that " the dauphin did not want to have his feet made clean with a damp cloth." Again there is silence until the 3rd March 1606. On that day, " at bedtime, the dauphin's legs were washed, in the queen's basin, for the first time." These two entries are the only occasions on which washing the child at bedtime is described, but one day " a pan of warm water with herbs in it was brought into his room to wash Mme de Montglat's legs in. He was very angry and had it taken away." The lady does really seem to have been lacking in a scrupulosity of taste.

We are left in doubt as to whether, on that 3rd March, it was the first time of washing in any basin or only in the queen's. On the 2nd August 1608, Héroard tells us that the dauphin " bathed for the first time; was put into the bath and Madame with him. He rubbed himself with vine leaves." Vine leaves and red roses were frequently added to baths to make the water wholesome, or perhaps we should say medicinal. The weather, we know, was extremely hot that August and the bath may have been used to cool the over-heated and perhaps feverish children. So far as the bath being for the first time we must accept the state-ment of a writer who appears to let no detail, however trivial, escape his pen. No further records of baths occur until 1610 when Louis had a bath on two con-secutive days. " June 27th. At half past seven in the morning the king was put into a warm bath, with vine leaves in it, in the great chamber. He stayed in it three-quarters of an hour; was put back to bed where he remained an hour; then dressed. June 22nd. At a quarter to eight was put into the bath, stayed half an hour. Washed his face. Went back to bed for an hour." From the recurrence of the bath on two consecutive days, the long time of immersion and the rest in bed afterwards, it seems likely that these baths were medicinal, although there is no mention of actual illness. It is pleasant to learn that the king washed his face. When he was still dauphin he once watched a play acted. " When put to bed he rubbed the black off his chin which the smoke of the *flambeaux* had deposited, and blackened the chins of those near him." Nothing is said about washing him clean. Perhaps the sheets of his bed rubbed his chin sufficiently but, of course, there may have been that useful damp linen. Or, again, if the

queen's basin were not available he may have had one
of his own. Basins and ewers in a bedroom were
considered an elegance, if not a necessity, in the
sixteenth and seventeenth centuries. In some of the
pictures of interiors of the time such toilet-basins can
be seen but they are dainty things, suitable only for
washing the face and hands. English travellers on
the continent fifty years ago, can recall their insular
disdain of the tiny basins provided for their morning
ablutions; nor were English basins earlier in the
century much bigger to judge by the size of the three-
cornered black mahogany wash-stands which survive
in such numbers in the antique shops to-day. No
doubt a considerable amount of cleanliness can be
achieved with the employment of a small quantity of
water, but, nevertheless these dainty little toilet sets
are small evidence of any great enthusiasm for washing.

Our studies of Louis and his household have not
often extended beyond 1610, but a few entries on this
subject from the later years of the doctor's journal
must find a place here. In July 1611, two baths are
recorded of much the same character as those in the
preceding June. No bath, by the way, is mentioned
between these dates. " July 11th. Waked at seven
and went to see the water put into his tub. Bathed
at half past seven. He sent for his little boats, made
them sail in his bath, loaded them with the red roses
strewn in the water. At a quarter to eight went back
to bed. July 12th. Got into his bath at seven o'clock.
Scattered the red roses over the water, had his little
boats fetched, loaded them with the wet petals and said
they were ships sailing from the Indies and Goa."
The editors of the printed journal add in a footnote
the further information, taken from the unpublished
part of the diary, that the king spent both of these

days in bed on account of the baths he had taken. There can be no question here that they were part of a medicinal treatment. If we look still further ahead, to the year 1617, we find, in a week of exceptionally hot weather, the young king indulging in an unprecedented amount of bathing. Not only did he bathe in the river on 25th and 27th July but he also had a bath in his room on the 31st and again on the 2nd August. During this last bath " he was painted by Ferdinand, an excellent painter, whilst in the water." This Ferdinand Elle was a Flemish painter of great repute in France; surely it must have been one of his oddest pictures.

Bathing in the Seine was a favourite pastime with Henri IV in hot summer weather, and it was a pleasure he taught the dauphin to enjoy in the last year they had together. The dauphin's first experience is thus described: " At half past four went with the king in a carriage to bathe in the river below Conflans, from the Ile Gauloise. It was the first time. He got into the water without showing any fear, thus winning a bet from M. de Bellegarde who had betted he would be frightened. The king poured hatsful of water over his head. M. de Paistry showed him how to swim, holding him under the chin. He wanted to go right under the water, swallowed some. Was in half an hour. Told me all about it at supper." We never hear of the girls bathing though the Vendôme boys shared in the fun. A little later in the century ladies must have grown bolder for there is an amusing account in Mme de Motteville's *Memoires* of Anne of Austria and her ladies bathing in the Seine near Fontainebleau one very hot summer, clad in long grey shifts. Montaigne, forty years before, in his account of mixed bathing in a Spa in the Vosges also describes these grey shifts so they must have been the proper style, just as heavy blue serge ones were in Victorian days. But with all these things we have really nothing to do, and we must go back to St Germain-en-Laye and the dauphin's toilet when he was a little boy.

Whatever is the truth about washing, combing his hair was a daily affair and generally a daily battle. Héroard rarely fails to note the days when Louis, whether as dauphin or king, allowed his hair to be combed in peace. On these rare occasions some reward was sure to follow; he was excused his morning lessons or let off a whipping for some naughtiness on the previous day. Sometimes wheedling was resorted to, not I imagine with much success. One morning " Mme de Montglat said, ' Monsieur, see what pretty fair hair Madame has because she lets it be combed quietly.' He replied, ' Black hair is best,' and told me to write in my book that he thought so." Another sort of argument was more successful. " Jan. 1st 1606. Covered up in his cloak he had his hair combed quietly because he was told that if he were naughty on New Year's Day he would be naughty the whole year through." Perhaps the dauphin was peculiarly sensitive to the pulling of his hair, as some children are. One funny little anecdote seems to point to this. " Whilst undressing him his nurse pulled out a tiny hair and he began to cry and wail piteously. ' But Monsieur, you cry so loudly for a little hair that you couldn't cry any louder for a sword-cut.' ' I shouldn't mind a sword-cut.' ' Why not, Monsieur ? ' ' Because I should be dead,' he said, just as if he were tired of life." It is a curious thing that Héroard only once mentions brushing the child's hair, and if, as is very possible, it was combed without being first brushed we cannot wonder that he made difficulties. Hairbrushes were in use; there is one in the Musée Cluny of the date together with a variety of combs, mostly toothed on both sides and made of bone or hard wood. They none of them look very comfortable to use but age may have warped them, and when we remember their antiquity we shall not judge them hardly. The one instance of the use of a brush occurred in the dauphin's babyhood. On the 22nd July 1602, " the dauphin was carried to the queen's room where both the king and the queen were. They wanted to see his hair. They had it brushed and all that day he was their pretty plaything." Three weeks earlier the baby's hair had been combed for the first time. " Its length was quite the width of three fingers." But the above is the only time when the doctor makes use of the word *brosser*. The insistence on combing the hair, so noticeable, when washing seems to be relatively of such slight importance, is an indication of the generally infested condition of people's heads. The Englishman's rule of " forty times from front to back " would go far to keeping the head free from vermin. There is plenty of proof that fleas and lice were common enough torments.

A baby's head was covered as soon as it was swaddled after birth, and was kept covered day and night for some years. As it grew out of early childhood the character of the cap changed ; lace and lawn were replaced by something stouter but the cap was not abandoned for a man's hat or a woman's headgear until the child was seven or eight years. When the dauphin was nearly five years old " a small cap of linen was put on his head, as his baby caps were to be given up and he was soon to wear hats. I said, ' Monsieur, now your baby caps have gone you will leave off being a little child and you will begin to grow up. You mustn't behave like a child any longer.' He listened and said ' I don't care.' " But the next day the queen came to see him and, like many a mother she did not like to see her baby growing up, so " she had his baby caps put on again and took away his little linen one." It would have been worn under his hat until he was of an age to wear manly clothes altogether. When he was still an infant the queen had sent to Italy for a straw hat for him because she was troubled by the swarthiness of his skin and wanted to keep the sun from browning it yet further. Winter air was not thought good for babies but when spring came one very fine day, " the dauphin was taken out for the first time by the chapel bridge, wearing his straw hat." He was six months old and still in swaddling clothes. This exit from the castle would lead him quickly out under the sunny south wall.

In the seventeenth century, as has already been said in a previous chapter, the habit of keeping the head covered both indoors and out was almost invariably observed. Men wore their hats and women whatever head-dress was proper for their rank and in vogue at the time, babies and little children had their heads close covered with lace or linen. A man only uncovered his head in the presence of his parents or superiors and this was a rule which held all over Europe. Those who are familiar with early Quaker memoirs will recall the troubles which befell the first Friends as a consequence of their refusal to show either parent or superior the deference they considered due only to God. Was not removing the hat a sign of respect for persons? a thing forbidden, and many were the beatings which they endured from infuriated father or outraged magistrate for their obedience to this biblical behest. The dauphin took off his hat in the king's presence and only replaced it if told to do so, and the respect he showed to his father he expected every one but the king to show to himself. It was a sore point that his half-brothers were allowed to wear their hats by the king's wish. One day when the dauphin was only four years old he saw that "M. de Vendôme had his hat on his head. 'Take your hat off. You mustn't wear your hat when I am present.' Someone told him Papa wished M. de Vendôme to wear his hat. 'Put it on, put it on,' he said." When he was a boy-king one of his favourite ways of annoying his governor was to object to his wearing a hat before him; but here M. de Souvré could get even with him. A governor might not wear his hat in his king's presence but he might, and frequently did, birch a refractory pupil. In truth, birchings went on even after Louis was considered old enough to be married. "'Madame,' he once said to the queen-regent when she curtsied to him, 'I could do with less reverence and fewer whippings.'"

In an earlier chapter we read of the white-satin jacket and cap which the baby dauphin wore over his swaddling-clothes, and of his first frock and petticoat and little shoes which he began to wear in the summer of 1602. In the Musée Cluny there is a case of little shoes and among them at least one pair with the square toes and broad flaps buckling across the instep which date the shoes as belonging to the days of Henry IV. As one looks at them one can feel some little child's pride in his new shoes reaching across the long gap of years; there are none, however, small enough to have been the dauphin's at nine months old. He was still very little when his portrait was painted wearing his toy "corselet under a gown of crimson velvet with gold trimming, his sword at his side, a pike in his right hand and his head covered with his baby's cap of white satin and a white feather in it." The sword was that Tom Thumb sword that *la belle Corisande* gave him. Children's frocks were worn very long and were often heavy with embroidery and tucks if they had the ill-luck to be born of parents rich enough to show off their wealth on their children's little bodies. More than once Héroard says the dauphin complained of the weight of his clothes, but like many others he liked to be fine, or at least he liked what he thought was proper to his rank. One hot May, when he was six, " he was given a tunic of white linen lined with taffetas and hose of the same. ' I don't want them; they are not pretty. I won't have them.' Mme de Montglat told him they were like the king's and that they were not to be worn always but only in the heat of the day. ' I won't wear them to-day and I won't wear them ever. I want a silk suit like féfé Chevalier. I want it red.' " At six years old he was not considered old enough to wear tunics instead of frocks, except as a relief in very hot weather. In the following October when he was turned seven, he had a new frock " of grey satin with a high collar, and left off wearing bibs." Pinafores, when he played in the garden, were still wisely put on over the satin and velvet; we have seen that the dauphin's were trimmed with lace while the luckier féfé Verneuil had plain linen ones. Christmas in this same year was to have been celebrated with a fine " dress of brown silk with gold and silver threads in it. Said it weighed more behind than in front. Nothing that they could do with it could please him, so it was taken off and the one he wore the day before was put on him." I rather think the colour of the frock may have displeased him. Héroard notes more than once his love of blue, or colours he associated with blue. He tells us that " Mme de Montglat looked at several pieces of silk to make a frock for the dauphin. She asked him which he liked best. Seeing a piece of violet velvet with gold in it, he said, ' That's my colour. There is blue in it.' " Nor was this the only time that he chose blue or violet for his clothes; red, perhaps, if féfé Chevalier had a red suit, but not brown. A brown dress could never have fitted comfortably just because of its brownness. Bibs had been discarded in October; at Christmas " he had a night-cap like a man. Put it on to go and see Madame in it. It is the first he has had of this sort." We should have liked to know the distinguishing difference between a baby's and a man's cap; greater simplicity and no strings tied under the chin we might guess. Besides the frocks, petticoats and shirts there were *chausses; bas de chausses* which were stockings, and *chausses* which covered the thighs as well as the lower part of the legs. *Haut de Chausses,* or trunk-hose, were only worn when the days of frocks were past. Breeches, or perhaps more properly drawers since they were worn under the frock, are spoken of but were only worn after the first early years and by no means regularly even then. The dauphin had stockings so soon as he left off swaddling-clothes. When a very small boy he " put on his stocking saying, ' There's a fine leg.' Mlle de Ventelet pulled it up and fastened it with a blue riband to the top of his petticoat." We may recall the day when the child tied his garter to his toy cannon and the other end to the belt of his pinafore and so dragged it along after him. It would have been such a riband that he made use of. *Chausses* as well as *bas de chausses* were also tied with long garters but when *haut de chausses* were worn, they and the *chausses* were often laced together and the garters treated as an ornamental part of the dress. How much they were in view we can see by the following story of Bompar, the dauphin's little page, a boy old enough to wear trunk-hose. One of the ladies in the dauphin's room sent Bompar on a message. The dauphin, offended at her freedom, called the boy back, but Bompar, not hearing his imperious master's voice, went on his way. " ' You'll be whipped, Bompar. Bompar will be whipped. A page called Par who wears red garters and blue stockings will be whipped,' the dauphin went on mumbling as he sat on Mme de Montglat's knee." Bompar's stockings were *chausses* reaching half-way up the thigh where they met the trunk-hose. When the dauphin was six years old he too was promoted to long hose, the first pair of which were made of yellow serge, but he did not always wear them. We may remember how he refused to do his lessons one day and, flinging his legs across his copy-book, exposed his bare thighs to Mme de Montglat's cane. He became restive over his frocks long before he was allowed to change them for the freedom of breeches. Early in January 1607, one bedtime after he had " said his prayers, he asked Mme de Montglat when he should have breeches to wear. Mme de Montglat told him when he was eight years old. ' Like féfé Chevalier? ' ' Yes, Monsieur.' ' But I'm big now.' ' Yes, Monsieur, you are six years old.' ' When shall I be eight ? ' ' In *two* years and a half.' " We must suspect here a misreading of the journal unless Mme de Montglat hoped to postpone the day when she would lose her charge until he was nearly nine. Whatever she may have wished the king had no intention of prolonging the dauphin's days of baby-hood. In the summer of 1608 preparations were made for turning the child into a miniature man. No half-way house seems to have been possible; frocks like a baby or the complete dress of a grown man. The only concession to youth was the ruff, which was at first replaced by a falling collar. " On the May 3rd the dauphin tried on a doublet and trunk-hose of satin. He skipped and jumped about and could hardly be persuaded to take them off, however much he was told that there was something which needed altering." It was June before everything was ready for the momentous change and when the day did come Héroard was unluckily away at his own country estate. The doctor, who on these rare absences replaced him, kept the diary posted but we always feel a certain meagreness of detail when he takes the pen. This is all he tells us: " June 6th. The dauphin was dressed in a doublet and trunk-hose instead of in frocks. Put on a cloak and a sword, the one M. de Lorraine gave him. His clothes were of scarlet satin and silver lace; M. de Verneuil was dressed exactly like him." A few days later Héroard himself writes, " I arrived from Vaugrigneuse. The dauphin took me to see his cloak and the cross on it. I pretended not to know him in his new clothes "; brief enough but we can see the little scene very clearly.

Little girls as they grew older lost instead of gaining liberty. Frocks from babyhood reached to the ground but stiff stays, ruffs and hair dressed high on the head were added at a very early age. Elizabeth and Christienne happily took pleasure in their finery and in the visits of the tailors and dressmakers from Paris, but any little modern girl would think their clothes a tyranny impossible to endure. Héroard does not often speak of the girls or their dresses but lets us know incidentally of various small feminine matters. There was the lady who put down her muff when she asked to hold the baby dauphin; the old pedlar woman who came with paints and powders for the ladies' faces; the masks which ladies wore when they went abroad. Mlle de Vendôme masked by the time she was twelve and even the women of far lower rank would not go into public places without a mask. Madame Christienne had a nurse with whom the dauphin played at being in love. He once "met her by the tennis court and made her take off her mask. 'Take it off, take it off. I want to kiss you.'" Patches we also hear about. One January "the dauphin had a little sore at the corner of his lip. I put a tiny bit of plaster on it and asked him if he would like to have a *mouche*. 'A *mouche*,' he said, laughing. 'I don't want to be made pretty. It is the Princesse de Conti who puts on *mouches* to make herself pretty.'" Their origin we shall see presently.

Parasols, as well as patches, seem to have been commonly in use. In 1607 "the king took the dauphin for a walk. On his return the dauphin wanted to beat Bompar, saying it was because he had not followed him but he held his tongue on his real reason. It was because Bompar had followed the king holding the dauphin's parasol over him. When Bompar came into his room he ran at him with the birch-rod in his hand and kicked him, would not forgive him whatever was said. Was threatened with a whipping. 'I shall beat him. I shall give him a hundred blows with a stick and pack him off to the kitchen.' He said this without passion but as if he meant it. To help him get over his obstinate fit of temper, I said, 'Monsieur, let Bompar finish up the rest of your drink.' He did so and began to laugh at seeing Bompar drink and so his ill-temper passed." The use of umbrellas against

TWO DOLLS IN LATE SIXTEENTH CENTURY

From L'Histoire des Jouets.   H. R. d'Allemagne

rain is, of course, much more modern than the use of parasols against the sun's rays, and it is therefore specially interesting to read that one day in May 1613 " a great storm of rain came on and the king put up his parasol and went on with his walk." It seems odd that a hundred years went by before the use of umbrellas as a protection from rain became habitual.

CHAPTER XI

OLD WAYS IN MEDICINE

As I have said elsewhere, the greater part of Jean
Héroard's diary still remains in manuscript " a volum-
inous collection, difficult to read, and the complete
publication of which would be neither possible nor
interesting," as the editors of the printed portion tell
us. Nor is there any reason to doubt the soundness
of their judgment. We know from other sources
that much of the journal consisted of notes on the
dauphin's daily physical condition, possibly useful to
his doctor for reference but absolutely without interest
to anyone else either then or since. It is certainly
curious that there should be so little to be learnt
about children's illnesses and their treatment from the
journal of a remarkably observant medical man; the
little that Messieurs Soulié and de Barthélemy have
included in their book is interesting enough to make
us regret that there is not more, but it may well be
that they have given us all there is. By careful gleanings
we can gather a few curious details on medicines, on
treatment for little hurts and pains and on the infectious
illnesses of children. Some illnesses, of which we
might expect to hear, are not spoken of. Perhaps
whooping-cough was not distinguished from the other
coughs and colds the children sometimes had; chicken-
pox may not have been distinguished from smallpox.
Once or twice " smallpox without fever " is mentioned,
and this might have been the milder chicken-pox.
L'Estoile in 1580 wrote of an " illness called *coqueluche* "

(whooping-cough) of which " ten thousand people in
Paris fell ill," the symptoms being those of a cold
with pains in the head, stomach, and kidneys and
extreme weakness, the best cure being to eat and drink
little and stay abed. After Paris he adds that not a
village in France escaped and that rumour said ten
thousand had died of the illness in Rome. It may
have been whooping-cough but it sounds like an outbreak of influenza. Nothing of the sort is described
by Héroard. On the whole health appears to have
been good among the children and medicines very few,
unless indeed all mention of them has been omitted
from the printed journal in the earlier years. We hear
a good deal about the two most infectious illnesses
among children, measles and smallpox, but neither
disease seems to have been really serious with any of
the king's sons and daughters. The *enfants d'honneur*
suffered their share as well as the children of the
various attendants and servants, but no death among
them is ever mentioned. On the other hand, since we
know that Héroard did not consider any other child
than the dauphin had any real place in his journal
this is not proof either way. Measles must have been
as worrying to Mme de Montglat as it is to-day in a
preparatory school. Catherine and Alexandre de
Vendôme had it when the dauphin was a baby but
were separated before they had spread the infection.
Little Madame caught it when she was three years
old but she does not seem to have been seriously ill.
" July 1605. While the dauphin was passing by the
chapel he and Madame met. They greeted each other
but when they were six feet apart his nurse said,
' Monsieur, you must not go any nearer to Madame.'
He stopped, his lip grew very long and at last tears
fell from his eyes and from Madame's too, as well as

from those of all the little company about them."
Other outbreaks of measles followed though none of
the king's children fell ill of it before Henri de Verneuil
in 1608. Apparently Héroard was not allowed to
attend the infectious illnesses of any children except
the queen's. So in March 1608, " M. Hubert, the
king's doctor, arrived to see M. de Verneuil who had
the measles. The dauphin asked what he was doing
at St Germain. ' Monsieur,' I said, ' he is coming to
live here instead of me.' Colouring up and smiling
he flung his arms round me. ' Oh! you are teasing.
I wouldn't let you go.' " The truth is that the king
had written to Mme de Montglat and sent the letter
by M. Hubert. Here it is : " Madame de Montglat.
I am very glad to see by your letter how careful you
are in giving me news of the health of all my children,
especially of my son de Verneuil; and since his illness,
although not dangerous, is infectious I thoroughly
approve of the separation you have made. And as
M. Héroard cannot attend him for fear of infecting
my son the dauphin and the other children, I have
sent Hubert, one of my own doctors, whom you know
and who brings you this letter, to take charge of my
son de Verneuil and do what he thinks advisable in
consultation with Héroard."

The dauphin must, after a moment's shock, have
been pleased to see Hubert coming to attend his féfé
Verneuil for he liked to consider Héroard as his own
exclusive property. A few days earlier than this
fresh appearance of measles Héroard says: " I told
the dauphin the king had commanded me to go and
see M. le Comte de Moret, and begged my congé from
him. He said ' Where is he. I don't want you to go.'
' Monsieur, the king has commanded me.' ' I don't
want you to go. Go away, you are a naughty man,

and don't ever come back.' He got as red as fire.
At supper he reproached me and said I was his doctor
and I'd gone to see that little Moret." The child was
ill with some childish ailment, not, we may be sure,
infectious. The dauphin escaped measles when de
Verneuil sickened in March 1608, as he had on
previous outbreaks among the children, but in the
following October his turn came. Héroard was away
at his own house when the child fell ill. " Oct. 31st
1608. I got back from Vaugrineuse. No one had
let me know that he was feverish, only said he had an
ordinary cold. I found he had fever, pulse full, even
and quick; he was hot and covered with a rash;
very restless both from fever and from the huge fire
they had made in his room of which he complained.
No one would listen to his complaints, half stifling
him in his bed with a curtain of serge all round it
and a heap of bed-clothes. I had him taken up and
his bed re-made. . . . Amused himself with painting
all the time he was ill of the measles." The child
was not ill long for in a week he was not only up but
was allowed to discard his invalid's furred gown and
slippers for doublet and hose. He also threw away
his night-cap and put his hat on for himself. But
though the illness was short it must have left him
fretful and liable to take cold, for a week or two after
" he got up at eleven o'clock his eyes running and
coughing; was dressed in his crimson-furred gown."
He seems to have been still ailing three days later,
" He began to yawn and went very pale, said he felt
ill and began to cry. The king came to see him and
as soon as he looked at him he said, ' You've been
crying, I can see.' The dauphin stopped short,
frightened, but seeing M. de Verneuil go up to the
king he ran up too, to kiss him. The king scolded

him for crying and asked why and what he wanted.
'I want to go to my room Papa.' The king was
annoyed and asked why. 'Because I am cold.' 'Oh!
what a story. You are a little liar,' said the king.
'You'll see if you take him to his room he'll run
about and play. But let him go.' Taken to his room
the dauphin did nothing but sob and cry. M. de
Verneuil came to see him and to tease him told him
he had had dinner with the king." Henri could never
endure tears from the dauphin and this is not the
only time that he made no allowance for a childish
indisposition causing a fit of crying. Héroard could
comfort the child but he could not make a wilful man
considerate.

If for tears the doctor had no cure but sympathy,
for other small woes we sometimes hear of a remedy.
One December he "sent for a chopped onion. It
was for M. d'Orléans whose thigh had a little burn
on it caused by a spark from the fire. I said it was
for Mercier who had burnt her finger. The dauphin
said, 'Look I burnt my finger the other day and I
just had a castor-oil plaster put on it and it got well
directly. Ask *Moucheu* Héroard. And I cut my
finger the other day in the garden and I put some
earth on it and it got well directly too.'" Castor-oil
plaster for a burn may be a good remedy but earth
for a cut! However, I think it was the little boy's
treatment and not the doctor's. Plasters were much in
use and of different sorts for a burn, a sore lip, an
aching tooth and others. For toothache a small black
plaster of mastic was frequently applied to the temples
and as the treatment was a common one for a great
number of years we must conclude that it did help
the sufferers. It is said that these plasters were the
origin of patches, *mouches*, for a lady, recovering

sufficiently from the pain of toothache to notice the effect of the little black patch on her fair skin, decided to retain it as an adornment when it was no longer needed as a cure. More care was taken of the teeth than we might expect, both for the sake of comfort and good looks. The English writer, quoted on the subject of the morning toilet, recommended the daily washing of the teeth with " certain dentifrices or cleansers." Here are a few recipes for making them taken from Gervase Markham's list of things a good housewife should know. " Take a saucer of strong vinager and two spoonsful of the powder *Moek allem* (Italian alum), a spoonful of white salt and a spoonful of hony, seeth all these till it be as thinne as water, then put it into a close viall and keepe it and when occasion serves wash your teeth therewith, with a rough cloath and rub them soundly but not to bleed." We might gather that it was not a daily habit. Sage and salt crushed to a fine powder could be used night and morning " to whiten yellow teeth," and powdered ivory and pimpernel " bruised well together " and laid to the teeth in a linen cloth would make loose teeth fast again. I have not come across a French recipe although care of the teeth was obviously taught to children. Montaigne wrote that " I have always had good teeth, even excellent I may say. I learnt in my youth to rub them with my napkin every morning and at the beginning and end of every meal." He would have done it too as he sat at table. Another French writer advises that " after meat you should wash your face and mouth with cold water and cleanse the teeth with an ivory or hartshorn or some other pick of pure gold or silver." We may recall that the dauphin was told that it was not pretty behaviour to clean his teeth with his fingers while at dinner.

Héroard never says anything about the washing of teeth any more than he does about washing the body, but this is, after all, again only negative evidence that they were not washed. He does twice speak of the cutting of teeth; that first tooth when he stood all night by the restless baby's cradle with the tiny hand in his big one, and again nearly five years later when " the dauphin's nurse, looking into his mouth saw that his twenty-first tooth had come through. He thought his nurse was going to hurt him and meaning to hit her hit Madame instead. He was so upset that he began to cry and beat his nurse; then he hugged and kissed Madame and then his nurse who pretended to be angry." Nurse Dondon cannot often have done more than pretend. Only on one occasion is toothache mentioned and that seems to have gone away after a " rest on Madame's bed," without recourse to any one of the many cures recommended in the old herbalists' books. The stopping of teeth was practised in the seventeenth century and even false teeth were worn, but these were only used to improve the appearance. It was not possible to make them fit well enough for mastication so that those who indulged their vanity by wearing them took them out at meal-times, only to replace them when eating was finished. After all, men have always found it easier to achieve adornment than comfort.

The only mention of giving the dauphin, or any of the children, medicine in their early years, occurs in 1608, when the dauphin was given half a rhubarb lozenge. As an infant Héroard had ordered the dauphin's stomach to be rubbed with oil of absinth and civet as well as washing him in oil of red roses, but apparently he did not dose his charges any more than he bled them. We know already what his colleague Dr

Guillemeau, "who would cheerfully bleed an infant of three weeks old," thought of Héroard's heresy on the matter of bleeding. So far did the heresy go that Louis was fourteen years old before he was bled for the first time. Since very little is said on the subject of medicine in the first nine years of the dauphin's life I have gathered what information I could from the early years of the child's reign. After Louis' accession the taking of medicine became fairly common, or if, as is possible, it had really been common earlier, we can at any rate read about it in the printed journal. Like hair-combing the taking of medicine was almost invariably accompanied by a fuss. Nor need we wonder when we read one of the prescriptions which the editors give us. "The king refused to take his medicine, preferred to be whipped; was well whipped but did not cry." The next day he "woke up quietly determined to take his medicine this time, but nevertheless, just like the day before, from seven to half past nine, neither force nor gentleness were of any use so much afraid was he of the draught." The prescription is as follows: One oz. of infused cassia, two drs. senna, four scruples rhubarb; half an oz. citron juice; a decoction of white chicory, sorrel, bugloss, agrimony, corinth raisins and fennel; some lemon and violet conserve. It had to be disguised by adding six oz. milk of sweet almonds and two drs. of diacarthemi. A year earlier the little king had objected to a simple infusion of camomile flowers with milk and white sugar. "He made a great fuss over taking it and said, 'Ask M. de Souvré if what one takes by force does one any good?' M. de Souvré threatened to whip him. This made him drink it. He said to M. de Souvré, 'If I had a birch-rod I'd make you drink too.'" After this little scene it is amusing to find him preaching a virtue he certainly did not practise. " The king went to see the queen who was taking medicine. He said, ' Be brave, Madame, come on Madame, be brave.' And as he said it he filled his pockets with melon comfits. ' Be brave, Madame, you have only to open your mouth and gulp it down.' " Modern children, who take their physic in tabloids, cannot really sympathize with these troubles of long ago; their still living grandparents can recall the horrors of black draught, of gregory-powder and of rhubarb.

When the dauphin left St Germain-en-Laye Héroard naturally went with him, and some other doctor must have been appointed to take charge of the family left behind. Cæsar de Vendôme had already left the *Vieux Château* to be married to Mlle de Mercœur; the Chevalier Alexandre de Vendôme, Henri de Verneuil and the *enfants d'honneur* followed the dauphin to Paris to be, as before, his playmates. Catherine de Vendôme seems also often to have been with the queen. At St Germain there remained the queen's five younger children, Gabrielle de Verneuil and the various children and babies belonging to the household, still quite a fair-sized family for Mme de Montglat to manage. Only one of the number gave any cause for anxiety in regard to health, the queen's second son, the Duc d'Orléans. He did not live to have a grand christening and a name of his own like his elder brother and sisters. When he was born the dauphin was proud of having a brother, " another servant for Papa." One of the prettiest of his letters was written about the new baby at Fontainebleau, where four of the queen's children were born. " Wednesday October 19th 1605. Mamma. I do so want to see you and to kiss my little brother Orléans, and

PORTRAIT OF LOUIS XIII AT NINE YEARS OLD

if you don't come soon I shall put on my white tunic and my hose and boots and I shall mount my little horse and I shall go troty-ti-trot. Mamma I shall start to-morrow quite early for fear of flies. Mamma they say you have something pretty for me and I do so want to see it. Come soon, dear Mamma, it is such fine weather and you will find me a very good boy. In the meantime I am Mamma your very humble and very obedient son and servant.   DAUPHIN."

After the dauphin went to live in Paris he liked to go out to St Germain to play with the others and sometimes one or other paid him a visit to the Louvre, and in summer-time they all met at Fontainebleau. Of course, when he was a king he became an immensely important person to the younger ones and a visit from him was an honour to be highly valued.   The last visit to his little brother d'Orléans was paid in November 1611, when the child was lying very ill and the doctors could do no more for him.   The account has a charm of its own which makes it worth reading, but apart from this it does throw some faint light on illness and doctors in those days.   Héroard and the king talked over this visit before they started. The king had recently been taking regular lessons in shooting with an arquebus and was proud of his skill. " He did me the honour to say to me, ' My sisters will love to see me shooting with an arquebus.   All the women will cry Jésu!   Mamanga will ask M. de Souvré why he lets me shoot and she'll go and tell the queen, my mother.'   Started for St Germain at half past one and arrived at five o'clock; went at once to see Monsieur, his brother, who was ill with convulsions and drowsiness.   The king said ' Good evening, brother.'   ' Good evening, *Papa petit*, you do me too

much honour to come and see me.' The king began
to cry and went away. He never saw him again. He
went to the *Nouveau Château* and had supper with
M. d'Anjou and Mesdames. While he was being put
to bed M. de Souvré talked to him about Monsieur's
illness. The king asked, ' Is there nothing that can
save him?' ' Sire, the doctors have done all they
can, but you must pray for him.' ' Yes, I will, but is
there nothing else I can do?' ' Sire, you must vow him
to our Lady of Loretta.' ' Yes, I will gladly. How is
it done? Where is my chaplain?' The chaplain
came and told the king he must have an image of
silver made of just his height. ' Send someone to
Paris this minute and tell them to hurry,' said the
king eagerly, and then began to say his prayers with
tears in his eyes. He waked up an hour after midnight and asked what the news was of Monsieur and
then went to sleep again. Two days later the Marquis
d'Ancre (Concini) told the king his brother was dead.
He was taken aback, went pale and stayed quiet for a
while; tried to play, told M. de Souvré to tell the
queen he did not want to give the holy water to
Monsieur; said it not from indifference but because
he was so sorry. At half past one got into his carriage
to return to Paris. Near the cross of Nanterre he got
out for he had on his boots, and went into a vineyard,
shot two shots with his arquebus and with each one
knocked down a finch on the top of a nut tree." And
so the visit began and ended with a boy's delight in
his skill with his gun, and yet the pleasure of shooting
finches covered a real sorrow for the little brother.
Perhaps if this Duc d'Orléans had lived they might
have remained friends. Gaston, Duc d'Anjou, now
become Duc d'Orléans and *Monsieur*, was never either
a companion in childhood nor a friend in manhood.

Old Ways in Medicine

We do not know what was the illness the little brother died of except that it was " slight convulsions and drowsiness." Besides measles only two other diseases are mentioned by name; smallpox and plague. Smallpox does not seem to have been severe with any of the children although none escaped it. Alexandre de Vendôme had it the same year as measles when the dauphin was a baby; Gabrielle de Verneuil fell ill in 1606 and was away a long time from the other children. About the same time several of the *enfants d'honneur* were taken to their own homes with the same malady. Henri IV was much worried over his daughter Gabrielle de Verneuil's illness, both on her own account and because of the infection among the others. As soon as he heard of the illness he wrote to Mme de Montglat two of his always characteristic letters.

" Sat. July 8th at Paris, two hours after noon. Madame de Montglat. You did quite right to separate my daughter Verneuil from my son and my other children, as she is sick with smallpox. I am sending you this by courier for the express purpose of bidding you to send both my son and my daughter to the *Nouveau Château*. As for my second daughter since she goes only where she is carried you can leave her in the *Vieux Château*. But I leave all this to you. Mme de Verneuil has asked permission to go and look after her daughter, which I have granted. You must prepare a room in the *Vieux Château* for her and allow my son de Verneuil to go and see her if she wants. Send me news of my son and my daughters by the courier. Adieu, Mme de Montglat."

Mme de Montglat, who never shared the king's feelings for his mistresses' children, was not full enough in her reply so that the king wrote again in haste.

Q*   243

" Sunday July 9th, 1606, at Paris. 9 o'clock in the evening. Madame de Montglat. The courier, whom I had dispatched to fetch me news of my daughter de Verneuil, brought me back your letter quite safely, but you did not tell me whether the smallpox has attacked her face or not, nor whether she is very ill, nor a great many other particulars which I wanted to know. This is my reason for sending this further letter by the hands of the lackey so that on his return he may bring me information on all these matters. Good evening, Madame de Montglat."

The little girl was not back with the other children till September. Clearly she had not permanently suffered in health, for here is our last glimpse of her in a letter of the king's to her mother, written in the following October.

" My all. I have let a day go by without writing to you because I left early in the morning and only got back by ten o'clock in the evening, so tired out that I could do nothing more. As for news this evening our daughter entertained my wife and me and all the company for three hours so that she nearly made us die of laughing. Compared with her Master William, the fool, is no good at all. I never saw anything like it. I wish you good night with a million kisses.

HENRY."

No more is said of smallpox at St Germain-en-Laye.
The real terror of life was plague and this gave the king and the doctor many an anxious thought for the children. During the sixteenth century Paris had seen five outbreaks of the terrible disease and early in the seventeenth yet another devastated the capital and the surrounding districts. We have already seen how

the king's children were kept at Fontainebleau for more than a year while the epidemic lasted. Even a slight knowledge of the condition of Paris and its streets is enough to prevent any surprise at a recurrence of the deadly illness. Most houses were without even the most primitive sanitary arrangements and the open gutters down the streets served as sewers. Regulations and city laws were not lacking for the paving of streets, the collecting of refuse by carts, the flushing of the gutters by the inhabitants, the forbidding of emptying slops out of the windows and so forth. Something indeed was actually achieved towards the better sanitation and cleansing of the city but far too little to prevent the outbreak of disease. Those who care to see what Paris in the seventeenth century was like, and who have not leisure to make their own research, can turn to M. Al. Franklin's volume entitled *L'Hygène* in *La Vie Privée d'autrefois*. They will not easily forget what they read. The habits of the people at that time were grossly indecent. Even at St Germain-en-Laye Mme de Montglat was driven into issuing a proclamation against fouling the Great Court, and instituting fines for any infringement of the rule. The dauphin himself was threatened with the penalty for his dirty habits. But this new order was not made until plague in Paris was bringing terror to all; perhaps it is some mark of grace that dirt and plague were linked together in men's minds. But more ancient beliefs still held the majority and *graisseurs*, smearers, evil men or phantoms or devils, who knew? were generally held responsible for the spread of plague. Héroard gives the account of a terrifying night at St Germain in the summer of 1606. The weather had been abnormally cold, vitality was low and people very despondent. " The 26th July was as cold as mid-winter with a bitter north wind blowing. It has been like winter for six weeks," says Héroard. L'Estoile, the diarist of Paris, also wrote : " The weather was so unseasonable, gloomy, rainy and cold that every one said that All Saints' Day fell in July this year; for it was such bad weather that the like was never seen in the memory of man. It caused a great deal of contagious illness in the town, where a general terror was worse than the disease itself with forebodings of evil to come . . . and even that the town would be swallowed up on the 27th of the month according to an almanac made by a Capuchin." And amid a sense of fear and gloom the devil's witchcraft got busy at St Germain. " July 23rd. Between midnight and one o'clock the sentinel on guard on the terrace saw, coming up the steps, a man in a white doublet, who would not stop whatever the sentinel said to make him go back. He hit him on the head with his sword three or four times but the man said nothing but ' Hé, Monsieur.' The sentinel was about to seize him by the collar but such a foul smell filled his nostrils that he had to let go. He thought it came from a box in the man's left hand and a rag round his arm. He ran for his pike but when he got back he saw the man going off towards Pecq. He believed it was a *graisseur*." Such men had been seen in Paris smearing the doors with plague-poison just as they had been seen in every bad outbreak since time began, smearers, plague spreaders. The sentinel's story made a great stir in the castle and the children heard all about it. There was no plague as yet in the little town without the castle walls but it might come any moment; the man with his box might have brought it. The dauphin shared in the fears of those around him. " Said he smelt rabbits in the moat. There were no rabbits and the window

is shut. 'There is something which smells bad.
I think it is that man with the box. I think it is in
the ditch. It smells of safran.' . . . Went into the
vineyard and picked green grapes to make verjus.
He saw me coming up the steps where the man with
the box had been. M. Birat carried him. He went
red with fear I should come to harm and called out
several times 'Moncheu Hé'ouad! Moucheu Hé'ouad!
don't go that way. It's where the man went.' "

With such fears added to the very real danger it
was time the family moved to Fontainebleau and to
the clean, safe air of the great forest. What security
from infection on the journey was possible Héroard's
medical knowledge was careful to supply. " I gave
the dauphin lozenges in which there was bezoar,
unicorn horn and other things which I told him he
must put in his mouth and let them melt. He said,
' I'll take one when I pass by a bad smell.' " Perhaps
bezoar, a popular antidote for poison, and other things
would be efficacious but I very much fear the unicorn's
horn was only powdered tusk of a narwhal.

Louis' health became steadily worse as he grew
older and in the later pages of the diary Héroard often
speaks of ailments; on one occasion he even describes
a curious fit the young king had which might make
us suspect epilepsy were it not that it seems to have
been a solitary instance. But with these later illnesses
we are not concerned. There is, however, one entry in
December 1610, to which, since it reveals a deep-
rooted medical superstition it is worth while to give
a word of explanation. Paris was infested with stray
dogs, ill-fed and diseased for the most part and rabies
was always a very present terror. One morning " the
king played in the garden of the Tuileries. A mad
dog got in who bit several other dogs, among them

his favourite, Gayan, and the man who had charge of his dogs too. The king hit the mad dog hard with his stick; it would have flown at him if it had not been stopped by the Sieur de Meurs, who would have killed it if the king, with his natural humanity, had not forbidden him. At half past ten he was taken home. He told the queen of the mischance which had befallen his dogs and implored her to send them all to the sea. At eleven o'clock he dined and did me the honour to tell me too all about it, with tears in his eyes when speaking of his dog-keeper and of Gayan, saying, 'I do wish I hadn't taken Gayan to the Tuileries to-day.'" L'Estoile describes more than one case of rabies and the terrible fate which befell those who were bitten, and Louis was never left in ignorance of things which might well have been kept from a child. For instance, in 1604, L'Estoile tells of "a young lady, newly wed, who having been bitten by a little dog was seized with raving, and because she was in terror of being smothered, as is the custom in these cases, it was agreed to give her a poisoned medicine so that she might die more easily. She took it willingly, though she suspected what it was, from the hand of her husband, who gave it with all the sorrow in the world, and died three hours later. In her terror she had implored her father not to leave her, 'for directly you go they will smother me,' and so they gave her the medicine." There were certain supposed antidotes but the only cure which gained any measure of credit was sea-bathing within nine days of the bite. Perhaps it may have been all the more believed in because of the difficulty which inhabitants of inland towns encountered in their efforts to get to the sea in time. A year before the above tragic death, L'Estoile describes the attempt of an unlucky page to carry out the cure. "A page having been bitten by a mad dog and setting out for the sea which is held to be the only sovereign remedy, passed through a wood where the brambles scratched him till the blood ran. When the poor page saw it and heard that the sight of his blood would drive him into immediate madness, which is held as a true and infallible fact, he implored his companions to smother him straightway as gently as they could; which they did, weeping and grieved to the heart." So that we now see why the little king begged that his keeper and his dogs should all be sent to the sea. Héroard says no more on the subject but since Gayan was still a favourite in May 1611, we may suppose that the dog who bit him was not really mad.

Being ill three centuries ago could not have been pleasant, but at least the king's children were blessed in a doctor not so wrong-headed as most.

L'ENVOI

In the beginning of this book I spoke of it as a tapestry where the central scheme of the composition is built up from many little scenes all contributing to the main subject. Two last pictures from Héroard will complete the weaving and my task is done. The first is dated on 27th September 1609, the dauphin's eighth birthday. " At eight o'clock he supped in M. Zamet's room to celebrate his birthday. The king drank to him saying, ' I pray God I may be able to give you a whipping twenty years hence.' The dauphin replied, ' No, please not.' ' What! don't you want me to be able.' ' No, please.' " On the tenth day of the following May Henri was stabbed to death as he rode in his coach through Paris and his eight-year-old son reigned in his stead. A week later, as the little king lay abed in the morning, " his nurse, who had slept by him, asked him what he was dreaming about. He answered, ' I was thinking,' and remained quiet a long time. His nurse said, ' But what are you thinking about? ' ' Dondon, I was wishing my father had lived twenty years longer.' The previous day he had said, ' I do so wish I was not king and that my father was still alive.' " Poor little king of eight years old. It is a tragic note to end on but in truth the underlying tragedy of the child's whole story led to a melancholy manhood. No one who has written of his later years has troubled to understand a king overshadowed in turn by worthless favourites and the dominating genius of Richelieu. Perhaps if his child-hood were better understood his cramped manhood

L'Envoi

could be more easily explained. However this might be, the curiously delicate insight into the ways of a little child shown by Jean Héroard brings before us Louis' early years with extraordinary vividness. Nor do we feel that it is the little dauphin alone who comes before us; it is rather the eternal child, without country and without century, with its infinite capacity for love and happiness, and for pain no less; with its whimsical dawnings of intelligence, its quick reactions to the surrounding world, its sure intuitions. Dr Jean Héroard, all unwittingly, describes for us in the pages of his diary the children whom we know to-day, whom our grandparents knew in the past, and whom our grandchildren will know in days yet to come. The old doctor possessed a wonderful gift of sympathy with childhood given to very few.

PRINTED IN GREAT BRITAIN BY THE EDINBURGH PRESS, EDINBURGH